The AS/400 & IBM i RPG & RPGIV Tutorial & Lab Exercises

*** THIRD EDITION ***

AS/400 & IBM i RPG & RPGIV Tutorial and Lab Exercises --
Stand Alone Tutorial Plus +++
Lab Book for College Text: <u>System i Pocket RPG & RPGIV GUIDE</u>
Provides Hands on Lectures, RPG & RPGIV Coding Exercises.
PowerPoint Slides for Textbook, Rich Student Libraries for Labs

– Learn RPG the easy way. This book assumes no RPG knowledge and it serves as a both a tutorial and a College / University RPG Laboratory Guide with a library full of Lab Objects to support the exercises. This tutorial starts with a simple program and continues to expand its scope to teach additional topics. Comprehensive Lab Book with many valuable examples / exercises for the new IBM i RPG/RPGIV Developer –

B R I A N   W .   K E L L Y

Published by: LETS GO PUBLISH!
Brian P. Kelly, Publisher
P.O Box 621
Wilkes-Barre, PA 18703
info@letsgopublish.com
www.letsgopublish.com
Library of Congress Copyright Information Pending

Book Cover Design by Michele Thomas; Editing by Brian P. Kelly

ISBN Information: The International Standard Book Number (ISBN) is a unique machine-readable identification number, which marks any book unmistakably. The ISBN is the clear standard in the book industry. 159 countries and territories are officially ISBN members. The Official ISBN for this book is:

978-0-9982683-2-3

The price for this work is :   ***$24.99 USD***

10	*9*	*8*	*7*	*6*	*5*	*4*	*3*	*2*
1								

Release Date: October 2007, February 2010, October 2016

Dedication

I dedicate this book to my wonderful wife Patricia, and our loving children, Brian, Michael, and Katie as well as the greatest pack of brothers and sisters, aunts and uncles, cousins, nieces and nephews that any person could ever hope to have in just one life. Thank you all for all your support.

Acknowledgments

I would like to thank many people for helping me in this effort.

I appreciate all the help that I have received in putting this book together as well as all of my other 79 published books.

My printed acknowledgments had become so large that book readers "complained" about going through too many pages to get to page one of the text.

And, so to permit me more flexibility, I put my acknowledgment list online, and it continues to grow. Believe it or not, it once cost about a dollar more to print each book.

Thank you and God bless you all for your help.

Please check out www.letsgopublish.com to read the latest version of my heartfelt acknowledgments updated for this book. Click the bottom of the Main menu!

Thank you all!

To sum up my acknowledgments, as I do in every book that I have written, I am compelled to offer that I am truly convinced that "the only thing you can do alone in life is fail." Thanks to my family, good friends, and a wonderful helping team, I was not and continue to be --- not alone.

Table of Contents

Table of Contents 7

Lecture A: Setting Up the IBM i for RPG Student Labs 1

Lecture B: Introduction to the RPG Tutorial Lab Book 7

Lecture C: Introduction to the RPG Language 9

Lecture D: System i Development Environment 13

Lab 1 System i Development Familiarity 17

Lab 2 Working with the Program Development Manager (PDM) 37

Lab 3 Write a Simple RPG Program.............................. 53

Lecture E: Understanding the RPG Fixed Logic Cycle............ 85

Lab 4 Using RPG Externally Described Files 95

Lab 5 RPG to RPGIV 107

Lab 6: Create a Payroll Register Report with RPG, Two Input Files Internally Described.......115

Lab 7: Create a Payroll Register Report with RPG, Two Input Files Externally Described......131

Lab 8: Payroll Register- Internally Described and Externally Desc. Converted to RPGIV 145

Lab 9: Multi-File Processing Using READ and CHAIN Operations 149

Lecture F: RPG Is Not Just the Cycle.................................... 181

Lab 10 Introduction to Interactive RPG Programming............. 183

Lab 11 Use Display Files with RPG Programs to Update DB Files.............................231

Lab 12 Adding Capabilities to the Payroll Program - Create Menu & Maint. Functions 239

Lets Go Publish! Books by Brian Kelly 267

Preface:

Finally, there is an affordable RPG and RPGIV tutorial with powerful Lab exercises. This book also doubles as a Lab Book for a College or University or Corporate RPG / RPGIV course. All that you need to learn -- the most used facilities in RPG and RPGIV --- are in this book.

If this were not designed as a tutorial, this book would serve as an excellent stand-alone Lab book. However, it was built to be both a language tutorial and the ideal Lab book for the AS/400 and IBM i RPG and RPGIV Developers' Guide, a recently released RPG text book that is soup to nuts in just over 600 8.5 X 11 pages.

With the Lab objects and the detailed lab instructions provided, the combination of the "Lab Book" and the AS/400 and IBM i RPG and RPGIV Developers' Guide as the text book, provide what is needed for a complete College/University Laboratory learning experience for RPG programming. The beauty is that the same environment can be established for corporate IT shops.

Having stated that, if I could buy just one and learning was the mission, I would buy this book. If reference and solid explanations were the missions, I would buy the Text Book!

That is not all. This, the third edition of this book has far better facilities than rounds one and two and it is designed to be part of a full learning environment. If your business or your school would like to run Moodle courses, or if not Moodle, you would like to have talking PowerPoints of all the lessons in the Pocket RPG Guide and an outline describing in detail how to accomplish the education mission, Lets Go Publish can make this phenomenal material available to you through our relationship with our distributors. In edition 3, just go to www.letsgopublish.com/files with your browser and bring down what you want.

Envision this, a downloadable lab set that once uploaded to your IBM i system is one touch away from a full install. Once the lab is installed, you create the user profile and add the startup program to the profile and the "smartcode" builds the complete environment for each student in your class. Students do not stumble over students as each has their own RPG / RPGIV learning environment.

If this were never designed as a Lab book, the set of lectures in this book and exercises would serve as an excellent RPG and RPGIV tutorial. Its twelve Labs and numerous in-stream lectures start you off with basic familiarization and take you on a journey that includes data structures, database access and interactive programming.

With the lab objects and the detailed Lab instructions provided in this book, the combination of the "tutorial" and any reference source that you choose -- from the AS/400 and IBM i RPG and RPGIV Developers' Guide to IBM's free online manuals -- provides you with what you need for a complete self-directed RPG and RPGIV learn-by-doing experience.

The first iteration of this book was good but I admit, I had my share of startup issues. The book was fine though there were some mistakes. The Labs were not easily installable. On my host system, I had all the libraries I needed and when I packaged everything in one library for shipment, on my system, it worked like a charm. For a brief period, I thought I was a genius. Then, the phone calls and emails came in and the CD originally shipped with the book required major work prior to being able to have a fully functional lab. Objects that were in other libraries on my system were found but were not shipped with the CD by mistake. So things that were necessary for the one-touch install created big issues for those trying to use the code as delivered.

My sincere apologies to all. In edition three just about all the kinks are ironed out and the libraries for multiple OS versions are downloadable from www/letsgopublish.com/downloads.

I went through the package as the faults were exposed by users and I created fixes for all of those but it made the installation experience multi-touch, though not difficult. But, that was not my goal.

Eventually, my university decided to offer RPG to our Business Information Technology. I used the opportunity to start from scratch to assure that my students had an effective working environment. I put all of my talking PowerPoint lectures on Moodle so I could be in lab with students every week for this three credit course and I lectured only when the talking Moodle lectures did not do the whole job. Learning programming is not easy but those who wanted to learn had a great experience and I was able to make the course better on the fly as students reported anomalies.

My students complained about the original book, which was all we had in the beginning and I gave them each a copy of the PDF of the new version as it was being built. I do not think it is perfect even in the third edition but it is pretty darn good. It introduces students to all aspects of RPG programming from the cycle to doing it yourself procedural programming -- interactive, batch, RPG/400 and RPGIV.

My students did not ask me to repeat a single lecture that they could view on "talking PowerPoints" as many times as they wanted. The talking slides added substantially to the learning environment.

While I was writing this book and had most of it completed, I read it and reread i t myself himself before completing it. The third with this edition time and having taught using this material recently to university students was the charm has helped perfect the book.

I wrote the book as a companion to my RPG textbook as noted above. So, in his initial writing for the hands-on Labs, he pointed out various reading assignments that were well explained in the companion RPG book. Rather than make the Lab book 1000 pages, Brian chose to use citations in the bigger text for the student to read. When he reread the Lab book, he found it less convenient to have to read the citations as part of the lessons. In fact it was actually cumbersome to need two books for a tutorial that was not guided by a professor or a syllabus in the classroom.

I discovered that by adding a few concise lessons / lectures and some in depth explanations of some of the Lab steps, this Lab book could be as almost as good of an RPG tutorial itself.

I added the necessary lessons as brief written lectures and expanded the explanation of the major learning steps in the lab exercises.

I am convinced that this is all you need to get started with RPG to be prepared for an entry level programming position. If you as a student of RPG / RPGIV are fortunate enough to have a professor, you will have a rich semester with this Lab Guide. If, on the other hand, as a student, you are learning RPG at your company in a self-directed style, the Lab lessons get you there. They build on one another and when taken one after another at your speed, you can quickly get to know the basics of how to program in RPG and RPGIV.

Please note that this book is not suggested as an advanced RPG tutorial / lab book. This book does not contain advanced topics per se. These are entry level topics, though any student who can write the almost 500 statement RPG program in the final exercise deserves a spot on somebody's IT staff. RPG subfiles, procedures, dynamic SQL, and Free Form RPG IV are not included in this lab/tutorial. These are not entry level topics. However, the full package from IT Jungle contains talking PowerPoints that address the advanced chapters of the "RPG Pocket Guide," which introduce this material.

So, these topics are included in the <u>AS/400 and IBM i RPG and RPGIV Developers' Guide</u> as well as a number of other advanced topics books that you may get from other sources. When you finish this book and all of the exercises successfully, you will be in a position to take an entry level RPG position, provided your background in other IT areas is sufficient. That's what this book can provide when read carefully and when the exercises are done faithfully.

When I wrote the <u>AS/400 and IBM i RPG and RPGIV Developers' Guide</u>, which is over 600 pages, I thought that I could condense all of the information in the IBM RPG manuals into a three or four hundred page book. I could not. Originally the book was almost 1000 pages because that's how much there is. This Tutorial/Lab Guide doubles as the Lab Guide for the <u>System i Pocket RPG and RPGIV Guide</u> or as noted above, it also can be a standalone tutorial. The Guide contains just about all you need to know to be pretty good in the type of RPG that Brian Kelly finds to be dominant in his consulting client accounts .

IBM manuals provide everything you need to know. Unfortunately, nobody actually learns from an IBM manual. This book contains what you need to know to be able to accomplish most of the tasks that an RPG programmer needs to do every day -- without overwhelming you. Therefore, there is lots about RPG that is not in this book. Again, the intention is to gently teach and exercise very specific skills to get you on board as quickly as possible.

There are lots of RPG books but there has never been an RPG book like this. Instead of arguing about the merits of RPG/400, the cycle, and the modern feel of ILE RPG (RPGIV), this tutorial / lab book teaches it all. You'll be pleased with all the valuable explanations and examples. You won't want to put down this comprehensive guide to learning **IBM i** RPG now that you've got your hands on it. This book is almost 50 years overdue.

In today's IT landscape, most **IBM i** shops support both RPG and ILE RPG (RPGIV). Besides its down-home writing style, the major benefit of this tutorial / Lab book is that it is built as an essential tool to teach anyone charged with the responsibility of maintaining and extending RPG code and converted RPGIV code. And that means a new approach to the historical cycle, RPG/400, and basic RPGIV interactive programming with sequential and random processing…And multiple file adds and updates. This Guide has a good example for nearly every type of RPG operation you can imagine from complex batch programming to interactive workstation programs.

I designed this book to show you how to use RPG by working with Lab exercises that you'll have to review over and over again. Additionally, for each example, the solution is included and the lab solutions are documented in source code. This is the first RPG book to hand to your new developers and some veterans who could use an RPG tune-up. More importantly, it is the right size tutorial (280+ pages) or Lab guide for any relevant modern business programming course at your nearby university or community college.

The original book package included a CD with all of the Lab exercises in this tutorial guide plus others as well as Lab setup programs and instructions. This is no longer distributed.

Both entry level and existing programmers will enjoy the easy to read, down home style of this tutorial / lab guide. The tutorial book shows how to begin developing and maintaining code to help get you started in learning RPG. Even if you are new to AS/400, System i, and IBM i, and you want to understand how to use RPG for programs that you now code in other languages, you can learn all you need to get the job done right from this tutorial or from the Lab book (same thing). It is written in a way that assumes very little prior RPG or even generic programming knowledge.

Go ahead and leaf through this book now. You'll see it is chocked full of examples. Many screen shots are included so you can code the RPG examples in the book right along with your AS/400 or IBM i server.

Who Should Read this book?

New programmers, existing programmers, supervisors, operation personnel, or any other person in your organization who needs to know how to program in basic or even advanced RPG or RPGIV. Many IT managers today are looking for ways to educate other staff in IBM i RPG. Look no further. If you plan to train operations people or PC people as AS/400 developers, or you want to help your staff better understand the marvels of System i RPG business-oriented programming, this is the right book.

With all of the smart PC technicians in every business and institution today, there are many who would appreciate the opportunity to learn the major IBM i business programming language – RPG/400 and/or RPGIV. Many of these would do very well as programmers if redeployed. This book can be all you need to move them off the mark.

If you've always wanted to be able to tell your team what you know about RPG, ILE, RPGIV programming on the AS/400 and System i, but you did not have the time, rest assured that Brian Kelly has done it for you with this book. He's said what you would have said if you had the time to say it. Moreover, the folks at *Lets Go Publish!* think you'll like what you would have said.

Consider creating a home-made RPG programmer with a minimal start-up investment. It may be a good deal for you and for your company.

Though rich in content, none of IBM's RPG reference and user manuals are built to teach you the language. They are for reference. There is way too much in IBM's manuals to learn it all but they are great detail references for specific topics. This Tutorial / Lab book in combination with fee or free reference material uses a different approach. It is your teaching / learning vehicle to RPG. It is your new tool to help you start solving programming problems with RPG coding. Once you have learned how to program in RPG, a new world will open to you.

There is no doubt that RPG and RPGIV together represent the finest business programming language ever developed. I wish you well in your RPG business programming endeavors, and I hope to see you again reading another Lets Go Publish Pocket Guide in the future.

Feel free to shop for this book and other LET'S GO PUBLISH! Books at Book Hawkers (www.bookhawkers.com), Amazon, Kindle, and other fine booksellers.

About the Author

Brian W. Kelly retired as an assistant professor in the Business Information Technology program at Marywood University, where he also served as the System i technical advisor to the IT faculty. Kelly developed and taught a number of college courses in the IT and business areas. He continues his active consultancy in the information technology field, Kelly Consulting. He is the author of 90 books; has written numerous articles about current IT topics, and has been a frequent speaker at the COMMON and other technical conferences and user group meetings across the United States.

Lecture A: Setting Up the IBM i for RPG Student Labs

Pre-Lecture & Pre Lab

This tutorial begins easy and finishes demanding that the student learn RPG. Any student who takes this tutorial once thoughtfully is well on his or her way to being an RPG programmer. Those of us in the industry know that there are both One's and Ten's in the RPG programming community toiling every day for the good of their organizations. The ingredients for a student to get off on the right path to becoming a #10 (the best) programmer are included in the basic packaging of this tutorial.

This book can be used then to become far better than average, more than just one step above your peers and former selves as learning RPG becomes a mission. This book greatly assists that mission. Additionally, there are other support materials, such as talking PowerPoints and a complete RPG & RPGIV Developers' Guide, as well as sample course syllabi that can extend the support for RPG education to all members of your shop's programming community. The materials can also serve as the basis for an extensive University course in RPG as we just recently completed here at Marywood University before I retired.

Students who are the most effective in learning from this tutorial, without being in a classroom setting, are clearly self-motivated. They may also be taking a college course with this material for credit as it is easily adaptable to a Moodle / Web/CT environment or a regular three credit course.

The bottom line is that this book is designed so that an individual wishing to learn how to be an RPG programmer can be an RPG programmer, and a fine one to boot. Nothing in life worth having is easy. When you become an expert, your life will change.

The best

IT'S Up To YOU!

Lecture A Continued:

This lecture is for System Administrators. Students may read it but it may not make as much sense as it would if you were an AS/400 -- IBM i System Administrator.

Before you can begin this tutorial, the LAB Exercises must be installed on the IBM i System that is to be used for this exercise. Your system administrator's job is to get this task accomplished for you. These instructions are for the system administrator.

The Original Method in the First Edition mandated that you install from CD. This method is no longer available.

----

1. Bring down the Save files

The Save files for the libraries at various release levels are on the **www.letsgopublish** Web site. The procedure in a nutshell is to bring the binary save file to your PC, and then upload it to the IBM i system and prepare it for a restore library (RSTLIB) command.

There are two files that are available for downloading, one is for V5R4, and the other is for V6R1. Either of these can be used for your IBM I system even if it is at V7.2. Bring the files down as soon as possible. -- RPGOBJ.....

To download the RPGOBJ Library from Lets Go Publish

Go to

www.letsgopublish.com

Pick Downloads from the main menu
Scroll down to the two choices -- V5R1 and V6R1

The V5R4 version has several objects that could not be brought back from V6R1 to V5R4. One of them is the RPGSTART program. Assure that you have compiled those programs that you need from the source file called SOURCE in RPGOBJ.

Treat the installation of the save files to the RPGOBJ library the same way as you would have restored from the CD. There is a nice and free FTP program called FileZilla if the files do not come down using the Web browser. FileZilla can then be used to upload the files to the IBM i System. See directions above.

The following procedures attempt to spell out the full process. If you know how to upload an IBM i SAVE file already and convert it to an IBM i library, then just glance through the rest of these instructions.

2. Create a SAVE File on your system called RPGOBJ in the QGPL library.

3. Use FTP to upload the proper file from Step 1 (RPGOBJ.SAV) or similar from your PC after downloading it from the LGP site to your PC. FTP permits you to "copy" the save file as downloaded from the Web to the RPGOBJ save file you built in QGPL.

Make sure that before you execute the FTP that you set the FTP transfer to binary from your PC.

4. If you have NETSERVER

Note: An alternative to performing an FTP from a PC to the IBM i system get the file uploaded, is to use NetServer. This is much easier if it works in your environment. Again, you will use the file(s) that you downloaded from the LGP site.

To use this method, first Create a directory called /RPGOBJ on the IFS. Map a drive to it from your PC. Do a point and click copy from your PC to the IFS into this directory.

You still must use FTP to get the save file from the IFS to a library. Once on an IFS directory, you can use the IBM i FTP client on your IBM i System to connect tothe IBM i FTP server on the same system. Then, copy the file from the IFS to the save file in the library/file system. Of course this will either be an FTP Put or Get, depending on how your system is set up.

This is at first a strange notion in that you are using the IBM i FTP client and talking to the IBM i FTP server. For example, if the save file were moved to the IBM i IFS, this would work if your settings are correct, assuming the file names are correct:

Type FTP then type Your IBM i local IP address

Sign on with your own user ID and password.

Type BINARY and Enter

Type PUT /RPGOBJ/RPGOBJ.SAV QGPL/RPGOBJ and Enter

If the settings are not right, you may have to use /QSYS.LIB/QGPL.LIB/RPGOBJ.FILE as the receiving location.

If you still have issues you may have ot use the NAMEFMT FTP command and first learn the settings and then change them to make them work for you.

4. With the save file in place, type RSTLIB RPGOBJ and hit F4

5. Complete the parameters for the restore and hit Enter to execute the RSTLIB command.

Now the Lab package is on your system in the RPGOBJ library..

6. To use the tutorial / lab package, you need to create a user profile and place a call to rpgobj/rpgstart as the user startup program in the profile. Make sure that there are no libraries on the system with the name of any student user profile or any user profile that needs to use this tutorial / lab package.

7. Once you test this and it works, create as many profiles as students who will be using the Tutorial / Labs.

When a user signs on, a complete lab environment is built in their library. The user's library list is displayed and the RPG programming menu is presented to the user. On subsequent sign-ons, the existence of the library is tested and if it is there, the environment build does not occur but the same menus are presented.

Profiles and Security

Once you have the software fully restored on your IBM i system, create user profiles for each of the members of the class or the individuals who will be taking the tutorial. Make sure that you use the RPGSTART program in RPGOBJ unless you first move it to another library. Once the user signs on, all of the files from RPGOBJ will be copied to the user's library and the user will be set up for the course. The second and subsequent times in, the library does not get built. SO, if a big issue occurs early in the course, you may delete the student's library and it will recreate itself automatically.

As a system administrator, my suggestion would be that you assign the profiles the most authority that your shop can afford so that they can actually learn how to do things.

That's easy for me to say. You are responsible for the security in your own shop. You may ultimately want to go into some of the programs and menus provided in this package (all shipped in RPGOBJ) and change anything that you need to make the tutorial run more securely in your environment.

In the University environment since my primary purpose was training, I made sure I was backed up, and could restore easily, I then gave all the users of the course *SECOFR authority. In a large class, it is easy to get messed up and lose the confidence of the students by having authorization issues. I would more than likely have used what is called adopt authority if I had to run on an existing system that was already being used for production.

If this is what you might like to use, the simple way to do it is to recompile RPGSTART from RPGOBJ and set the **USRPRF attribute to *OWNER.** Then for each profile you create, grantobjaut to RPGSTART for that user. If the person taking the course is trusted, and already has SECOFR authority then you are OK to go with no additional work.

Additional Setup Work

Years ago Power Systems with IBM i were called AS/400s and they were too slow to permit programmers to work interactively. Thus, much programmer work, such as the submission of compiles was done in batch. The PDM default for submissions is batch. As a suggestion, because it is much easier for a student to know immediately whether their work is correct, change the defaults (PDM Option 18) so that compiles are not submitted in batch. Your boss may not be happy about that but the students will.

Startup

When the student signs on, the program RPGSTART begins and establishes a full use environment. Administrators should check it out in the SOURCE File of the RPGOBJ library to gain the proper perspective.

Lecture B: Introduction to the RPG Tutorial Lab Book

Use this Tutorial / Lab Book for all your IBM i RPG Labs.

As a companion to this Tutorial / Lab Guide, you should consider purchasing a spiral notebook to keep your notes or you should open up a Microsoft Word document on your first day and you can copy in the intermediate steps that you perform to solve the labs. More importantly, you can write yourself notes about things you learned -- especially what I like to call light-bulb learning. Light-bulb learning is what happens to you when after struggling on a problem for a length of time, and you do something differently and all of a sudden the solution comes to you. Actually the "light-bulb" can turn on in a dream or while you are a passenger in a car -- please don't be thinking of these labs while you are driving- or anywhere, anytime. Write down what you learn when you learn it because you will be so drenched in knowledge, you will be able t come back rather than figure it out again.

Copy the parts that are necessary for your solution and any other results, questions, concerns, and light-bulbs into a Microsoft word document and label it properly for your benefit. Keep adding to the same document throughout all the labs -- using separator lines between the exercises. Use this document to store all of your exercises and all the notes that accompany your solutions. Depending on whether you are using this book as a tutorial or a lab guide, your instructor may demand that you keep a log of your activities. The notebook / document approach works well. The document approach is far better since it can be easily emailed to your instructor no matter where they may reside.

Keep you document complete but separate it by Lab Exercises and by syllabus week so that you will have a running reminder of the work that you have performed from week to week. If this were my class, I would ask that you submit your document to me every week to assure that you will have created it and to assure that you are advancing as a student properly through the course. If you are booming through this as a tutorial, hopefully you can email this to somebody in your company so they can help assure that you are on track.

For your information

Many of you have used Web browsers and therefore you may be familiar with the http://www.host.domain.com nature of the Internet. There are more high level domain names than just com. For example, the university where I teach is marywood.edu.

Since our server is not necessarily part of the domain system, it is easy for you to directly address it with an IP (Internet Protocol) address. You may already know that all host/domain names are resolved to IP addresses on the Internet via domain name servers and these servers provide a real IP address to your browser or other facility when you are accessing a site.

In other words, all sites are addressed via an IP address, not via a name. Using names actually adds more processing overhead to each request since the name must be resolved to an IP address before the user can actually work with the selected site.

Our server has two IP addresses for classroom purposes and we will use them directly. In other words, we will not be using names. Verify this information for your server.

Internally the address for the IBM i server is (specify -- your remote server IP or web address)

See your instructor or your system administrator for this address

We call this a private address. Nobody from the Internet can directly access any computer in the world whose address begins with a ten prior to the first dot.

Because at our university we provide off campus access for students for certain functions, the IBM i server also has a public address. This address is   (specify)

See your instructor or your system administrator for this address

Because most colleges and companies have firewall protection , only some functions within this address may be permitted permitted.

To access the IBM i server from home or work, you will have to download one of several free 5250 protocol telnet servers (TN5250). Some URLS for this are in Lab 1. Look up TN5250 on Google. The IBM i Access program in most of the labs on our campus should provide this telnet facility for you when you are on campus. Once you download the TN5250 program to your mobile or home or residence hall system, configure it to connect to the external address and you should have little trouble getting in.

BTW, Another name for IBM i is the System i as well as iSeries as well as the AS/400.

Lecture C: Introduction to the RPG Language

What is RPG?

RPG began as an acronym for Report Program Generator, which was descriptive of the original purpose of the language: generation of reports from data files, including matching record and sub-total reports.

Check out this brief history article at IT Jungle: "RPG: A Great Language with a Greater History" -- http://www.itjungle.com/tfh/tfh081709-story01.html. Either type in the URL or type the title into Google for a nice crisp read.

RPG was not created to be a general-purpose programming language. Many consider this the basis for its power. Underlying every early RPG program was the 407 Accounting Machine sequencing algorithm, hardwired into the software, relieving the programmer of the burden of controlling the input process procedurally. Early textbooks called RPG a problem oriented language because it was designed to solve simple business problems – especially reporting. These texts compared RPG to COBOL, which was characterized as a procedural language in which the programmer used input output commands inside of the program to perform the functions that were inherent automatically in the RPG language. Thus, early COBOL programs were always substantially longer than early RPG programs.

The RPG programming language initially used fixed-format cards. When the cards had been used within the context of the 407 Accounting Machine, the control panel would pick up the data from various card columns, perhaps add the data to accumulators and then print a line on a report. By mimicking this electromechanical machine, original RPG programming was little more than a fill-in-the-blanks operation. For example, if columns 47-53 of a transaction card held a part number, which was used as a control field, a two character designation in RPG was all you had to provide to make it happen.

The original RPG programming language used only a fixed processing cycle it was designed to process cards. In many ways, the design of the original RPG language had many similarities to what are called fourth generation languages or 4GL languages.

The simplicity of RPG made it easy to learn. In fact, it was so easy to learn that many early RPG programmers were taken from other areas of the business and trained. This method was very effective and even today some companies choose to pick a person who knows the business to be their computer expert for the company.

To simulate the functions of the fixed cycle of the 407 Accounting Machine, IBM adapted its RPG language. The System/3 had two card hoppers in its multi-function card unit (MFCU) package so RPG II was enhanced to be able to directly access both of these card reader / punches in one program. Since both card hoppers could read and both could punch, RPG II was given the ability to punch data into the same card that was read.

Additionally, RPG programs could also punch out new decks of cards from blanks. Since the MFCU could not print on cards, RPG did not gain this ability either. However, any card output that required interpreting was sent through the 96-column card keypunch unit that IBM called its 5496 Data Recorder.

Early IBM Computers Used RPG & RPGII

Though the RPG language design for the card-only System/3 models was not much different from that which preceded it, technically it became known as RPG II. In addition to being able to perform the "RPG Cycle" that imitated the 407 Accounting machines, RPG II added many more programmer tools to the language, making it appropriate for interactive programming as well as report writing.

With its new disk drives, the 1970 version of System/3 RPG II was a much more capable programming language. The major operators included for DISK were the CHAIN and the EXCPT, which are explained briefly in this book and are used extensively in the tutorials and labs. By introducing these operation codes, for the first time in RPG, programmers were able to access and update/add disk records both randomly and by key (index files) within the confines of the RPG calculations specification form. These operations, in essence were the very first operations in RPG that did not depend on the RPG cycle for execution. RPG was well on its way.

In 1977 IBM enhanced RPG II by adding the WORKSTN device to the language. This was a real phenomenon. IBM defined the notion of a display screen. The displays screen was defined externally to the program and was manipulated within the program using normal RPG operations against screen names. An extension was added to the RPG File description specification to permit what was called a format member to be compiled along with the program. From this member, the programmer could select screen names for output / input to interact with a user.

Prior to the native WORKSTN device support for the System/34, display terminals were not ever integrated into compilers. In fact, terminals were supported only via special add-on support in the form of the Communication Control Program (System/3 CCP) or the Customer Information Control System (System/370 CICS). Both CCP and CICS had their own system generation process and specialized operation codes such as Get and Put. Moreover, these tools required skills above and beyond that of a normal programmer. The WORKSTN file was so easy to use that many who had become adept at CCP or CICS could not believe that it could possibly work. It worked, and it made the RPG language the easiest to use for business full screen at a time interactive processing.

RPG III

In 1978, IBM introduced a machine that was so architecturally elegant that it would take the company almost another two years to deliver its first customer's shipment. It was called the IBM System/38 and it was a minicomputer class machine but IBM liked to call it a small business computer. The System was built to be the replacement box for the IBM System/3. It was clearly the most advanced general-purpose computer of its day, complete with a built-in relational-like database management system and natural workstation facilities that were far better than even the System/34.

With the System/38, IBM introduced the RPG III language which brought a host of new functions to the language, among these, a nearly complete set of structured programming operations (e.g., IF-THEN-ELSE, DO). With these new features, programmers were able to define RPG programs, which did not require understanding a hint of the RPG cycle.

The System/38 permitted the input and output of files to be described externally such as in a workstation file object or a database file object. The RPG compiler was enhanced to work directly with database files -- both relational tables and views. At compile time, the programmer merely added a switch in the File Description Specification to tell the compiler that the input and output specs (from a database or other file) were to be obtained from an external object (the file itself). The compiler would then dutifully go to the object and bring the specs into the program, provide them in the compiler listing and make them available for use within the program. This saved the programmer massive amounts of time.

In 1988, IBM introduced the AS/400 and the company provided another new compiler package called RPG/400. The package contained the RPGII, RPGIII, and the new RPG/400 RPG compilers.

RPG IV – Best Language on any Platform

In 1994, IBM introduced a significant update to the RPG language —ILE RPG a.k.a. RPG IV. The introduction of RPG IV marked the first time ever that the RPG specifications had been significantly revamped. A new data definition specification was added and the File Extension specification form was eliminated from the new language.

With RPG IV, IBM also eliminated virtually all of the perceived limitations of previous versions of RPG. With RPG IV, for example, there are natural expressions in the language. Mathematics and conditioning capabilities were enhanced and leading edge DATE and TIME arithmetic operations were made available. .

This latest version of RPG is, by far, the richest language in existence. Though it is more capable and therefore more complex than the RPG of the 1960's, it is still easy to learn and it offers a ton of functions for day-to-day, general-purpose business applications. With its reasonably new free form facilities and its many built in functions, and its effective use of sub-procedures for modular programming, RPGIV also has an affinity to the type of languages most preferred by the computer science community -- block structured languages.

With RPGIV supporting these programming language characteristics, it makes it easier for System i programming shops to train today's college graduates for a career as a System i IT professional. Moreover, with RPGIV, the concepts learned are applicable to other programming languages.

The list of RPGIV improvements is large. The top nine enhancements brought by RPGIV include the following:

1. Larger internal constructs. All RPG specs were enhanced to provide for variable names of up to 10 characters (up from 6 in RPG/400) and longer operation codes and other enhancements.

2. New 'D' Specification: In addition to the specifications for RPG/400, IBM introduced a new specification form called the Definition 'D' spec. All non-external data definitions can now be coded using the new 'D' spec that is new to ILE RPG. In addition you can define "named constants" that greatly simplify coding these in the C-spec's.

3. New Operations: A number of new operations have been added and the op codes on others have been enhanced to make them more readable. For example, the Lokup op is now Lookup. Semi-free form formula capability was added to the language to make it easier to include expressions.

4. Modularity: With ILE, you can now write modules (non-executable) in several languages and bind them together into a single ILE program. This program can be an RPG IV program. You can also use RPG modules in other language programs.

5. Larger Spec sheet and field size: With RPGIV, the RPG spec has been widened to 100 characters to accommodate up to ten character field names and larger operation codes.

6. Date fields / operations: One of the first major differentiations between RPG/400 and RPGIV is the new compiler's ability to deal with the date data type. For example operations exist to subtract a duration from a date and get a duration or to subtract two dates and have the result presented as a duration.

7. Procedures: IBM has also built into the language the notion of callable procedures – implemented with subprocedures and functions.

8. Built-In Functions (BIFs): Many built-in functions or BIFS have been added to the RPGIV language including *%date, % days, %months, %years, %diff, %abs, %editc, %subdt, %DEC, %INT, %UNS, %FLOAT, %error.* These fit nicely in expressions

9. Free format RPG specifications: With RPG FREE form, IBM has given the RPG programmer the opportunity to code without the typical columnar boundaries of RPG/400. The Once and Future RPG

Lecture D: System i Development Environment

RPG Program Development

RPG programmers develop, code, compile, and test their programs. In this course, we teach about the RPG language but if there were no way to develop, code, compile, and test programs, there would be no way to deploy RPG programs or any other programs for that matter. The tool that continues to be most popular in an IBM i shop is the aging Program Development Manager or PDM. It was introduced in 1988 with the AS/400. For a green screen development platform, it still is first class and it helps make RPG programmers very productive.

IBM is currently promoting a very nice Windows based development tool called WebSphere Development Studio Client (WDSC). In the past year most of the pieces of this product have come together but there are still a few holes, such as an integrated screen designer that is, however, on the promised list. Consequently, for this and other reasons, among those that the PDM is just so easy and immediate to use with no PC setup, this tool has not been adopted yet by most of the System i community.

In this next lab, you will learn about PDM since it is more widespread than WDSC and it does a nice job of aiding the development process, though it is green screen based.

Programming Development Manager (PDM)

PDM is part of the Application Development Tool Set (ADTS) which had been a staple for application development on the AS/400 since 1988, when they were announced. In early 2000, the whole ADTS was repackaged and it became part of the WebSphere Development Studio for IBM i product set. PDM is, therefore, not an island. It works with all of the other tools in the tool set including the following:

1. Source Entry Utility (SEU)
2. Screen Design Aid (SDA)
3. Data File Utility (DFU)
4. Advanced Printer Function (APF)
5. Report Layout Utility (RLU)

PDM Features

In order to enter a program into a System i source file, the major tool used is called the Source Edit Utility or SEU. This is # 1 in the above list and it is a very important tool. From PDM, when you choose to edit a source member, PDM invokes SEU to get the job done for you. PDM is a menu driven productivity tool for programmers. SEU is launched from the PDM panels. For a more detailed explanation of the development environment on the System i, you may want to read a book I wrote called the IBM i Pocket Developer's Guide, available at both IT Jungle and MC Press.

PDM provides a focal point and an integrated environment for using the development tools available to the programmer on the IBM i system. It works with lists of items to be developed or maintained. Virtually all types of objects can be accessed using PDM interfaces, though it is most commonly used for programs, display files (or screens), and data base objects (or files).

The IBM i operating system is an object based system and so you will hear the term used in this book quite often. In its natural state, the IBM Power System operating system IBM i manages objects through a directory structure known as a library. So, we say that objects such as files, output queues, and programs are "stored" in libraries. Just as nothing is stored "in" a directory, we really mean that the library is a means of locating the objects.

A special type of file called a source file is used with IBM i and PDM to store your source programs. A file on System i has some of the characteristics of a subdirectory in that a source file can contain many source members. If you write fifty source programs (program before it is compiled and translated into machine code), each source program is identified by its own name within the source file.

The structure of a file in IBM i permits what are called members (individually identified files with the same shape as the major file definition) to reside inside of a file structure. A source file then is a normal IBM i database file that is shaped so that it is a natural for storing source. Each source program that you write in RPG/400 for example would be stored in a sub-object called a member which is a component of a file. The file is stored in a library.

PDM then is a list manager that can work with lists of libraries, objects including file, and members and it can help you create objects and run programs on the system. To be a programmer on System i, you must understand PDM and the source editor, SEU.

References:
The AS/400 & IBM I RPG & RPGIV Developers Guide
A slide set for this book is available at www.letsgopublish.com/files
The IBM i Pocket Developer's Guide
http://publib.boulder.ibm.com/pubs/html/as400/online/v4r5eng.htm
http://publib.boulder.ibm.com/infocenter/IBM i/v5r4/index.jsp
http://publib.boulder.ibm.com/infocenter/IBM i/v6r1m0/index.jsp
http://www.ibm.com/support/knowledgecenter/ssw_ibm_i_71/welcome.html

The first IBM Link above takes you to the V4R1 (Version 4, Release 1) Soft Copy Library. Green screen oriented programmer development manuals have not been substantially changed since V4R5. IBM suggests these tools are stable and new development in IBM i programming tools is dedicated towards the GUI WebSphere Development Studio Client - WDSC package. Thus, these manuals are not included in IBM's Web based Infocenter, where all current manuals are kept.

So, if you looked for these on your own, it would be really hard to find them. Once you get to this site, click on "Search or View All V4R5 books. This will take you to a list of books that you can scan. Or, instead of scanning, to get to the Program Development Manager Manual (PDM), for example, type in PDM in the search Window and it will fetch you the PDM manual from the IBM site. To find the Source Entry Utility Editor (SEU), type SEU and likewise for Screen Design Aid (SDA), and Data File Utility (DFU). Without purchasing any of my books or anybody else's you have more than enough information to look up anything that you may not understand in this tutorial / Lab Exercises.

The second and third and fourth IBM Link above takes you to the IBM InfoCenter where all current manuals are kept (Link 2 = V5R4 and Link 3 = V6R1 and Link 4 = V7R1). Take any of these links to find any of the RPG manuals. The RPGIV manuals are referred to as ILE RPG and the regular RPG manuals are RPG/400.

When you get to the InfoCenter scroll down the left side until you see Programming. Open this up until you see RPG. Pick RPG and you will see ILE RPG and RPG/400. Pick each in turn. There are two main RPG manuals for each link. There is the RPG Reference guide which you use to look things up and find out what they do and how you code them. There is also the RPG Users Guide which teaches you how to do specific things in RPG. When you find any operations or code in the labs that you do not understand or need more information about, go to this manual and the information is definitely

When I wrote the <u>AS/400 & IBM i RPG and RPGIV Developers Guide</u>, it was almost 1000 pages in a 5.5 X 8.5 footprint. I had once thought that I could condense all of this information in these manuals into a three or four hundred page book. I could not. This Tutorial/Lab Guide is the Lab Guide for a very comprehensive book that I wrote called the System i Pocket RPG and RPGIV Guide in its first iteration. In its new incarnation, it is called AS/400 & <u>IBM i RPG and RPGIV Developers' Guide</u> The Guide contains just about all you need to know to become pretty good in RPG and RPGIV.. IBM manuals provide everything you need to know but they are not instructional in nature.

This Tutorial book contains what you need to know to be able to accomplish most of the tasks that an RPG programmer needs to do every day without overwhelming you. Along with the PowerPoint slide sets, the question bank, the RPGOBJ Lab library that is included and the <u>RPG and RPGIV Developers' Guide</u>, you have a full complement of materials to learn or to teach RPG and RPGIV in your shop. Therefore, there is lots about RPG that is not in this tutorial book because it is designed to teach you how to get started as an RPG programmer. From there you can grow your knowledge. The intention of this book therefore, is to gently teach and exercise very specific skills to get you on board as quickly as possible.

Lab 1 System i Development Familiarity

Lab 1 Exercise 1
Introduction to Traditional Development

Objective: Introduce the student to the look and feel of IBM i traditional interface and a sample application set.

The IBM i operating system is multi-user. It is not client server. Instead of a PC talking to a Windows server with special Windows software, the PC uses a special package on IBM i systems known as IBM i Access. It was formerly known as Client Access. Among many other tools, there is what IBM calls an emulator included in the toolset icons for IBM i Access. This permits your PC to talk to the IBM i system in much the same way as if it were a native terminal physically connected to the machine.

Thus, In most cases, already on your PC, there will be an icon that may say AS400 or IBM i, System i, or Power System with IBM i. If none of these are there look for an icon that says IBM i Series Access for Windows. It is the same thing. It may be small picture symbolizing the system or it can be a nice big blue icon that you have to click to get to the IBM 5250 emulator. . If this does not exist on your PC, ask your system administrator to arrange your PC so that it does exist.

If you can access the system from home, you can download what is called a TN5250 emulation package from the Internet. In this case, you will have to establish your own desktop icon for it. You will also have to plug into the emulator the IP address for your system or the DNS (domain name) such as *system.mygreatcompany.com* so that your PC can reach the IBM i system.

Some sites for downloads if your PC does not use IBM IBM i Access:

http://tn5250.sourceforge.net/
http://www.freedownloadmanager.org/downloads/tn5250_software/)
http://www.freedownloadscenter.com/Best/free-tn5250.html

Once you launch your TN5250 emulator, whether it is part of IBM i Access or anybody's TN5250 program, and your administrator has set up the labs as noted in Lecture A, you are ready to go.

Start this lab by connecting to the AS/400 (System i or IBM i) from your college or university lab machines, your companyPC, or your at home personal unit. If you are taking this as part of a class, and you may ultimately work off campus. First sign on to a campus machine so you know what to expect when you try to make this environment work at home or from your office. If you are taking this course at your office or using your office IBM i system, again, it would be better to sign on locally first.

Your instructor or your system administrator will give you a user id and a password. Sign on with your user profile and password to replace YOURID and YOURPASSWD in Figure 1-1 below: This should be all you need to get going

Figure 1-1 Sign on Screen

```
                            Sign On
                                      System  . . . . . :   YOURSYS
                                      Subsystem . . . . :   QBASE
                                      Display . . . . . :   BONZO1


        User  . . . . . . . . . . . . .     YOURID
        Password  . . . . . . . . . . .     YOURPASSWD
        Program/procedure . . . . . . .
        Menu  . . . . . . . . . . . . .
        Current library . . . . . . . .
```

Press Enter after typing your information in Figure 1-1 and the next panel will appear very similar to that shown immediately below in Figure 1-2.

Figure 1-2 Display of Sample Library List

```
                        Display Library List
                                              System:   YOURSYS
Type options, press Enter.
  5=Display objects in library
                            ASP
Opt  Library      Type    Device      Text
     QSYS         SYS                 System Library
     QSYS2        SYS                 System Library for CPI's
     QHLPSYS      SYS
     QUSRSYS      SYS                 System Library for Users
     YOURLIB      CUR
     QGPL         USR                 General Purpose Library
     QTEMP        USR

                                                            Bottom
F3=Exit    F12=Cancel    F17=Top    F18=Bottom
(C) COPYRIGHT IBM CORP. 1980, 2005.
```

This is the first panel you see. The next set of screens including this one come about because I wrote a program called RPGSTART and it first walks you through a series of displays such as the one in Figure 1-2. If you were to type a command in on the IBM i command line to see this panel, you would type DSPLIBL, and then hit ENTER. This command is called display library list.

YOURLIB is shown in the middle of the panel, your ID will appear since each student will have his / her own library. Notice that there is a "CUR" following YOURLIB. This signifies that your library is the current library. Since a library is like a directory, your current library is much like your home directory. Whatever objects you place in this library, the system will be able to find them for you, based on your sign-on information. As you will soon see, there are lots of objects already placed in your library when you begin the machine exercises.

When you press ENTER your next panel will look like the one below in Figure 1-3. This is the second panel shown by the RPGSTART program.

Figure 1-3 Continue Decision Panel

```
                    Marywood University RPG Class


    Hello Mr. / MS.    STUDENTNAME



        Do You want to continue? (Y or N)        Y
```

Type a Y in the blank space to continue. As you can see, the Y is already filled in above. If you want to exit the process and sign off, type an "N."

Press ENTER and you will see the panel in Figure 1-4.

Figure 1-4 The RPG Programming Menu with no options selected

```
RPGMENU                        RPG Programming Menu

 Select one of the following:

      1. Work with output queue
      2. Refresh Files After Creation
      3. Start PDM
      4. Start SQL
      5. Display Library List
      6. Run AS/400 Query
      7. Display Submitted Jobs
      8. Start Screen Design Aid (SDA)
      9.
     10. Run Some Programs
     11. Signoff
Selection or command
 ===> _____
 F3=Exit    F4=Prompt    F9=Retrieve    F12=Cancel
 F13=Information Assistant  F16=AS/400 main menu
```

This is your RPG GREEN Screen Main Menu for this tutorial / lab. This menu object is part of the tutorial lab system downloadable from the Internet.

Let me walk you through the options now very briefly. Most of these options will be used in this course.

1. Work with output queue

An output queue is like a windows print queue. In Windows, you find out that such a thing exists when you have a printer malfunction and the things you printed are still there. In my classes I print nothing. Students thus need access to their own queue to be able to see the result of their work. When you pick this option, you get to see what happened when you selected a compile option.

2. Refresh Files after Creation

In some early labs, we intentionally wipe out files and data and this option restores them.

3. Start PDM

This is how you invoke the Program Development Manager

4. Start SQL

If your instructor gives you RPG/SQL assignments, this option will help. These assignments are advanced and are not included with this tutorial.

5. Display Library List

This will produce a display whenever you want similar to the one you see when you sign on (Figure 1-2)

6. Run AS/400 Query

Some of the early Labs use AS/400 Query to show you how to get formatted printouts of database data. Pick this option to do that.

7. Display Submitted Jobs

If your system administrator chooses not to permit compiles interactively, this option will show you the work that you have done and form this option, you can see your compile printouts.

8. Start Screen Design Aid (SDA)

When you get to the interactive RPG assignments, you will need to use this tool to build screen panels.

9.

10. Run Some Programs

There are three programs that can be run here and this option is requested in early labs.

11. Signoff

When you are ready to wrap it up and go home, sign off the system using this option.

In this exercise (lab 1 Exercise 1), you will use the Program Development Manager (PDM) to compile a number of items and to run a few programs. The purpose is to familiarize the student with the most common development environment on an IBM i system. Though a GUI development environment is available as noted in the lectures, it requires a very fat client and it also requires significantly more instructions to understand how to use it. Therefore, we will use the timeless green screen oriented IBM Program Development Manager for this course.

There is an IBM GUI Development Environment which may be installed on the Education / Lab systems. It is called WDSc. You can alternatively use this to make changes to programs and databases. The green screen panels that you will see when you run these programs may be converted in other courses to run in a Web environment under WebSphere. Because every IBM i system has RPG and the PDM tools, and most programmers still use them, we have opted to focus on this non-GUI style as a teaching tool.

Figure 1-5 RPG Menu with Option 10 selected to run sample programs

```
RPGMENU                         RPG Programming Menu

  Select one of the following:

        1. Work with output queue
        2. Refresh Files After Creation
        3. Start PDM
        4. Start SQL
        5. Display Library List
        6. Run AS/400 Query
        7. Display Submitted Jobs
        8. Start Screen Design Aid (SDA)
        9.
       10. Run Some Programs
       11. Signoff

  Selection or command
  ===>10_____

  F3=Exit    F4=Prompt    F9=Retrieve    F12=Cancel
```

Start the first option:

Select option 10 from the panel in Figure 1-5 and press Enter. You will return to the above panel in Figure 1-5, after you pick option 10 to run the three programs that are already in

your library. In this exercise, you will delete these objects by recreating them and you will
notice a big difference when you run them

Run Sequence for Programs

You will come back later in this exercise to this panel to run the programs again after you
recreate the objects in the below exercises. You will also return to run the programs after
you refresh the files using a menu option. Thus, you will see this panel three times to
successfully complete the Lab exercise

Select option 10 by typing it in as above. You will be taken to the panel as shown in Figure
1-6 below:

Figure 1-6, The Program Launch Screen

```
                        Marywood University RPG Class

  Hello Mr.  /  MS.    YOURUSERID


         Want to run    GRNCLIENT1? (Y or N)          Y



         Want to run    HELLOAR001? (Y or N)          Y



         Want to run    HELLOAC001? (Y or N)          Y
```

Type "Y" for each of the options to run the programs. In other words, type "Y" three times
as shown in the above panel. One at a time, each program will start and present a panel to
you. In this scenario, you asked for three programs to run, including GRNCLIENT1. You
may run them one at time also which is preferred. Place a Y next to GRNCLIENT1, Enter;
then HELLOAR001, Enter; then HELLOAC001with a final press Enter.

Please note that when you place a Y to run each program at once, all three programs will
run... but one at a time. It may be difficult for you to understand while this is happening
when one program ends and another program begins. Please remember that all of these
programs end (one at a time so this happens 3 times) by your pressing Function Key 03 on
your PC keyboard. These programs are **not** controlled by your mouse.

The first program, named GRNCLIENT1 represents an application that we call Download
INC. This is a green screen version of what could be a Web program. In a WebSphere /
WebFacing course this program would provide a good sample to be converted to a
WebFacing program.

The essence of GRNCLIENT1, which is not very pretty in its green screen form, is to accept new registrants, such as you, from the Web to be able to use the Download Inc Application. Even if you have not registered, you can press F9 and you will see a list of the database of people and companies who have something to offer for downloading. Do not spend any time registering for a more full use of this program. It will be confusing. So, just hit F9 to see a piece of the database. Use the page up and page down keys to roll through the data. Then, hit F3 twice to end the program. Now, you should be in the first of two Hello World panels. We'll come back here shortly.

Granted, the GRNCLIENT1 application is a little hoaxy but it has many of the ingredients of a typical Web application in that if you registered then later, you could log in to be able to access restricted functions. If you registered and logged in, you could then use your user id and password to add or change or delete customers (download places) from the big database. DO not do this but be aware that these functions exist and this program is written in RPG.

The ENTER key has little facility in this application. For example, if you click F10 to Log In, you would get the Login Panel. After you log in, you could press ENTER, instead of F10 again. The same panel will appear with your information blanked out. The analyst designed this program so that you must hit F10 on the Login Panel in order to Log in. Enter will not do it.   Registration and other panels are similar in behavior. In the WebSphere course, when this application is WebFaced and prepared to run on the Web, the Function keys become buttons to be clicked and this makes more sense for a Web application. Anyway, you should be looking at the first Advanced Hello World Panel Now. You may recall that you put in 3 Y's.

The second Y For program named HELLOAR001 is an RPG language version of a program that we call Advanced Hello World. From time immemorial, programmers have written Hello World programs to test their skills in new programming languages. Advanced Hello World is very simple but more advanced than the original hello world. It has a small database file with language names for FRENCH, SPANISH, and GERMAN, and it has a language not found routine so it knows if you typed correctly. It also has what we AS/400 developers call a display file to make the program interactive. When you use this program, type in the three languages and then type in a fourth language that is not on file and watch what happens

Most AS/400 programs end with F3 so that's how you end these.

The third program runs exactly the same as the second. However, it is a different program completely. It is a program named HELLOAC001. Again, this program (third "Y" does the same exact thing as HELLOAR001 (second "Y"). However, it is written in COBOL. It does use the exact same display file to interact with the screen panel and it uses the same LANGUAGE database file.

Feel free to exercise this program as you did the RPG version.

In fact, feel free to exercise each program until you feel comfortable with the notion of green screen applications. If you get messed up in the GRNCLIENT1 program, don't feel bad, it has a very rigid set of rules. Remember that you will be asked to run three programs in this exercise.

When you have had enough of each program, press F3. When you press F3 the first time, if you have selected all three programs, you will see the initial panel of the next program. Since program 2 and three use the same panel, be careful that you don't forget that you hit the F3 key already.

If you have not typed in a Y for each program, then the program processing the "Y's" will run as many (up to three) programs as you selected. If you select one program for example, each time that you press F3, you will be taken back to the main RPG menu that got you there.

When you come back to the RPG menu SHOWN in Figure 1-5 above, and you have exercised (run) each program, type a "3" (in place of the 10 as shown) to run PDM. Press ENTER and you will see a panel similar to that shown in Figure 1-7 below:

Figure 1-7 System i PDM MAIN PANEL

```
                AS/400 Programming Development Manager (PDM)

Select one of the following:

     1. Work with libraries
     2. Work with objects
     3. Work with members

     9. Work with user-defined options




Selection or command
===> 2

F3=Exit        F4=Prompt        F9=Retrieve         F10=Command entry
F12=Cancel     F18=Change defaults
                           (C) COPYRIGHT IBM CORP. 1981, 2002.
```

Working with Objects in PDM

From the PDM Main panel as shown in Figure 1-7, take option 2 by typing 2 at the bottom and pressing ENTER. You will see the panel as shown in Figure 1-8 below:

Figure 1-8 PDM Panel to Specify Objects

```
                       Specify Objects to Work With

  Type choices, press Enter.

     Library  . . . . . . . . . .    *CURLIB    *CURLIB, name

     Object:
       Name . . . . . . . . . . .    *ALL       *ALL, name, *generic*
       Type . . . . . . . . . . .    *ALL       *ALL, *type
       Attribute  . . . . . . . .    *ALL       *ALL, attribute, *generic*,
                                                *BLANK
```

When you get this panel, look at it and then after digestion, press ENTER and it will show the first page of all the objects in your current library.

FYI: A library is very much like a folder or a directory on PCs. It contains objects

There are many types of objects, including files, programs, output queues, etc.

If an object is a physical database file, it can "contain" thousands of members, just as DOS directories can contain subdirectories and Windows folders can contain subfolders. So, a file in some ways resembles a subdirectory or subfolder and the members to which it points actually contain the data records. You will see soon that a file named SOURCE has many smaller files called members.

Most files, such as the customer file would have just one member containing the customer data records. However, database files may contain many members. An invoice file, for example can be set up for 2010, and theoretically may contain one member for each of the days of the year (365 or 366 members). This file could be processed as one file with all member records being accessible or one member at a time can be processed, at the programmer's discretion.

There are special uses for certain database files called Source files. For these IBM pre defines the file with three different fields or data elements. These are (1) date, (2) the data or program information, and (3) the date last changed. The file named SOURCE that you are about to work with is such a file. It has a number of different members that are visible with the Work with Members panel..

After you hit the ENTER key on the panel in Figure 1-8, you will be taken to a panel very similar to that shown in Figure 1-9. The items on the list will not be the same since your author and your instructor have been adding things to your library since the time that this panel represented all the objects that you would see. However, these objects are in your library along with a lot of others. To view all of the objects, page down and after a few screens, you will come across all of the objects as shown in this panel. Please note that type *PGM or programs come before type *FILE. Prior to the sample solutions for all of your programming applications being built in your library by your author or your instructor, there

were just not as many programs. Now, there are many. Scroll down until you see
CUSTOML3 on your screen panel similar to that shown in Figure 1-9.

Figure 1-9 Work with Objects - Delete the Logical File CUSTOML3

```
               Work with Objects Using PDM              YOURSYS

Library . . . . .    YOURLIB        Position to . . . . . . . .
                                    Position to type  . . . . .

Type options, press Enter.
  2=Change        3=Copy         4=Delete      5=Display      7=Rename
  8=Display description          9=Save       10=Restore     11=Move ...

Opt  Object       Type         Attribute    Text
     GRNCLIENT1   *PGM         RPGLE
     HELLOAR001   *PGM         RPG          Advanced Hello World, RPG/400, Pgm1,
     CUSTAUTH     *FILE        PF-DTA       Customer Download Authentication File
     CUSTOMER     *FILE        PF-DTA       Customer physical file (used to compi
     CUSTOMER1    *FILE        PF-DTA       Customer physical file (used to compi
  4  CUSTOML3     *FILE        LF           Customer file by customer number
     GREENSCRN    *FILE        DSPF
     LANGUAGE     *FILE        PF-DTA       LANGUAGE File For Hello World
                                                                    More...
Parameters or command
===>
F3=Exit          F4=Prompt          F5=Refresh          F6=Create
F9=Retrieve      F10=Command entry  F23=More options    F24=More keys
```

These are a lot of objects already in your library as you can see. Some of them, you will be
recreating in Labs. Do not proceed until you see a panel similar to Figure 1-9. A number of
these files and programs will be replaced in this exercise. Also, make note that the panel
above says, "Work with Objects," and not "Work with Members." This is a key point to
understanding PDM and also IBM i.

By placing a 4 next to the CUSTOML3 file, you will prepare to delete it. When you hit the
enter key, it will be deleted. But not yet! Notice the LF next to *FILE next to CUSTOML3.
This says that this is a *FILE object but it is a logical file (LF) and not a physical file (PF).
Logical files can perform the same functions in RPG programs as physical files.
Programmers or DB administrators create logical files to make the underlying data in the
physical file easier to use.

For example if the physical file named CUSTOMER upon which this logical file is based,
did not have a key of say customer number (which btw, it does.), the programmer or DB
administrator could create a logical file (a.k.a. logical view or simply view) that placed a key
on the file -- in the fashion of an alternate index. So, an RPG programmer needing to process
the CUSTOMER file by key would use the CUSTOML3 file instead in her program -- rather
than the CUSTOMER file. It would behave as if the key were actually on the CUSTOMER
file.

It's OK if you delete it. We will shortly recreate it. So, type a 4 next to CUSTOML3 now
but do not hit ENTER yet. Instead, hit the page down key on your PC keyboard to see more

objects. The "4" will still be there but you won't see it. Your panel will look like that shown below in Figure 1-10 (without the 12):

Figure 1-10 Preparing to Work With Members of "SOURCE" File

```
              Work with Objects Using PDM                    YOURSYS

Library . . . . .   YOURLIB          Position to . . . . . . . .
                                     Position to type  . . . . .

Type options, press Enter.
  2=Change         3=Copy          4=Delete        5=Display       7=Rename
  8=Display description            9=Save         10=Restore      11=Move ...

Opt  Object      Type       Attribute    Text
__   PANEL       *FILE      DSPF         Display File Panel For Advanced Hello
__   QCBLSRC     *FILE      PF-SRC       FILE FOR COBOL SOURCE
__   QDDSSRC     *FILE      PF-SRC       dds source
__   QRPGLESRC   *FILE      PF-SRC       Longer SRC
__   QRPGSRC     *FILE      PF-SRC       RPG Source
__   REGFILE     *FILE      PF-DTA       Web users
12   SOURCE      *FILE      PF-SRC       Source File For Marywood Students
__   SOURCEBU    *FILE      PF-SRC       BU Source File For Marywood Students
                                                                      Bottom
Parameters or command
===>_____

F3=Exit            F4=Prompt           F5=Refresh           F6=Create
F9=Retrieve        F10=Command entry   F23=More options     F24=More keys
```

Work with Members from Work with objects

Type in the 12 as shown above next to the word SOURCE and hit the ENTER key once. Keep in mind that you have placed a 12 (work with) next to your SOURCE file. PDM will execute one line command at a time in sequence. Since it encounters the 4 (delete) command first, the next panel you see looks very similar to that shown below:

Figure 1-11 Delete Confirmation while Preparing to Work With Members of "SOURCE"

```
                    Confirm Delete of Objects

  Library . . . . . . . :   YOURLIB

  Press Enter to confirm your choices for Delete.
  Press F12=Cancel to return to change your choices.

  Object      Type       Attribute    Text
  CUSTOML3    *FILE      LF           Customer file by customer number




                                                          Bottom
  F12=Cancel            F19=Submit to batch
```

When you see this panel, you may hit the ENTER key again. This action will delete the object CUSTOML3, selected with (4) on the prior panel. Now, remember that you selected to work with the SOURCE file above by placing a 12 next to it. PDM remembers that you entered two commands. When the delete (4) is completed, PDM will execute the work with command against the SOURCE File.

The next thing you see will be the *Work with Members* Panel for the SOURCE file that you picked above. It no longer says, "Work with Objects."

Important: This did not just happen for no reason at all.   It happened because you placed a 12 next to SOURCE above. The Work with Members panel will appear and show you what is in the SOURCE file and permit you to work with any of the members of that source file.

So, from the Work with objects screen, you selected an object, SOURCE, a file, and you asked to work with it by typing in an option 12. SOURCE contains members so, by placing the 12 next to the SOURCE file and pressing the ENTER key you cause the action to occur. Option 12 therefore takes you on a trip inside the SOURCE database file.

Since a source file is always created by IBM I default to be able to contain multiple members, and your author and/or your instructor have loaded this source file up with database descriptions as well as RPG program source, your trip inside the source file should be quite adventurous. You will find a number of data definitions and source programs as shown in Figure 1-12.

Figure 1-12 Work with Members in SOURCE File

```
                    Work with Members Using PDM              YOURSYS

File  . . . . . .      SOURCE
   Library . . . .     YOURLIB                 Position to  . . . . . .

Type options, press Enter.
  2=Edit           3=Copy  4=Delete 5=Display        6=Print      7=Rename
  8=Display descr  9=Save  13=Change text  14=Compile  15=Create module...


Opt   Member      Type        Text
5     CUSTAUTH    PF          Customer Download Authentication File
_     CUSTOMER    PF          Customer physical file
_     CUSTOMER1   PF          Customer phys file (used to compile customer)
_     CUSTOML3    LF          Customer file by customer number
_     GREENSCRN   DSPF
_     GRNCLICOPY  RPGLE       COPY of program from WFACE
_     GRNCLIENT1  RPGLE
_     HELLOAC001  CBL         COBOL VERIFICATION PROGRAM
                                                              More...
Parameters or command
===>_____


F3=Exit           F4=Prompt           F5=Refresh          F6=Create
F9=Retrieve       F10=Command entry   F23=More options    F24=More keys
```

Check Out Some Members!

The overall objective of this next phase is for you to review the source objects in your library according to a list that is presented below. Upon reviewing the source objects (by placing a 5 next to each member noted, you will observe the contents of the source member used to create the object originally. In other words, the SOURCE file contains the descriptions and source rules for a number of to-be-created or re-created objects. Option 5 opens the object for viewing just like clicking on a word document opens up Word. Option 2 opens it for editing but let's not do that now.

This exercise is easy but it will take you some time to complete because you will be learning about a structure that is unlike any with which you have ever worked unless you are already a System i expert. For each member in the SOURCE file, open it up by placing a 5 next to it, one at a time, and then press ENTER.   Start with CUSTAUTH as shown below in Figure 1-12. Place a 5 next to it and press ENTER. You will then see a panel similar to the one shown below for CUSTAUTH and for each other member that you select with option 5. Again do one at a time.

While you are completing this exercise remember that all of the members you are examining are in the Source file which you opened by placing a 12 next to it and pressing the Enter key. You can also look at members by choosing option 3 on the Main PDM menu as shown in Figure 1-7. Option 3 is the way you will typically get into the Work with members mode but there is nothing wrong with coming in with an option 12 (open) on the source file that you choose from the Work with Objects list panel.

Remember your assignment is to open up and review the source statements in each of the source members in the source file named SOURCE. So, if you started with CUSTAUTH, your members' panel would look similar to that shown in Figure 1-12. Option 5 says to display the source member. It does not permit you to change the source member. Option 2 does permit you to change the member while you are looking at it but there is no need for that right now and it might mess you up in future labs so do not select option 2 against any of the members right now.

Since you will be looking up lots of members, you will see Figure 1-12 many times during this process. You will repeat option 5 on each individual descriptor until you see all of the members in the file. Once you take option 5 and hit enter, depending on which member you select, the contents will be different. For example, when you select CUSTAUTH (option 5) and Enter, SEU will open up in display mode and show you the contents of CUSTAUTH, which happens to be the data definition for the CUSTAUTH file.

To repeat for effect, please notice the very top line of this panel compared with the last panel you saw like this (Figure 1-10). This (Figure 1-12) says Work with Members. The last PDM panel said Work with Objects (Figure 1-10). (If you want to go back to the last panel, hit F12 and then take option 12 on SOURCE again.) In Figure 1-12, you are looking at the members that are stored in the object file named SOURCE that is in your library.

Now, when you press ENTER, because you typed a 5 next to CUSTAUTH, you will be taken to the panel as shown in Figure 1-13 below:

Figure 1-13 --- What's Inside the CUSTAUTH Member of SOURCE File

```
Columns . . . :   1  71            Browse                    MWOOD/SOURCE
 SEU==>                                                         CUSTAUTH
 FMT A*  .....A*. 1 ...+... 2 ...+... 3 ...+... 4 ...+... 5 ...+... 6 ...+... 7
        *************** Beginning of data *********************************
0001.00    A* DOWNLOAD INC. CUSTOMER AUTHORIZATION FILE
0002.00    A           R CUSTAUTR
0003.00    A             CUST#         7              COLHDG('Customer numbe
0004.00    A             CONAME        40             COLHDG('Company name')
0005.00    A             USERNAME      30             COLHDG('Name')
0006.00    A             USID          8              COLHDG('User Id')
0007.00    A             PASWD         8              COLHDG('Password')
0008.00    A             AUTHQ         70             COLHDG('Authent Quest.
0009.00    A             AUTHR         70             COLHDG('Authent Respon
0010.00    A           K CUST#
        **************** End of data ***********************************
```

If this member had more than 10 statements, it would have a *more* indicator in the bottom right. If this were the case, as in RPG and COBOL source programs also, you would be able to page down to see the next page.

This is not an RPG program. It is a database definition using DDS that is already built in your SOURCE file. You can get a sense of what type of database file this is by reading the field names (names of data elements) and the column headings on the right side. This is the way databases are described on the System i without using SQL. In other words, a programmer or DB administrator types those field names and definitions into a source member in a source file as you are observing.

Though we are not teaching database concepts in this RPG tutorial / lab, you will be working with various pre-built databases in this tutorial / lab set. Figure 1-13 shows the DDS statements that were typed in by the original developer to define the CUSTAUTH (customer authorization) file.

Press F3 when you have seen enough of the CUSTAUTH database description. Please note that what you are looking at, is not the CUSTAUTH database. However, it is the source description of the CUSTAUTH database as typed in by the programmer.

When the developer chooses to create this database, they would select the create object (option 14) in PDM (We'll show you later) and this would actually create the CUSTAUTH database with no records (no data). It would have the fields as shown in the panel above.

So, the description of the database as typed by the programmer and shown in Panel 1-13 is not the database. However, it is the means that the programmer has to tell the database compiler on the server what the exact shape the CUSTAUTH database is to be when it is created.

So, let's take F3 now to exit the Source Entry Utility Display. When you hit F3, you are taken back to the Work with Members panel shown in Figure 1-14.

Panel 1-14 Work with Members in SOURCE File

```
              Work with Members Using PDM              YOURSYS

File . . . . . .    SOURCE
  Library . . . .   YOURLIB            Position to . . . . .

Type options, press Enter.
 2=Edit        3=Copy  4=Delete 5=Display      6=Print      7=Rename
 8=Display descr  9=Save  13=Change text  14=Compile  15=Create module...

Opt  Member      Type       Text
 __  CUSTAUTH    PF         Customer Download Authentication File
 __  CUSTOMER    PF         Customer physical file
 __  CUSTOMER1   PF         Customer phys file (used to compile customer)
 __  CUSTOML3    LF         Customer file by customer number
 __  GREENSCRN   DSPF
 __  GRNCLICOPY  RPGLE      COPY of program from WFACE
 __  GRNCLIENT1  RPGLE
 __  HELLOAC001  CBL        COBOL VERIFICATION PROGRAM
                                                              More...
Parameters or command
===>  _____

F3=Exit         F4=Prompt        F5=Refresh        F6=Create
F9=Retrieve     F10=Command entry F23=More options  F24=More keys
```

Before we do anything more, press F18 (upper shift and a 6) You will see the panel shown in Figure 1-15.

Figure 1-15 Change PDM Defaults for your session

```
                     Change Defaults
Type choices, press Enter.

  Object library . . . . . . .    *SRCLIB      Name, *CURLIB, *SRCLIB
  Replace object . . . . . . .    N            Y=Yes, N=No
  Compile in batch . . . . .     N            Y=Yes, N=No
  Run in batch . . . . . . .     N            Y=Yes, N=No
  Save session defaults . . .    Y            Y=Yes, N=No
  Save/Restore option . . . .    1            1=Single, 2=All
  Job description . . . . . .    QBATCH       Name, *USRPRF, F4 for list
    Library . . . . . . . . .      *LIBL      Name, *CURLIB, *LIBL
  Change type and text . . . .   Y            Y=Yes, N=No
  Option file . . . . . . . .    QAUOOPT      Name
    Library . . . . . . . . .      QGPL       Name, *CURLIB, *LIBL
  Member . . . . . . . . . . .    QAUOOPT      Name
  Full screen mode . . . . . .    N            Y=Yes, N=No
                                                      More...
F3=Exit     F4=Prompt     F5=Refresh     F12=Cancel
```

As shown above, if your environment permits, change the third line here in "Compile in batch" to "N" as highlighted above, and press Enter. This helps in your debugging of programs. If your system administrator tells you not to do it this way, listen to them since you may be working on a production machine. However, if you are on a test machine, try to convince the administrator to let you make this change.

You will come back to the Work with Members panel as shown below:

*****

Start the repetition here. Look at each source member using the option 5 as shown in Panel 1-12 and Panel 1-16 below. Go through each of the members and see what the contents are and when finished continue from this point in the tutorial / lab exercise.

Figure 1-16 Selection to look inside source members to see the descriptions /programs

```
                        Work with Members Using PDM              YOURSYS

File  . . . . . .      SOURCE
  Library . . . .      YOURLIB                Position to  . . . . .

Type options, press Enter.
 2=Edit          3=Copy  4=Delete 5=Display        6=Print     7=Rename
 8=Display description  9=Save  13=Change text  14=Compile  15=Create module...


Opt  Member       Type       Text
 __   CUSTAUTH     PF         Customer Download Authentication File
 5    CUSTOMER     PF         Customer physical file
 __   CUSTOMER1    PF         Customer physical file (used to compile customer)
 __   CUSTOML3     LF         Customer file by customer number
 __   GREENSCRN    DSPF
 __   GRNCLICOPY   RPGLE      COPY of program from WFACE
 __   GRNCLIENT1   RPGLE
 __   HELLOAC001   CBL        COBOL VERIFICATION PROGRAM


                                                              More...
Parameters or command
===>
F3=Exit          F4=Prompt           F5=Refresh          F6=Create
F9=Retrieve      F10=Command entry   F23=More options    F24=More keys
```

Since you already done with CUSTAUTH, now let's look at the description of the Customer database description by placing a 5 next to it as in Figure 1-16 and continue by pressing the ENTER key. After reviewing all of the source members using this process, you will be back to the panel in Figure 1-16. In between, you will have completed a lot of work.

Pay special attention to the contents of the following program source members:

GRNCLIENT1 -- The big Download Inc RPG program
HELLOAR001 -- The Small Hello World Program in RPG
HELLOAC001 -- The Small Hello World Program in COBOL

The HELLOAR001 (RPG) and HELLOAC001 (COBOL) program perform the same Advanced Hello World Function. Note how much different a COBOL program is from an RPG program. Note also how much bigger a COBOL program is to perform the same functions. Both this RPG and COBOL program are old style programs so if you happen to show these examples to experts in your company, you may tell them that we are starting at the basics and working up.

There is a major similarity between the RPG and COBOL versions however. Both of them use the same display file. A Display file is a separate System i object that, just like native databases, is built with DDS. The Advanced Hello World panel named GREENSCRN that you can see in Figure 1-16 was built from DDS. There is nothing that prevents a display file from being used in an RPG program and a COBOL program -- even at the same time. Take a look at the display file DDS (source description) and notice that the line and column of the display are coded for each prompt or variable that the program displays.

As an aside, the DDS for display files typically gets created using a facility called Screen Design Aid (SDA). In later labs we will describe SDA and use it to create panels for our later RPG lab programs. Developers paint the screen with the prompts and the variables they want to be depicted on the panel and then the SDA function creates the DDS. This saves lots of keying. Additionally, SDA takes the DDS after it creates it and it builds the display file object in the developer's (your) library.

Table 1 shows the list of members that you should examine in this step – just as you did with CUSTAUTH and CUSTOMER. Place a 5 next to each in PDM and take a look at each. Of course you may look at each member but after looking at all of these, that may be more than enough to have a good feel for this exercise.

Table 1-17 List of members to View and one to recreate

```
Perform Display (option 5) operations on members in this sequence
CUSTAUTH
CUSTOMER
CUSTOML3
LANGUAGE
GREENSCRN
REGFILE
PANEL
HELLOAC001
HELLOAR001
GRNCLIENT1
```

When you type the 5 next to CUSTOMER member in Figure 1-16, you will see a panel such as that shown in Figure 1-18 below

Figure 1-18 Work with Members in SOURCE File

```
. :     1 100                                        Browse

.A*. 1 ...+... 2 ...+... 3 ...+... 4 ...+... 5 ...+... 6 ...+... 7 ...+..
*********** Beginning of data **********************************************
A* CUSTOMER FILE
A          R CUSTOM01
A            CUSTNO        7              COLHDG('Customer' 'Number')
A            CUSTNA        40             COLHDG('Company name')
A            REPNO         5              COLHDG('Sales' 'Rep ID')
A            CONTAC        30             COLHDG('Contact' 'Name')
A            CPHONE        17             COLHDG('Telephone')
A            CFAX          17             COLHDG('Fax')
A            CADDR         40             COLHDG('Address')
A            CADDR1        40             COLHDG('Address1')
A            CCITY         30             COLHDG('City')
A            CSTCD         2              COLHDG('State' 'Code')
A            CCOUNT        20             COLHDG('Country')
A            CZIP          10             COLHDG('ZIP Code')
A            CZIPLO        1              COLHDG('PC location')
A                                         VALUES('1' '2' '3')
A          K CUSTNO
************* End of data **************************************************
```

Press F3 to return to the work with members PDM panel as shown in Figure 1-19.

Figure 1-19 End of look inside source members to see the descriptions /programs

```
                    Work with Members Using PDM              YOURSYS

File . . . . . .     SOURCE
  Library . . . .    YOURLIB              Position to . . . . .

Type options, press Enter.
  2=Edit         3=Copy  4=Delete 5=Display     6=Print       7=Rename
  8=Display description  9=Save  13=Change text  14=Compile  15=Create module...

Opt  Member      Type       Text
     CUSTAUTH    PF         Customer Download Authentication File
     CUSTOMER    PF         Customer physical file
     CUSTOMER1   PF         Customer physical file (used to compile customer)
     CUSTOML3    LF         Customer file by customer number
     GREENSCRN   DSPF
     GRNCLICOPY  RPGLE      COPY of program from WFACE
     GRNCLIENT1  RPGLE
     HELLOAC001  CBL        COBOL VERIFICATION PROGRAM
                                                            More...
Parameters or command
===>
F3=Exit          F4=Prompt              F5=Refresh           F6=Create
F9=Retrieve      F10=Command entry      F23=More options     F24=More keys
```

To repeat the lab instructions for effect, go through each of the other members in the list shown in Table 1-17 above, starting with CUSTOML3 just to see what is in there. In the exact above sequence, place a 5 next to the source member (CUSTAUTH file and CUSTOMER files have been previously selected.) Do this one at a time. To go to the next page of this display file, press Page Down. To come back, press Page Up. As you can see, all of the members cannot be shown on one panel.

Each time that you press ENTER with a 5 next to a member, you will be taken to the browse source facility of the Source Entry Utility (SEU). With this, you will be able to roll through all of the source lines in these data descriptions or source programs.

For your edification, you will be looking at the contents of various different source objects. Some are data descriptions for CUSTAUTH and CUSTOMER and CUSTOML3 and others. GREENSCRN is the DDS of a display file, which has the many panels that you saw before in Figure 1- 6 above. PANEL is the name for a set of DDS in the same fashion as GREENSCRN but much smaller. It is used in the Advanced Hello World program as noted above.

As you may recall, GRNCLIENT1 and HELLOAR001 are RPG programs and HELLOAC001 is a COBOL program. When you look at the source for these programs, you will be able to see a major difference between RPG & COBOL.

Hit F3 when you have viewed your last source description (DDS or RPG or COBOL) to return to the PDM member list as in Panel 14. You may move on to Lab 2.

Lab 2   Working with the Program Development Manager (PDM)

Lab 2 Objectives:

Introduce the student to developing System i traditional applications with the Program Development Manager (PDM).

Lab 2 -- Exercise 1

Recreating Program and File Objects by Re-compiling with PDM

Figure 2-1A Recreate the object by compiling its description from the source member

```
                       Work with Members Using PDM                    YOURSYS

 File  . . . . . .     SOURCE
    Library . . . .        MWOOD            Position to  . . . . .

 Type options, press Enter.
   2=Edit            3=Copy  4=Delete 5=Display        6=Print       7=Rename
   8=Display description  9=Save  13=Change text  14=Compile  15=Create module...

 Opt  Member       Type        Text
 14   CUSTAUTH     PF          Customer Download Authentication File
      CUSTOMER     PF          Customer physical file
      CUSTOMER1    PF          Customer physical file (used to compile customer)
      CUSTOML3     LF          Customer file by customer number
      GREENSCRN    DSPF
      GRNCLICOPY   RPGLE       COPY of program from WFACE
      GRNCLIENT1   RPGLE
      HELLOAC001   CBL         COBOL VERIFICATION PROGRAM
                                                                      More...
 Parameters or command
 ===>
 F3=Exit           F4=Prompt            F5=Refresh          F6=Create
 F9=Retrieve       F10=Command entry    F23=More options    F24=More keys
```

Figure 1-10 shows you how you get to the point in which you were able to examine the panel in Figure 2-1A. However, if you do not come in via a Work with Objects and then an option 12 on the SOURCE file to get you to the Work with members screen, you can take the Work with Members directly as shown in Figure 1-7, You pick option 3 --Work with Members, instead of Option 2 --Work with Objects. This takes you to a panel in which you need to fill in the blanks. It looks like the screen shown in Figure 2-1B

Figure 2-1B Specify Work with members -- Source file Name, Library.

```
                     Specify Members to Work With

  Type choices, press Enter.

      File  . . . . . . . . . .    _____      Name, F4 for list

         Library . . . . . . . .    *LIBL       *LIBL, *CURLIB, name

      Member:
        Name  . . . . . . . . .    *ALL         *ALL, name, *generic*
        Type  . . . . . . . . .    *ALL         *ALL, type, *generic*,
                                                *BLANK
```

Fill in the blanks as in Figure 2-1C and you will be in the SOURCE file, just as you were
back in Figure 1-12

Figure 2-1 C Filled in panel for specifying the SOURCE file and the current library

```
                     Specify Members to Work With

  Type choices, press Enter.

      File  . . . . . . . . .     SOURCE__       Name, F4 for list

         Library . . . . . . .     *CURLIB      *LIBL, *CURLIB, name

      Member:
        Name  . . . . . . . .     *ALL         *ALL, name, *generic*
        Type  . . . . . . . .     *ALL         *ALL, type, *generic*, *BLANK
```

Press ENTER from here and you will be back to Figure 2-1D, which is a repeat of Figure 2-
1A for your convenience.

Figure 2-1D Recreate the object by compiling its description from the source member

```
                    Work with Members Using PDM                    YOURSYS

 File . . . . . .     SOURCE
   Library . . . .    MWOOD              Position to . . . . .

 Type options, press Enter.
  2=Edit        3=Copy  4=Delete 5=Display      6=Print    7=Rename
  8=Display description  9=Save  13=Change text  14=Compile  15=Create module...

 Opt  Member      Type       Text
 14   CUSTAUTH    PF         Customer Download Authentication File
      CUSTOMER    PF         Customer physical file
      CUSTOMER1   PF         Customer physical file (used to compile customer)
      CUSTOML3    LF         Customer file by customer number
      GREENSCRN   DSPF
      GRNCLICOPY  RPGLE      COPY of program from WFACE
      GRNCLIENT1  RPGLE
      HELLOAC001  CBL        COBOL VERIFICATION PROGRAM
                                                                     More...
 Parameters or command
 ===>
 F3=Exit          F4=Prompt          F5=Refresh          F6=Create
 F9=Retrieve      F10=Command entry  F23=More options    F24=More keys
```

For each of the members that you have already viewed above in Figure 2-1D, with option 5, take option 14 to create the object from the source description. You can do them one at a time or all at once.

Take option 14 on CUSTAUTH as shown in Panel 14 and hit ENTER. You will see the following panel:

Figure 2-2 Confirm Compile which will delete the former object and replace it

```
                      Confirm Compile of Member

The following object already exists for the compile operation:

   Object which exists  . . . . . . . . :    CUSTAUTH
      Library . . . . . . . . . . . . . :    MWOOD
   Object type . . . . . . . . . . . . :     *FILE

   Member to compile  . . . . . . . . . :    CUSTAUTH
   File . . . . . . . . . . . . . . . . :     SOURCE
      Library  . . . . . . . . . . . . :     MWOOD

Type choice, press Enter.
Press F12=Cancel to return and not perform the compile operation.

   Delete existing object . . . . . . . .    Y    Y=Yes, N=No












F12=Cancel
```

Where it asks, "Delete existing object…," as shown above, say yes by typing a Y. You will be re-creating the CUSTAUTH file later. It is OK to tell the machine it is OK to get rid of the old one for the labs will guide you to replace it wand repopulate the data later. Please note that if there is data in CUSTAUTH right now. It will be destroyed. For now, this is OK because you will replace it when instructed with the exact directions.

Type the Y for CUSTAUTH and press ENTER. You may delete the other physical file objects also but remember that the data does go away when the object goes away. In other words, take option 14 and in the panel question as shown in Figure 2-2, type a Y even if it is PF type source member. The database physical file creation (compilation) will proceed and you will get comfortable in understanding what this means.

If the data in CUSTAUTH and other files is valuable as in real-life, you would say "NO." But, this is a learning environment and you will refresh this data later as part of the course. Ask your instructor how the refresh will occur if there is one guiding you during your labs. Otherwise, continue Please note that when you take the "Y" for delete, it is not the source member shown in Figure 2-1 that gets deleted, it is the compiled object as shown in Figure 2-2 that is replaced with a new version and the new version has none of the data as the old version.

Figure 2-3– First part of recreation is the deletion – do not normally delete these members!

```
                   Work with Members Using PDM             YOURSYS

File . . . . . .    SOURCE
  Library . . . .   MWOOD                Position to  . . . . .

Type options, press Enter.
 2=Edit           3=Copy   4=Delete 5=Display      6=Print      7=Rename
 8=Display description  9=Save 13=Change text  14=Compile  15=Create module...

Opt  Member      Type        Text
     CUSTAUTH    PF          Customer Download Authentication File
     CUSTOMER    PF          Customer physical file
     CUSTOMER1   PF          Customer physical file (used to compile customer)
     CUSTOML3    LF          Customer file by customer number
     GREENSCRN   DSPF
     GRNCLICOPY  RPGLE       COPY of program from WFACE
     GRNCLIENT1  RPGLE
     HELLOAC001  CBL         COBOL VERIFICATION PROGRAM
                                                             More...
Parameters or command
===>
F3=Exit           F4=Prompt              F5=Refresh           F6=Create
F9=Retrieve       F10=Command entry      F23=More options     F24=More keys
Object CUSTAUTH in YOURLIB type *FILE deleted.                         +
```

Notice at the bottom of the panel that your old file was deleted. If you place the cursor on that message and hit the page down key, you will see the next message which is buried underneath. So, the CUSTAUTH object is deleted when you recreate it from the CUSTAUTH member in SOURCE which contains the data definition. It is important to understand the difference between definitions of data and data base objects. It is the same notion as source and object on other systems. The refreshed panel showing the results of the page down is shown in Figure 2-4 below:

Figure 2-4 CUSTAUTH panel recreated - message

```
                    Work with Members Using PDM              YOURSYS

File . . . . . .      SOURCE
  Library . . . .     MWOOD              Position to  . . . . .


Type options, press Enter.
  2=Edit          3=Copy  4=Delete 5=Display      6=Print      7=Rename
  8=Display description  9=Save  13=Change text  14=Compile  15=Create module...


Opt  Member      Type         Text
     CUSTAUTH    PF           Customer Download Authentication File
     CUSTOMER    PF           Customer physical file
     CUSTOMER1   PF           Customer physical file (used to compile customer)
     CUSTOML3    LF           Customer file by customer number
     GREENSCRN   DSPF
     GRNCLICOPY  RPGLE        COPY of program from WFACE
     GRNCLIENT1  RPGLE
     HELLOAC001  CBL          COBOL VERIFICATION PROGRAM
                                                              More...
Parameters or command
===>
F3=Exit          F4=Prompt          F5=Refresh          F6=Create
F9=Retrieve      F10=Command entry  F23=More options    F24=More keys
File CUSTAUTH created in library YOURLIB.                          +
```

Go back to Figure 2-1D and recreate the next object using the next member (option 5 to view and option 14 to recreate)

Repeat the process. However, please do not recompile CUSTOMER (option 14) or CUSTOML3 (option 14) since there is a logical file involved and there is a precise way of handling this type of recompilation that is beyond the scope of this early RPG Lab exercise. Go through all of the other panels.

Go through all of the other noted source members, if you did not view them in Lab 1, then view them now. Then with option 14, unless PF, create the objects using the techniques shown in panels above, beginning with the panel in which you first placed a 14 next to CUSTAUTH.

When you have finished, press F12 and / or F3 to return to the RPG Programming Menu as shown in Figure 2-5 below.

Keep hitting F12 until you return to the Main eBusiness Menu as shown in Figure 2-5 below:

Lab 2 -- Exercise 2

Run New Programs

Figure 2-5 RPG Programming Menu with Option 10 selected to run sample programs

```
RPGMENU                         RPG Programming Menu

 Select one of the following:

        1. Work with output queue
        2. Refresh Files After Creation
        3. Start PDM
        4. Start SQL
        5. Display Library List
        6. Run AS/400 Query
        7. Work with Submitted Jobs
        8. Start Screen Design Aid (SDA.
        9.
       10. Run Some Programs
       11. Signoff




 Selection or command
 ===> 10

 F3=Exit    F4=Prompt    F9=Retrieve    F12=Cancel
```

To run your programs again, just as we did above, take option 10

When you select option 10 from the RPG Programming Menu, just as above, you will be taken to the panel as shown in Panel 18 below:

Figure 2-6 Running Recompiled Programs with No Data (if you took Y above)

```
                        Marywood University RPG Class

 Hello Mr. / MS.   YOURUSERID




        Want to run   GRNCLIENT1? (Y or N)          Y



        Want to run   HELLOAR001? (Y or N)          Y_



        Want to run   HELLOAC001? (Y or N)          Y_

```

Type "Y" again for each of the options one at a time to run the programs. One at a time, each program will attempt to start and present a panel to you. Document what actually occurs.

If you have completed your exercises to this point properly your applications will not run as they did before because all the files are empty – because you deleted them and recreated them earlier in this Lab 3.

Feel free to exercise each program. When you no longer want to see what the program does, press F3 to come back to the RPG Programming main menu

You should notice a number of things this time.

For example, in Advanced Hello World, the database file has no records so even FRENCH will return a not on file message.

If you registered above, then by recreating the REGISTER file, you are no longer in the file. Even the refresh option (coming up next) will not bring your record back because the program uses a copy of the file taken before you registered.

Lab 2 -- Exercise 3 Refresh Files after Recreation

Now, go back to the RPG Programming Menu as shown below:

Figure 2-7 RPG Programming Menu with Option 2 selected to refresh files

```
RPGMENU                        RPG Programming Menu

 Select one of the following:

      1. Work with output queue
      2. Refresh Files After Creation
      3. Start PDM
      4. Start SQL
      5. Display Library List
      6. Run AS/400 Query
      7. Work with Submitted Jobs
      8. Start Screen Design Aid (SDA.
      9.
     10. Run Some Programs
     11. Signoff




 Selection or command
 ===>  2

 F3=Exit    F4=Prompt    F9=Retrieve    F12=Cancel
```

Select Option 2 in Figure 2-7 and press ENTER to refresh the data into the files that you just created. They will be populated with data again from data copies stored elsewhere on the system. If all data is not refreshed, you may ask your administrator to add those files into the DBRFSH CL program.

Press Enter and after the copies complete, the panel is refreshed and looks again like as in Figure 2-7.

Now, for the third time, try to run the programs. This time you will be using files that you created earlier that have now been re-populated with data (during the refresh). Select Option 10 and follow the procedure as you did the two previous times.

Have fun with this third iteration.

Lab 2 -- Exercise 4 Run a Query/400

Before we move to RPG programming per se, in the next lab, let's run one Query/400 query.

Query/400 is an "almost-end user tool" that permits data to be brought to a report format quite easily.

Start Query/400 by taking option 6 on your RPG Programming Menu as shown in Figure 2-7.

You will see a menu as follows in Figure 2-8.

Figure 2-8 QUERY1 Operation

```
QUERY                        Query Utilities
                                                    System:   YOURSYS
Select one of the following:

  Query for AS/400
     1. Work with queries
     2. Run an existing query
     3. Delete a query

  DB2 for AS/400
    10. Start DB2 Query Manager for AS/400

  Query management
    20. Work with query management forms
    21. Work with query management queries
    22. Start a query
    23. Analyze a Query for AS/400 definition
                                                          More...
Selection or command
===> 1


F3=Exit   F4=Prompt   F9=Retrieve   F12=Cancel   F13=Information Assistant
F16=AS/400 Main menu
(C) COPYRIGHT IBM CORP. 1980, 2002.
```

Take Option 1 and you will be taken to a panel similar to that in Figure 2-9.

Figure 2-9 QUERY2 Operation

```
                      Work with Queries

Type choices, press Enter.

  Option  . . . . . .      1          1=Create, 2=Change, 3=Copy, 4=Delete
                                      5=Display, 6=Print definition
                                      8=Run in batch, 9=Run
  Query . . . . . . .    FIRSTQRY     Name, F4 for list
    Library . . . . .    YOURLIB      Name, *LIBL, F4 for list




3=Exit        F4=Prompt      F5=Refresh      F12=Cancel
                                       (C) COPYRIGHT IBM CORP. 1988
```

Type in FIRSTQRY for name and type your library name and then press ENTER You will see a panel similar to Figure 2-10.

Figure 2-10 QUERY Operation Define the Query Panel

```
                          Define the Query

Query . . . . . . . :     FIRSTQRY         Option . . . . . :     CREATE
  Library . . . . :       YOURLIB          CCSID . . . . . . . :  65535

Type options, press Enter.  Press F21 to select all.
  1=Select


Opt     Query Definition Option
 1      Specify file selections
 _      Define result fields
 1      Select and sequence fields
 1      Select records
 1      Select sort fields
 _      Select collating sequence
 _      Specify report column formatting
 _      Select report summary functions
 _      Define report breaks
 _      Select output type and output form
 _      Specify processing options


F3=Exit            F5=Report            F12=Cancel
F13=Layout         F18=Files            F21=Select all
```

Place 1s as shown in Figure 2-10 and press Enter. Remember the words next to the ones because the reason you will see the next set of panels is because of those 1s. As you can see, the last 1 is for sorting instructions.

Figure 2-11 QUERY4 Operation File Selections

```
                      Specify File Selections

 Type choices, press Enter.  Press F9 to specify an additional
   file selection.

     File . . . . . . . . . .     customer      Name, F4 for list
       Library  . . . . . .       yourlib       Name, *LIBL, F4 for list
     Member . . . . . . . .       *FIRST        Name, *FIRST, F4 for list
     Format . . . . . . . .       *FIRST        Name, *FIRST, F4 for list


 F3=Exit          F4=Prompt        F5=Report          F9=Add file
 F12=Cancel       F13=Layout       F24=More keys
```

Fill in your screen as above in Figure 2-11 and press ENTER (substitute your library for YOURLIB). This picks the customer file from yourlib (change accordingly) and it uses the first member (typically only 1 member in a DB file) and it uses the first format. Only logical files have multiple formats.

When you do as instructed, the system will go inside the database to get information and it will display the member and the format name (already filled in.) Press ENTER again. You will see the next panel

Figure 2-12 QUERY5 Operation

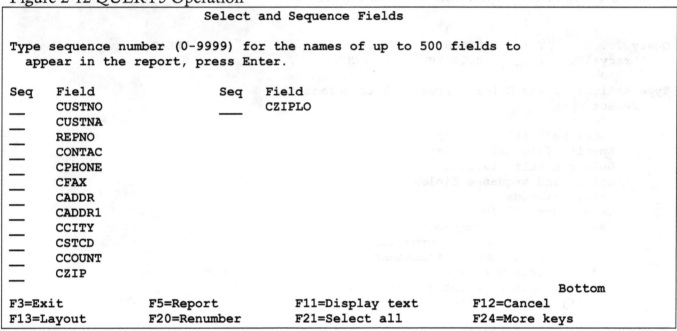

```
                    Select and Sequence Fields

Type sequence number (0-9999) for the names of up to 500 fields to
  appear in the report, press Enter.

Seq    Field                Seq    Field
___    CUSTNO               ___    CZIPLO
___    CUSTNA
___    REPNO
___    CONTAC
___    CPHONE
___    CFAX
___    CADDR
___    CADDR1
___    CCITY
___    CSTCD
___    CCOUNT
___    CZIP
                                                          Bottom
F3=Exit          F5=Report        F11=Display text    F12=Cancel
F13=Layout       F20=Renumber     F21=Select all      F24=More keys
```

If you want to select specific fields from the database, you would do so on this panel by placing a number representing the left (low number) to right (high number) sequence of the fields in the spaces next to the fields. This permits you to rearrange the fields from the database for report presentation. Instead, for this query, hit the F21 key to select all fields. The fields will all light up with default numbers next to them. Press ENTER to continue and you will see the next panel as in Figure 2-13.

Figure 2-13 QUERY6 Operation Enter Selection Criteria

```
                        Select Records

Type comparisons, press Enter.  Specify OR to start each new group.
  Tests:  EQ, NE, LE, GE, LT, GT, RANGE, LIST, LIKE, IS, ISNOT...

AND/OR  Field            Test    Value (Field, Number, 'Characters', or ...)
        CSTCD            EQ      'PA'

                                                          Bottom

Field            Field            Field
CUSTNO           CFAX             CCOUNT
CUSTNA           CADDR            CZIP
REPNO            CADDR1           CZIPLO
CONTAC           CCITY
CPHONE           CSTCD
                                                          Bottom
F3=Exit          F5=Report        F9=Insert        F11=Display text
F12=Cancel       F13=Layout       F20=Reorganize   F24=More keys
```

Select the State Code for Pennsylvania. By testing for CSTCD = to 'PA" as shown in Figure 2-13. Then press ENTER and you will go to the Sorting panel. In Figure 2-14.

Figure 2-14 QUERY7 Operation Select Sort Fields

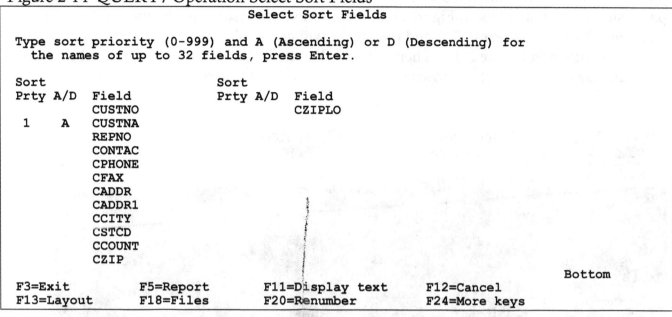

```
                              Select Sort Fields

  Type sort priority (0-999) and A (Ascending) or D (Descending) for
    the names of up to 32 fields, press Enter.

  Sort                      Sort
  Prty A/D  Field           Prty A/D  Field
            CUSTNO                    CZIPLO
    1    A  CUSTNA
            REPNO
            CONTAC
            CPHONE
            CFAX
            CADDR
            CADDR1
            CCITY
            CSTCD
            CCOUNT
            CZIP
                                                              Bottom
  F3=Exit          F5=Report        F11=Display text    F12=Cancel
  F13=Layout       F18=Files        F20=Renumber        F24=More keys
```

Take a one to select the CUSTNA (Customer name) field for sorting and an A for ascending sequence. If more than one field is to be sorted (not in this example) you would place a 2 in the next most important field for the sort and a 3 and then a 4 etc. In this case, after placing the 1 and the A, press ENTER. Press ENTER one more time to confirm. 1

Figure 2-15 QUERY8 Operation Back to Query Definition

```
                              Define the Query

  Query . . . . . . :    FIRSTQRY            Option . . . . . . :   CREATE
    Library . . . . :    BKELLY              CCSID . . . . . . . :   65535

  Type options, press Enter.  Press F21 to select all.
    1=Select


  Opt     Query Definition Option
        > Specify file selections
          Define result fields
        > Select and sequence fields
        > Select records
        > Select sort fields
          Select collating sequence
          Specify report column formatting
          Select report summary functions
          Define report breaks
          Select output type and output form
          Specify processing options


  F3=Exit             F5=Report
  F13=Layout          F18=Files            F21=Select all
  Select options, or press F3 to save or run the query.
```

After your selections, Query will come back with greater than > signs in the areas that you selected options (Figure 2-10). Press F5 any time to run an intermediate query to see how you are doing. Do this now. You will see the panel below... almost. Actually, you will see a panel similar to that below in Figure 2-16. Position your cursor near the end of the Company Name field. Press F21 and the Query will go to split screen mode. The split version is shown in Figure 2-16. Then, hit F20 (Window Right) several times until PA and USA appear in your panel as shown in Figure 2-16 (QUERY 9) below.

Figure 2-16 QUERY9 Operation Display the Query Report

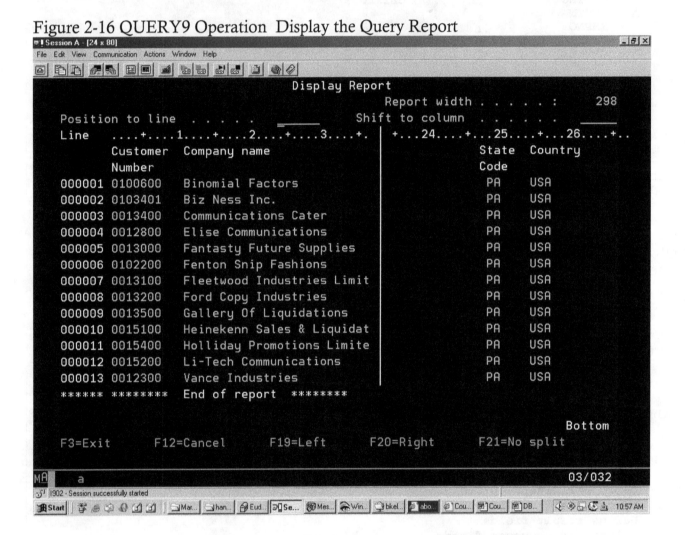

Hit ENTER and you will come back to the main Query panel. Hit F3 to end Query and you will get the next panel Figure 2-17 (QUERY10) below.

Figure 2-17 QUERY10 Operation Exit Query

```
                              Exit this Query

Type choices, press Enter.

   Save definition  . . .     Y                Y=Yes, N=No

   Run option . . . . . .     1                1=Run interactively
                                               2=Run in batch
                                               3=Do not run
   For a saved definition:
      Query  . . . . . . .   FIRSTQRY          Name
         Library  . . . . .   YOURLIB          Name, F4 for list

      Text . . . . . . . . Your First Query -- Against Customer File

      Authority  . . . . .  *LIBCRTAUT         *LIBCRTAUT, authorization list name,
                                               *CHANGE, *ALL, *EXCLUDE, *USE

F4=Prompt        F5=Report        F12=Cancel          F13=Layout
F14=Define the query
```

Save the Query in your library as shown in Figure 2-17. With these options, it will run again immediately. Press ENTER and you will be taken to Work with Query panel. Hit F3 and you will see the Main Query panel. Hit F3 again to get back to the main RPG panel for the course.

That's it for the first green screen lab

What was the purpose of the lab?

There were five major purposes:

1. Demonstrate the Program Development Manager PDM environment, which AS/400 professionals use to create and maintain production computer applications. As we learn the WDSC programming environment later in the semester, it will help you understand the magnitude of the change for AS/400 developers, who now have a choice of staying with the older and more stable PDM or moving to the new WDSC Intelligent Development Environment.

2. Demonstrate the difference between AS/400 file objects and database members.

3. Demonstrate that the recreation of database files removes the old data and thus one must be very careful before performing such functions.

4. Demonstrate the various source types that are used in a program development environment. For example, the option 5 exercise as begun in Panel was used so that the student could view the contents of the various member types such as DSPF – display files, PF – physical files, LF – Logical files, RPGLE – RPG IV programs. CBL – COBOL program. When a create command (PDM Option 14) is used referencing these various source types, the system takes the description from the member and creates an AS/400 object in a library using the description to build the object's structure.

5. Introduce the two applications, Advanced Hello World and Download Inc., so that the student is familiar with these applications. Advanced Hello World is used in a later lab.

If you do not feel that these objectives were accomplished in this Lab, please review the Lab again. If you have an instructor, ask any questions of your instructor that you believe may help your understanding.

Lab 3 Write a Simple RPG Program

Objectives:

Gives student opportunity to enter a program from scratch.

Lab 3 -- Exercise 1

Enter and create a new RPG program to create a simple employee list. Please note that in your library within the source file called SOURCE in your library, is a full solution to this programming problem. It is contained within the member named LAB03PS. The S stands for solution. Do not work with the solution but feel free to take option 5 every now and then when you are stuck to see the proper coding for this lab exercises. It's like having the teacher right next to you. Of course, you will learn more if you try several times yourself before you check out the solution.

How to do this Lab?

Learning anything new is frustrating. Chicken or egg syndrome sets in. Things that need to be discussed for the matter at hand may actually not be in the correct order of the language you are teaching. I have tried to direct you through the things you need to do in these labs so that in the end, you can go back and take them again and say, "ah! hah! Got it!"

So, have a little faith as I tell you to do certain things. If you come back after you are done, you will know why. So, in tutorial fashion, you will be requested to do things like only a dummy would do. After you do them once and you are a smarty, and you come back and do them again and you understand them.... you won't feel so dumb -- and perhaps more importantly, you won't think I am so dumb for directing you in this fashion.

Program Specifications

List the employee file with report and column headings

Figure 3-1 is a look at a record in the EMPMAST file with its default column headings. Use these headings for your report. Figure 3-1 shows a record in EMPMAST and its field contents. Figure 3-2 shows the data description specifications (DDS) that were used to define the EMPMAST database file. Figure 3-3 shows a query list of the data in the EMPMAST file that you will be using in your Labs. Figure 3-4 shows a Query listing of the data in the TIMCRD file that you will be using in your labs. Figure 3-5 is the report layout (without spacing) that you need to use to get your print positions correct in your program modifications.

Figure 3-1 EMPMAST Data Record

```
WORK WITH DATA IN A FILE                    Mode . . . . :    CHANGE
Format . . . . :    EMPR                     File . . . . :    EMPMAST


EMP NBR:            1
EMP NAME:          BIZZ NIZWONGER
EMP RATE:           780
EMPLOYEE CITY: WILKES-BARRE
EMP STATE:         PA
EMP ZIP:           18702
SAL CODE:          N
DEPT CODE:         PING
```

Figure 3-2 Data Description for EMPMAST

```
Columns . . . :    1  71        Browse              YOURLIB/SOURCE
SEU==>                                              EMPMAST
FMT PF .....A..........T.Name+++++RLen++TDpB......Functions++++++++++++++++++
     *************** Beginning of data *************************************
001.00      A         R EMPR
002.00      A           EMPNO       3S 0      COLHDG('EMP' 'NBR')
003.00      A           EMPNAM     30         COLHDG('EMP' 'NAME')
004.00      A           EMPRAT      5S 2      COLHDG('EMP' 'RATE')
005.00      A           EMPCTY     20         COLHDG('EMPLOYEE' 'CITY')
006.00      A           EMPSTA      2         COLHDG('EMP' 'STATE')
007.00      A           EMPZIP      5S 0      COLHDG('EMP' 'ZIP')
008.00      A           EMPSCD      1         COLHDG('SAL' 'CODE')
009.00      A           EMPDPT      4         COLHDG('DEPT' 'CODE')
010.00      A         K EMPNO
     ***************** End of data ********************************************
```

Figure 3-3 Query Listing of EMPMAST File Data

```
        EMP EMPNAM              EMP EMPCTY        EMP  EMP
        #                       RAT               STA  ZIP
000001   1 Bizz Nizwonger      7.80 Wilkes-Barre PA   18702
000002   2 Warbler Jacoby      7.90 Wilkes-Barre PA   18702
000003   3 Bing Crossley       8.55 Scranton     PA   18702
000004   4 Uptake N. Hibiter   7.80 Fairbanks    AK   99701
000005   5 Fenworth Gront      9.30 Fairbanks    AK   99701
000006   7 Bi Nomial           8.80 Fairbanks    AK   99701
000007   8 Milly Dewith        6.50 Juneau       AK   99801
000008   9 Sarah Bayou        10.45 Juneau       AK   99801
000009  10 Dirt McPug          6.45 Newark       NJ   07101
****** ********  End of report   ********
```

Figure 3-4 Query Listing of TIMCRD File Data

```
        EMPNO  EMPHRS
000001    1    35.00
000002    2    40.00
000003    3    65.00
000004    4    25.00
000005    5    33.00
000006    6    40.00
000007    7    39.00
000008    8    40.00
000009    9    40.00
000010   10    35.00
****** ********    End of report   ********
```

Figure 3-5 Spool File Look of Program Printed Report Output

```
                        Display Spooled File
File  . . . . . :   QPRINT                  Page/Line   1/6
Control . . . . .                           Columns     1 - 78
Find  . . . . . .
*...+....1....+....2....+....3....+....4....+....5....+....6....+....7....+...
        THE DOWALLOBY COMPANY EMPLOYEE LIST       BY STATE        6/09/07
   ST   CITY                    ZIP    EMP#  EMPLOYEE NAME              RATE
   PA   WILKES-BARRE            18702  001   BIZZ NIZWONGER             7.80
   PA   WILKES-BARRE            18702  002   WARBLER JACOBY             7.90
   PA   SCRANTON                18702  003   BING CROSSLEY              8.55
   AK   FAIRBANKS               99701  004   UPTAKE N. HIBITER          7.80
   AK   FAIRBANKS               99701  005   FENWORTH GRONT             9.30
   AK   FAIRBANKS               99701  007   BI NOMIAL                  8.80
   AK   JUNEAU                  99801  008   MILLY DEWITH               6.50
   AK   JUNEAU                  99801  009   SARAH BAYOU               10.45
   NJ   NEWARK                  07101  010   DIRT MCPUG                 6.45
   NJ   NEWARK                  07101  011   BANDAID JONES              4.50
               HASH TOTAL OF THE RATES            78.05
```

1. Start your Lab exercise by signing on to the system and after a few panels you will see your RPG Programming Menu. This is the menu you will use for all of your RPG programming needs in all labs. It will be assumed after this Lab that you know how to invoke your class RPG Programming Menu. If you need a refresher, just comeback to this lab.

After you sign on, of course, you will see a panel showing your library list and then a panel asking you if you want to continue or end. Once you say that you want to continue by typing a Y and enter, you will be right here in the sequence of things and the menu you will be looking at on your screen is that shown below in Figure 3-6.

Figure 3-6 Your RPG Programming Menu

```
RPGMENU                          RPG Programming Menu

Select one of the following:

      1. Work with output queue
      2. Refresh Files After Creation
      3. Start PDM
      4. Start SQL
      5. Display Library List
      6. Run AS/400 Query
      7. Work With Submitted Jobs
      8. Start Screen Design Aid (SDA)
      9.
     10. Run Some Programs
     11. Signoff

Selection or command
===> _____


F3=Exit    F4=Prompt    F9=Retrieve    F12=Cancel
F13=Information Assistant  F16=System main menu
```

2. Continue this startup by taking option 3 and pressing Enter to start the program development manager (PDM). You will see a panel such as that shown in Figure 3-7.

Figure 3-7 PDM Main Panel

```
                    Programming Development Manager (PDM)

Select one of the following:

      1. Work with libraries
      2. Work with objects
      3. Work with members

      9. Work with user-defined options


      Information about new tools - press F1 for details

Selection or command
===>  3 _____

F3=Exit        F4=Prompt        F9=Retrieve        F10=Command entry
F12=Cancel     F18=Change defaults
                          (C) COPYRIGHT IBM CORP. 1981, 2005.
```

3. From here (The PDM main panel), choose the Work with Members option # 3 as shown in Figure 3-7. Press Enter.

Figure 3-8 Entry Panel for SEU from the PDM Option 3

```
                    Specify Members to Work With

Type choices, press Enter.

   File  . . . . . . . . .     SOURCE        Name, F4 for list

      Library . . . . . . . .    YOURLIB      *LIBL, *CURLIB, name

   Member:
     Name   . . . . . . . .    *ALL          *ALL, name, *generic*
     Type   . . . . . . . .    *ALL          *ALL, type, *generic*, *BLANK



F3=Exit      F4=Prompt      F5=Refresh      F12=Cancel
```

4. Type in SOURCE and your library name and press ENTER. When you get to the Work with members panel similar to the one shown in Figure 3-9, scroll until you find the LAB03P shell as shown in Figure 3-10. You will not use it at this point but you should be able to find it and see it in the list as shown in Figure 3-10. The panels you see may not be exactly the same as those below but they will be close.

Figure 3-9 Work with Members Using PDM

```
                    Work with Members Using PDM                BUS400

File  . . . . . .      SOURCE
   Library . . . .     RPGOBJ              Position to  . . . . .

Type options, press Enter.
  2=Edit           3=Copy  4=Delete 5=Display      6=Print     7=Rename
  8=Display description  9=Save  13=Change text  14=Compile  15=Create module...

Opt   Member      Type       Text
      AREADME1ST  TXT        Read Me 1st Installation Instructions
      ARRAY5      RPGLE      Sample Program
      CUSTAUTH    PF         Customer Download Authentication File
      CUSTOMER    PF         Customer physical file (used to compile customer)
      CUSTOMER1   PF         Customer physical file (used to compile customer)
      CUSTOML3    LF         Customer file by customer number
      DBREFRESH   CLP        Refresh RPG Files
      DBREFRSH    CLP        Refresh the data in five files
                                                                More...
Parameters or command
===>
F3=Exit          F4=Prompt           F5=Refresh           F6=Create
F9=Retrieve      F10=Command entry   F23=More options     F24=More keys
```

Figure 3-10   Scroll to Page of Members Display in Which LAB03P is Contained.

```
                    Work with Members Using PDM              YOURSYS

File . . . . . .     SOURCE
  Library . . . .    YOURLIB                    Position to . . . . .

Type options, press Enter.
 2=Edit            3=Copy  4=Delete 5=Display      6=Print      7=Rename
 8=Display description  9=Save  13=Change text  14=Compile  15=Create module...


Opt  Member      Type        Text
     INSTRUCT    TXT         MWOOD Installation Instructions
 3   LAB03P      RPG         Code from Book - Internally Described Problem
     LAB03PS     RPG         Solution for Lab 03 program described
     LAB03PY     RPG         Lab 03 RPG Internally Described
     LAB04EY     RPG         Lab 04 RPG Externally Described
     LAB05E4Y    RPGLE       LAB 05 RPGIV Externally Described
     LAB06P      RPG         LAB 06 Internally Described Problem
                                                          More...


Parameters or command
===>
F3=Exit            F4=Prompt              F5=Refresh           F6=Create
F9=Retrieve        F10=Command entry      F23=More options     F24=More keys
```

Note: For all subsequent labs, use the steps 1 to 4 as shown above to get to the work with Members Display in the Program Development Manager. This is a good starting point for your programming activity.

5. Begin a PDM copy of member LAB03P to create the LAB03PY member. The "Y" stands for you. You will do your Lab 3 work in this copy. When the next panel of the copy comes up make sure the To-Member is LAB03PY in the SOURCE file in your library. Note that in Figure 3-10, there is already a LAB03PY but in your actual lab's member list this will not be there. SO, in essence the picture in Figure 3-10 is really an after look of the member list -- after the copy.

6. Make sure that in the report shown in Figure 3-5 (the objective output of this program) that you space each field on the report so that it looks similar to the report shown above in Figure 3-3. The reason for this is that the line spacing in Figure 3-5 does not show in the spool file display but it does show on the actual printout. Additionally, when you really print the report, in addition to the proper spacing, the spool file output at the top of Figure 3-5 will not appear on the real report. You would not want it and it does not appear.

7. Your mission to repeat is to Write the LAB03PY internally described program to print the employee list as shown above in Figure 3-5. My recommendation is to use the LAB03P shell as discussed earlier as the basis for your program though you can try to write it from scratch if you wish. The process will be much easier if you choose to use LAB03P. For additional learning, you may want to come back after making LAB03P work and you may create a blank source member called LAB03P2 and try to type the whole program from scratch. See if you can write it once you actually make the shell work. Optional.

8. The input is the EMPMAST file shown above and the output is a printer file. Use QPRINT for the file name.

9. Calculate the record length (required by RPG) for EMPMAST by using the DSPFD command (Display File Description) at the command prompt. or by looking at the DDS which is resident in the SOURCE file.. A method for achieving this is described in the next paragraph.

Type DSPFD on a command line and press Enter. You will see a panel similar to that shown in Figure 3-11 below. To get to this panel from the first panel you first see in Figure 3-11, scroll three times and the record length is on the fourth panel of the file description. While you are there, you can get an appreciation of the difference between a PC file and an AS/400 or System i or IBM i File Object. All of the information on all of those panels comes from inside the file object... and there is even more. Note that a PC file has only data. The stuff below is called metadata which is data about data.

Note that in Figure 3-11 we enlarged the part you should find to make it easier to spot.   So, 70 is your record length... for the EMPMAST file. See Figure 3-11.

Figure 3-11 Fourth screen of the DSPFD command shows record length.

```
                        Display Spooled File
 File . . . . . :   QPDSPFD                  Page/Line   2/2
 Control . . . . .                           Columns     1 - 78
 Find . . . . . .
 *...+....1....+....2....+....3....+....4....+....5....+....6....+....7....+...
      Access path size . . . . . . . . . . . . : ACCPTHSIZ  *MAX1TB
      Access path logical page size . . . . . . : PAGESIZE   *KEYLEN
      Maximum key length . . . . . . . . . . . :               3
      Maximum record length . . . . . .        70
      Volatile . . . . . . . . . . . . . . . . :             No
      File is currently journaled . . . . . . . :           No
   Access Path Description
      Access path maintenance . . . . . . . . . : MAINT      *IMMED
      Unique key values required . . . . . . . : UNIQUE     No
      Key order . . . . . . . . . . . . . . . . :           Not specified
      Access path journaled . . . . . . . . . . :           No
      Access path . . . . . . . . . . . . . . . :           Keyed
      Constraint Type . . . . . . . . . . . . . :           NONE
      Number of key fields . . . . . . . . . . :             1
      Record format . . . . . . . . . . . . . . :           EMPR
        Key field . . . . . . . . . . . . . . . :           EMPNO
                                                              More...
  F3=Exit   F12=Cancel   F19=Left   F20=Right   F24=More keys
```

10. The record length for the QPRINT file should be 78. Figure out how to make the report print using this record length. Hint (no end position can be past column 78)

11. Use the RPG cycle - make EMPMAST a primary file - program described

12. Use indicator 01 to recognize a master record on the input cycle

13. Skip to line 6 before printing the report title.

14. Space two spaces after printing the report title

15. Print the report title on the first page and on any overflow lines

16. Condition a line of column headings as shown in Figure 3-5 above spacing 3 after each heading... Note again that in the sample printout above, you do not see the proper line spacing

17. Space 1 before each detail line

18. Each record that is read should turn on indicator 01 and should cause the EMPRAT field to be totaled in an accumulator field called TOTRAT that is size 7 with 2 decimal places.

19. Define this field, TOTRAT as a new field in RPG calcs.

20. The shell program named LAB03P (p = program described) is available for your use. It is in your source file and you may have viewed it in an earlier exercise. When you start PDM create a new member and call it LAB03PY -

The Y designator means that you created the program

Once you are in the empty program with SEU, you may use the SEU COPY facility to copy the shell code for LAB03PY into your program.

The next set of steps outlined show you how to accomplish this SEU copy

21. Go back and look at Figure 3-10. The steps to get you actually moving again in this Lab are shown below beginning with this next step. You have already started PDM and you are looking at the members list.

22. If you have already copied LAB03P to LAB03PY then, place a 4 next to it and delete it. Continue with these directions. When there is no LAB03PY in your member list, press F6 to create a new member that you will call LAB03PY

You will see the following panel:

Figure 3-12 Start SEU Panel for New Source Member

```
                    Start Source Entry Utility (STRSEU)

Type choices, press Enter.

Source file  . . . . . . . . . > SOURCE        Name, *PRV
  Library  . . . . . . . . . . > YOURLIB       Name, *LIBL, *CURLIB, *PRV
Source member  . . . . . . . .   LAB03PY       Name, *PRV, *SELECT
Source type  . . . . . . . . .   RPG           Name, *SAME, BAS, BASP...
Text 'description' . . . . . .   LAB03PY Program Described Employee List Program



                                                                 Bottom
F3=Exit    F4=Prompt    F5=Refresh    F12=Cancel   F13=How to use this display
F24=More keys
```

23. Fill in your library name if not already done and make sure the panel looks like the one in Figure 3-12 and then hit the ENTER key. You will then be taken to the main SEU entry panel

Figure 3-13 Main SEU Edit Panel

```
 Columns . . . :   1  71            Edit                    YOURLIB/SOURCE
 SEU==>                                                     LAB03PY
 FMT H   .....H........1..CDYI....S.............1.F...........................
         *************** Beginning of data ************************************
 ''''''''
 ''''''''
 ''''''''
 ''''''''
 ''''''''
 ''''''''
 ''''''''
 ''''''''
 ''''''''
 ''''''''
         **************** End of data **************************************
 F3=Exit    F4=Prompt    F5=Refresh    F9=Retrieve    F10=Cursor   F11=Toggle
 F16=Repeat find         F17=Repeat change       F24=More keys
 Member LAB03PY added to file YOURLIB/SOURCE.                             +
```

24. Notice there is no source at all in this source member. You have created a member with the above action but there is no source in the member (Figure 3-13). There is no RPG code yet in this member because you typed none yet. You may choose to type in the program source code from scratch to solve the problem outlined above (employee list) or you may choose to copy the shell called LAB03P into this member so you do not have to do as much keying and so this first programming lab goes more smoothly for you.

In this example, choose to use the records copy facility within SEU. Please note that this is different than the member copy that is available in PDM that you completed successfully in step 5. Select the method below to learn more about SEU and its facility.

25. To copy the shell into the program take the following action: Press F15 for the COPY / Include Menu and you will see a panel similar to that panel as shown below in Figure 3-14

Figure 3-14 Browse / COPY before Pic for LAB03PY Source

```
                        Browse/Copy Options

Type choices, press Enter.

     Selection . . . . . . . . . .      1               1=Member
                                                        2=Spool file
                                                        3=Output queue
     Copy all records . . . . . . .     N               Y=Yes, N=No
     Browse/copy member . . . . . .     LAB03PY          Name, F4 for list
       File  . . . . . . . . . . .      SOURCE          Name, F4 for list
         Library . . . . . . . . .      YOURLIB         Name, *CURLIB, *LIBL

     Browse/copy spool file . . . .     LAB03PY         Name, F4 for list
       Job . . . . . . . . . . .        LAB03PY         Name
         User  . . . . . . . . . . .    Youyou          Name, F4 for list
         Job number  . . . . . . .      *LAST           Number, *LAST
       Spool number  . . . . . . . .    *LAST           Number, *LAST, *ONLY

     Display output queue . . . . .     QPRINT          Name, *ALL
       Library . . . . . . . . . .      *LIBL           Name, *CURLIB, *LIBL


F3=Exit         F4=Prompt         F5=Refresh         F12=Cancel
F13=Change session defaults     F14=Find/Change options
```

Figure 3-15 Browse / COPY -- Type Changes for SEU COPY for LAB03PY Source

```
                        Browse/Copy Options

Type choices, press Enter.

     Selection . . . . . . . . . .      1               1=Member
                                                        2=Spool file
                                                        3=Output queue
     Copy all records . . . . . . .     N               Y=Yes, N=No
     Browse/copy member . . . . . .     LAB03P           Name, F4 for list
       File  . . . . . . . . . . .      SOURCE          Name, F4 for list
         Library . . . . . . . . .      YOURLIB         Name, *CURLIB, *LIBL

     Browse/copy spool file . . . .     LAB03PY         Name, F4 for list
       Job . . . . . . . . . . .        LAB03PY         Name
         User  . . . . . . . . . . .    YOURLIB         Name, F4 for list
         Job number  . . . . . . .      *LAST           Number, *LAST
       Spool number  . . . . . . . .    *LAST           Number, *LAST, *ONLY

     Display output queue . . . . .     QPRINT          Name, *ALL
       Library . . . . . . . . . .      *LIBL           Name, *CURLIB, *LIBL


F3=Exit         F4=Prompt         F5=Refresh         F12=Cancel
F13=Change session defaults     F14=Find/Change options
```

26. When you see the panel in Figure 3-14, it looks almost exactly as this. Modify the first group of lines under the word "Selection" so that it looks exactly like Figure 3-15. as follows:

A. Leave the default of N to not copy all records this time.

B. Make sure your library is the one designated. (change YOURLIB) to your library.

In addition to showing you the SEU full copy of a source member's contents since it is early in the course and you can use all the tips you can get, we are advising that you take the N option as noted. A correct option is also to replace the N with Y but not this time. This time we are choosing the selective copy because it is used quite frequently by programmers in practice. If you use the Y option the whole shell will be copied to LAB03PY. Instead as directed, type the N as above press ENTER and you will see a split screen panel like the one in Figure 3-16 below. This is a powerful SEU feature. Two source members are in the one editor at the same time.

Figure 3-16 Split Screen for Selected Source Program Copy

```
 Columns . . . :    1  71              Edit                YOURLIB/SOURCE
 SEU==>                                                         LAB03PY
 FMT H   .....H........1..CDYI....S..............1.F.........................
         *************** Beginning of data ***************************************
         ***************** End of data ******************************************




 _                                                          _____
 Columns . . . :    1  71              Browse              YOURLIB/SOURCE
 SEU==>                                                          LAB03P
         *************** Beginning of data ***************************************
CC01.00       H* RPG HEADER (CONTROL) SPECIFICATION FORMS    LAB03PS
0002.00       H* SOLUTION FOR LAB03
0003.00       H
0004.00       F*
0005.00       F* RPG FILE DESCRIPTION SPECIFICATION FORMS
0006.00       F*

 F3=Exit   F4=Prompt   F5=Refresh   F9=Retrieve   F11=Toggle   F12=Cancel
 F16=Repeat find       F17=Repeat change          F24=More keys
```

27. Though it is hard to see, the cursor is in the bottom half of the panel. The split portions of this panel are individually controllable depending on where you position the cursor. Position the cursor now using the arrow keys on the keyboard to the bottom part of the panel. Arrow keys do not change any of the data on an SEU panel.

28. Type in CC for group copy as shown on line 0001.00 in Figure 3-16 above. Do not hit Enter yet. Then scroll (page down) to the end of the program and place a CC on the last line as shown in Figure 3-17 below:

29. Type CC on the very last line above "End of Data." This may or may not be line 51 of the shell program but does appear as line 51 above. In the event that a programmer would have modified this source subsequent to taking the snap shown in Figure 3-17, the line # may be different. This CC sandwich (CC in line 01-- first line and a CC in line 51 --last line) identifies the first and the last lines to be copied from the shell to your SEU source edit session. When you have done you have told SEU the "From" part of the SEU COPY facility. This demonstrates some superb PDM power that will come in handy for you as a

developer. As a side note, these facilities are also available in the new Rational GUI editors available through IBM..

30. So, we are going to copy a block of code from one member to another. From which line in that "from" member should the copy begin?   For the destination line command we like to use A for *After line*, and B for Before line. In this case, place an A for "After" on the beginning of data line in the **top half** of the panel as shown in Figure 3-17. Then Press Enter for the COPY to occur. .

Figure 3-17 Preparing for the block copy from member to SEU work space

```
 Columns . . . :    1  71            Edit             YOURLIB/SOURCE
 SEU==>                                                    LAB03PY
 FMT H   .....H........1..CDYI....S.............1.F................
A         *************** Beginning of data *********************************
          *************** End of data *********************************



 Columns . . . :    1  71            Browse          Pending . . . . . :   CC
 SEU==>
0048.00       O                         EMP   1   77
0049.00       O          T 22     LR
0050.00       O                              'HASH TOTAL OF THE RATES '
CC51.00       O                         TOT   1
          ***************** End of data *********************************



 F3=Exit    F4=Prompt    F5=Refresh    F9=Retrieve    F11=Toggle   F12=Cancel
```

Figure 3-18 Shell source named LAB03P Copied into new Member LAB03PY

```
 Columns . . . :    1  71            Edit             YOURLIB/SOURCE
 SEU==>                                                    LAB03PY
 FMT *   ..... *. 1 ...+... 2 ...+... 3 ...+... 4 ...+... 5 ...+... 6 ...+... 7
          *************** Beginning of data *********************************
001.00        H* RPG HEADER (CONTROL) SPECIFICATION FORMS    LAB03P
002.00        H* SHELL FOR LAB03
003.00        H
004.00        F*
005.00        F* RPG FILE DESCRIPTION SPECIFICATION FORMS
006.00        F*

 Columns . . . :    1  71            Browse           YOURLIB/SOURCE
 SEU==>                                                    LAB03P
048.00        O                         EMPRAT1    77
049.00        O          T 22     LR
050.00        O                              51 'HASH TOTAL OF THE RATES '
051.00        O                         TOTRAT1    72
          ***************** End of data *********************************
```

31. You now have the shell program in LAB03PY in your SEU Edit panel as shown in Figure 3-18. Now, that the program is ready and the tools are all set (PDM, SEU etc.), it is OK to begin the edit process to solve the programming problem as defined at the beginning of this lab.

32. For the edit session to change to full screen from split screen to full screen for editing, press F12 and you are now ready to complete the assignment. Figure 3-19 shows the entire program as it exists in your source file. As you can see on your own machine, however, just one page of this program is in your edit window. To see the rest on your machine, scroll to the end one page at a time.

The program LAB03PY is now ready for you to modify. In essence the contents of the shell source program LAB03P has been copied using the SEU line copy function from the shell member -- LAB03P to the member that you are about to modify -- LAB03PY.

Please note that there are a number of double XXs in the code. These are there instead of blanks so that you can see and think through the entries that should go there to assure your program compiles and runs.   I can assure you of one thing at this time: without modification, your program LAB03PY will not compile. The syntax checker will not like those double XXs.

When you finish editing the XXs into the codes as they should be applied to this program, and you are reasonably assured that the program will run, end your SEU session by pressing F3 and you will come to Figure 3-24 to end the SEU editor. It is not time to do not do this step just yet. Let's make some other changes first.

Figure 3-19 The Whole LAB03PY Program with XXed out areas.

```
0001.00      H* RPG HEADER (CONTROL) SPECIFICATION FORMS    LAB03PS
0002.00      H* SOLUTION FOR LAB03
0003.00      H
0004.00      F*
0005.00      F* RPG FILE DESCRIPTION SPECIFICATION FORMS
0006.00      F*
FMT **    ...+... 1 ...+... 2 ...+... 3 ...+... 4 ...+... 5 ...+... 6 ...+.
0007.00      FEMPMAST IXX X       XX        DISK
0008.00      FQPRINT  O  F        78    XX    PRINTER
0009.00      I*
0010.00      I* RPG INPUT SPECIFICATION FORMS
0011.00      I*
0012.00      IEMPMAST AA   XX
0013.00      I                                        1   30EMPNO
0014.00      I                                        4   33 EMPNAM
0015.00      I                                       34  382EMPRAT
0016.00      I                                       39   58 EMPCTY
0017.00      I                                       XX   XX EMPSTA
0018.00      I                                       XX  XXXEMPZPP
0019.00      I                                       XX   XX SALCOD
0020.00      I                                       XX   XX DEPT
0021.00      C*
0022.00      C* RPG CALCULATION SPECIFICATION FORMS
0023.00      C*
0024.00      C            ADD   EMPXXX      TOTRAT  XX
0025.00      O*
0026.00      O* RPG OUTPUT SPECIFICATION FORMS
0027.00      O*
0028.00      OQPRINT  H  XXX   XX
0029.00      O        OR  XXX   OF
0030.00      O                            XX  'THE DOWALLOBY COMPANY'
0031.00      O                            XX  'EMPLOYEE LIST      BY '
0032.00      O                            60  'STATE'
0033.00      O                  UDATE X   77
0034.00      OQPRINT  H  X     XX
0035.00      O        OR  3     OF
0036.00      O                             4  'ST'
0037.00      O                            13  'CITY'
0038.00      O                            37  'ZIP'
0039.00      O                            XX  'EMP#'
0040.00      O                            XX  'EMPLOYEE NAME'
0041.00      O                            XX  'RATE'
0042.00      O        D 1     XX
0043.00      O                  EMPSTA      X
0044.00      O                  EMPCTY     29
0045.00      O                  EMPZIP     39
0046.00      O                  EMPNO      XX
0047.00      O                  EMPNAME    78
0048.00      O                  EMPRAT1    XX
0049.00      O        T XX     XX
0050.00      O                             5X 'HASH TOTAL OF THE RAT'
0051.00      O                  TOTRAT1    7X
```

33. Take the LAB03PY simple RPG programming lesson that begins immediately below and ends at Step 35. Then, you will have learned almost enough to modify the program to make it work and to produce the output in Figure 3-5.   This is a big lesson and sets the groundwork for you RPG knowledge.

The LAB03PY Simple RPG Programming Lesson (This whole lesson is Step 34)

34. Now, before you end anything since you have not changed anything, let's talk about this simple program that exercises the RPG cycle. At the end of this Lab, there is a short tutorial on the RPG cycle. It is important for you to read this now even before you take this simple programming lesson. So, please take an abrupt cut to the end and pick up this tutorial and then come back to right here....

RPG and RPG IV are specification driven. Each specification has its own format. Right in line with the notion of INPUT >> PROCESS >> OUTPUT, RPG has an Input specification (I) a processing spec called the Calculations or Calc spec (C) and an Output spec (O).   RPG has a six character limit to the names that can be read from database files or display files. RPGIV's limit is 10. Therefore, names cannot be extremely specific and meaningful.

Since database files and screen files (called workstation files) can be used with RPG, there must be a way to tell the compiler where these files exist and how they should be used. RPG provides a File Description specification (F) for this and we will describe the file types and specifications for this tutorial as we encounter them.

There is also a specification originally called File Extension (E) where things like execution time tables and arrays can be defined. Today this specification is called merely the Extension Spec. Because RPGIV introduced the definition spec to define the unique attributes of various structures without requiring extension or input specs, the extension spec is not needed as all of this work is performed in RPGIV by the "D" spec.

There is a line counter spec in RPG (L) to describe printed report forms. as well as a header specification.(H) to introduce global conditions for the program. RPG IV introduces the notion of keywords for special items that needed column spaces on RPG forms. Thus, the L spec is replaced by forms keywords in RPGIV and the Header specification has no columns. It is all keywords.

As you can see in Figure 3-19, the specifications as shown in column 6 that are used in this program are H, F, I, C, and O. This is the sequence in which they are specified.

Decoding the Program

To learn about a program, it helps to decode solutions. The solution for this is in your Lab Library and is called LAB03PS if you need to take a sneak peek every now and then. Let's look at the shell program and talk about some options for the various specification forms for the program to work properly. If you must refer to the source program LAB03PS don't stare too long so that you can actually learn this.

Starting with the H specification, notice that there is nothing specified in the H spec. The asterisk in column 7 means that the H specs are comments. The H spec with no comment at line 3 means that no global specifications are being made in this program.

RPG OUTPUT is First

From the tutorial you may recall that output is done before input. The RPG cycle does all of the record reads without the programmer needing a READ or CHAIN statement. However, even before the first read, so that the program can print report titles and column headings, RPG first produces output. When RPG is ready to produce output, it will write to the device specified all of the lines defined that are unconditioned or those conditioned lines whose conditions are met.

Note after the second QPRINT that there is an OR situation. The "R" in OR occupies the same position as H, D, or T and it ORs the line directly above. So, there is a condition XXed out on the first line and on the second line with the OR, the print line is conditioned on the print overflow. Print overflow of course means that the printer has passed the forms length and now should be printing on the next page.. This line makes that happen when print overflow occurs.

Note the second QPRINT. It as an H designation. Following that is another OR and then a D and then a T. Notice the line #s in Figure 3-20 are from the LAB03PY program that we are correcting. building.

Figure 3-20 RPG Output Lines Defined in LAB03PY

```
0025.00        O*
0026.00        O* RPG OUTPUT SPECIFICATION FORMS
0027.00        O*
FMT **     ...+... 1 ...+... 2 ...+... 3 ...+... 4 ...+... 5 ...+... 6.......
FMT O      .....OName++++DFBASbSaN01N02N03Excnam.............................
0028.00        OQPRINT   H   XXX    XX
0029.00        O         OR  XXX    OF
0034.00        OQPRINT   H   X      XX
0035.00        O         OR  3      OF
0042.00        O         D 1        XX
0049.00        O         T XX       XX
```

The H, D, and T stand for Heading, Detail, and Total. RPG can print Heading, Detail, or Total Lines at various times during the cycle. The programmer sets up lines to be used for headings, for record data listing, and for totals. The designation, D, D, or T is specified in column 15 of the output specification and it signifies the definition of a print line.

The actual fields or headings that are printed are defined after these "line definitions." QPRINT is a standard name for an IBM i printer file definition that is available for everyone's use. Once you specify the printer file name in output, all subsequent line specifications (H, D, or T) refer to that particular printer file since more than one printer file can be defined in an RPG program.

Notice the FMT line after statement 27 in Figure 3-20. This shows the column numbers in which the various RPG coding is placed. For example, the xxx in line 28 is located in positions 18 to 20 of the RPG output and the XX on the same line is in positions 24 and 25.

In column 17, you can specify the # of lines to space **before** printing the current line. In column 18, you can specify the # of lines to space **after** printing the line being defined. In columns 19 and 20, you specify the line to which the printer should skip before printing the current line and in columns 21 and 22, you specify the line # to which the printer should skip after printing the current line. The space and skip before and after designations are very handy in controlling the output of fixed format forms that have sections such as headings, bodies, and totals.

Our report wants 2 lines to start printing on line 06 (skip to 6) and it wants to space 2 lines skip after it prints the first line. It wants to space 3 lines after printing the second heading line. The detail line wants to space 2 before printing each line (Single spacing) and after printing all the details, the total line wants to space 2 before printing and space 2 more after printing (though admittedly the 2 after does no real good).

So, looking again at columns 19 and 20, we learn that in these areas, you specify to which line on a form the printer should stop at before it prints a particular report line. Typically a report prints six lines to an inch on 11 inch paper and the first print line is about line 06 as is the case for our report. The other lines spacing is governed by the space entries. There is also a skip after in columns 21 and 22 so that if the programmer needed to skip to the middle of say a pre-printed form, RPG provides that ability.

There is another trick used for printing. It is called overflow. Notice in lines 29 and 35 the letters OF are used. This stands for overflow indicator in this program. A number of different two character combinations beginning with O can be used such as OA. The entry made in the printer file in File descriptions determines which entry is used in output. So, if there were an OA in File descriptions, there would be an OA used in Output.

There's another trick that you don't have to guess that helps condition the heading at first page or heading at overflow printing of the title and column heading print lines. Notice on lines 29 and 35 the word or in column 14 (discussed above). When you want a line to print when either condition occurs, you can specify a second line condition and print specs as in 29 and 35 and link the two print line conditions with an OR as done in this program.

Figure 3-21 RPG File Descriptions LAB03PY

```
FMT **    ...+... 1 ...+... 2 ...+... 3 ...+... 4 ...+... 5 ...+... 6 ...+.
FMT O     .....OName++++DFBASbSaN01N02N03Excnam.............................
0049.00      O        T XX        XX
0007.00      FEMPMAST IXX X         XX              DISK
0008.00      FQPRINT  O   F        78        XX     PRINTER
```

Getting back to output, the area in the output format shown as N01N02N03 (figure 3-21) in columns 23 to 31 is where the programmer can specify conditioning indicators. This means that only if the conditions are met will the line print. Unconditional lines print every time their respective cycle is performed. So and unconditioned detail line would print every time a record was read.

Header output is typically conditioned by two types of indicators -- an indicator that designates the first page and an indicator that designates that a full page has printed and new titles are needed (overflow indicator). The first page indicator is 1P and the overflow indicator in this program is already specified as OF. Therefore, you now have enough information to fill in statement 8 and statements 28, & 29, 34 & 35.

What indicator should be used to condition the printing of the detail line as in line 42, shown in Figure 3-22? The answer to this is the same indicator that is assigned to the input record that is read. The EMPMAST file is the input file for the program. We know that because as shown in Figure 3-22, it is designated in column 15 with an I.

Figure 3-22 Detail Line Printing

```
0012.00      IEMPMAST AA   XX
0013.00      I                                           1     30EMPNO
0014.00      I                                           4     33 EMPNAM
0015.00      I                                          34     382EMPROT
...
0042.00      O        D 1      XX
0043.00      O                        EMPSTA      X
0044.00      O                        EMPCTY      29
0045.00      O                        EMPZIP      39
0046.00      O                        EMPNO       XX
0047.00      O                        EMPNAME     78
0048.00      O                        EMPRAT1     XX
```

We have input specifications defined for this file from statement 12 to 20. These are internally described specifications (programmer types the input specs rather than the DB providing them.) Therefore, we know that this file is not externally described and it should be coded with an F in File descriptions column 19 (Figure 3-21) just as the printer file description below it.

Back to the question, what indicator should be used to condition the printing of the detail line as in line 42? The answer is the indicator assigned on line 12 where the XX's are. So if we were to say this were 01 (which happens to be in the solution but any indicator would work), then we would specify the same indicator on line 42 to condition the printing of the line. It makes sense. When a record is read, it turns on the indicator so that at printing time it can be used to print the record that was read.   So much for the detail line.

Now, how about the total line?   The answer to the question when do we want it printed is needed to know what indicator to use on line 49. When you look at the report in Figure 3-5, you can see that this is a final total. When RPG automatically reads an input file, at the time it tries to read a record and has none because it has already read them all, it knows it must shut down the program. To make you aware of this condition, RPG provides an indicator called 'last record' or LR that you can use to get this job done. So at total time you can use the LR special indicator to cause the final totals to be printed.

Figure 3-23 RPG Output Field Definitions -- for Constants and Variables

0030.00	O		XX	'THE DOWALLOBY COMPANY'
0031.00	O		XX	'EMPLOYEE LIST BY '
0032.00	O		60	'STATE'
0033.00	O	UDATE X	77	

Now after examining the output record print line specifications and how a particular line gets printed in this program, take a look at the output field definition specifications to show what gets printed when a particular line gets printed.   We start with XX in the "print line ending position' for the first two lines of the report heading / title in lines 30 and 31 repeated above for your convenience. We're going to give you these from the solution rather than make you borrow some fingers and thumbs to count print positions using the information in Figure 3-5. You would have to check out the printout in great detail and get the spacing right in order to know what print ending position to plug in after knowing that the constant (literal) used for the heading for STATE on line 32 ends at print position 60. Use 32 and 55 for these two sets of XXs and you'll have it right.

So that's how we create report titles that are constant in nature. Right on the output field specification you specify where the information is to be printed and then within quotes -- notice the quotes, you specify the actual words you want printed constantly -- each and every print line. So, how do you handle variables?

The answer to this question is in line 33. The field happens to be one that we are not reading in from the employee master. It is called UDATE and it is a special variable that goes into the system and retrieves the date. As you can see, this variable or field as we like to call them ends in position 77 of the first report line. Take a look at Figure 3-5 to see what actually prints. Where did those slashes come from? RPG has what are called special edit codes that can be used to format various types of data much like Excel can format columns with numbers different than columns with letters. Again, we are going to give you this one. Place a Y where the single X is located. The Y edit code says insert slashes at the right spot in a date field. To find out more about edit codes Google edit codes, RPG or check your references.

So we have now explained the first of four different print lines. Looking at 3-18, the rest of the field definitions for the other print lines are basically repeats of this. The rest are basically the same. In lines 43 to 48 of Figure 3-18, you see the fields from the EMPMAST that are selected to print on the detail line (once every time a record from EMPMAST is read). See how that looks in the middle of the report in Figure 3-5. Use Figure 3-5 to help you figure out what print positions to specify in place of the Xs in the r print lines other than the first heading as described in detail above.

Primary File Description

After RPG does its heading work on the very first cycle, when indicator 1P is on, it goes to step 2 of the cycle to read in a record from the files defined either as primary or secondary in column 16 of file description. It reads the contents of the record into the input buffer. When a programmer uses a P or an S in column 16 of a file used for input (I) or update (U), that is how RPG knows to use the cycle.

When there are two files in a program that is to use the cycle, one gets designated as primary and the other gets designated as secondary. The third fourth and fifth files, tertiary, quaternary, and quinary and any others that are in the mix are also coded as S for secondary. The third file listed in the program is tertiary, the fourth is quaternary, the fifth is quinary etc. When no matching fields are specified for the files, all the records in the primary are processed followed by all the secondary's, followed by all the tertiary's, followed by all the quaternaries, followed by all the quinary file records.

Every program that processes using the cycle must have a primary file. So, with just one file for input and the cycle in play, we now know how to code column 16 of the EMPMAST file in File Descriptions. Column 17 should have an E in it to tell the program not to end until at least all the records from this file are read. This obviously has more meaning in programs that have more than one file. So, designate the file as s.

Input Happens in INPUT

We have input specifications defined for this file from statement 12 to 20 as shown below isolated from the program first introduced in Figure 3-18. As noted, these are internally described specifications (programmer types the input specs rather than the DB providing them.) Internally described means that there are input specification field statements, such as those shown from 13 to 20 below in Figure 3-24.

Figure 3-24 RPG Input Specs for Record and Internally Described Field Definitions

```
FMT *     ..... *. 1 ...+... 2 ...+... 3 ...+... 4 ...+... 5 ...+... 6 ...+..
FMT I     .....IFilenameSqNORiPos1NCCPos2NCCPos3NCC........................
0012.00      IEMPMAST AA   XX
FMT J     .....I................................................PFromTo++DField+L1M1FrP1M
0013.00      I                                          1   30EMPNO
0014.00      I                                          4   33 EMPNAM
0015.00      I                                         34   382EMPROT
0016.00      I                                         39   58 EMPCTY
0017.00      I                                         XX   XX EMPSTA
0018.00      I                                         XX   XXXEMPZPP
0019.00      I                                         XX   XX SALCOD
0020.00      I                                         XX   XX DEPT
```

As noted previously and repeated for effect, we know that this file is not externally described. Thus, you have already been instructed to code column 19 of the EMPMAST file description specification with an F just as the printer file description below it. So that the input specifications relate to the input file described in file descriptions, statement 12 repeats the name EMPMAST so that the compiler knows that the input specs relate to the EMPMAST file described in the F spec above it. We have already determined that the XX in statement 12 columns 19 & 20 should be 01 to reflect the notion of a record identifying indicator which is spelled out in detail in the coming Lecture topic. In Lecture E.

In the input blow-up above, notice that there is a statement that says FMT I and a statement that says FMT J. The "I" stands for the record format for the input specs and the J stands for the field format. Note in the J format, nothing is required until column 43 and our file has nothing that requires a P in column 43. If the data were packed (a special form of data) we would use the P in 43 on the field to designate it as a packed field. Then, in column 44 the "from position in the record" begins (goes to 47) and in column 48 the "to position in the record" begins (goes to 51). In column 52, if the field is numeric, you place the # of decimal places -- from 0 to 9. If no decimal places are used, then the field is defined in the program as alphabetic, alphamerical, or character, all of which mean the same thing.

In column 53, you specify the 6 character field name for the file as used in this program. Since this program uses internally described input, it is OK but not desirable to use field names in the program for EMPMAST that are different than those defined to the EMPMAST database. However this is not recommended because the external definition is the more desirable and using an internal definition that is different from the DB definition makes it more difficult o make the transition to externally described data in programs -- again the more desirable state.

In column 59 and 60, you see in the J format, the characters L1 and following that in columns 61 and 62, you see M1. This is where you would specify the match fields for programs that have more than one input file. You will need this information for future labs. That wraps up the input specifications.

Figure 3-25 Calculation Specifications -- Where Processing Is Done

```
FMT *      ..... *. 1 ...+... 2 ...+... 3 ...+... 4 ...+... 5 ...+... 6 ...+.
FMT C      .....CL0N01N02N03Factor1+++OpcdeFactor2+++ResultLenDHHiLoEqComments
0021.00       C*
0022.00       C* RPG CALCULATION SPECIFICATION FORMS
0023.00       C*
0024.00       C                        ADD   EMPRAT    TOTRAT  72
```

Getting Processing Done

The Calculations specification is used to get processing done. Everything from detail calcs to total calcs to conditioned calcs to resulting indicators to field definitions can be done in calculations. Level calculations (occur in a control break) are performed when an entry is placed in column 7 & 8 that is L1 through L9 or LR. Any statements so coded execute at total calculation time in the RPG cycle. From 9 to 17, you can specify indicators and an N preceding the indicator if you want a calculation to occur on a NOT condition of an indicator. All indicator conditions tested for must be true in order for the line to execute. Therefore, on this line, the three conditions are "ANDed" together. Using multiple lines, these three conditions can be "ANDED" or they can be "ORed" with other conditions to determine whether a particular calculation statement is executed or not executed each cycle.

Line 24 shows that there is no Factor 1 used in the statement but there is an entry in the Op code, Factor2, and the Result field. If Factor 1 were used and it is OK but longer to use it, it would look like this:

The way an ADD statement works follows:: The operation ADD adds to the value stored in the variable or the constant in Factor1, the value in the variable or the constant in factor 2 and it stores the result in the variable in the Result field. Thus, the employee pay rate (EMPRAT) in factor 1 in the above calculation would be added to the accumulator variable (TOTRAT) in factor 2. The result of the ADD operation would then be stored in the accumulator in the result field called TOTRAT.

Since the field named TOTRAT (total of all the rates in all master records) is not defined in Input, it must be defined in Calculations either before or during its use in this operation. As you can see above, it is specified as 7 positions long,. It is a numeric data type since # of decimals is specified, and it is to hold two decimal places.

There is another shorter form to the add statement. If the result field and Factor 1 are the same, you do not need to specify anything in Factor 1. Thus, the following is a valid replacement for the above ADD operation:

```
0024.00        C           TOTRAT    ADD   EMPRAT    TOTRAT   72
```

This once over on the ADD operation and the use of the Calculations specification should be enough for our other labs. To gain more information on this topic, use the reference material or just Google RPG calculation specification and you will get enough information to satisfy your curiosity. For example to use the subtract operation in RPG, type the following into Google:

subtract opcode RPG IBM as400 boulder

From the IBM link, you select from the Google page, you may have to search for the word subtract, or multiply or chain or read or whatever but, if you change the first word of this set of search values, you are fairly sure that you will hit the correct IBM page to learn as much about the operation as you will need to know. So, in future labs, when the operation is not fully explained to your satisfaction, take this Google search and you shouldn't be disappointed.

In this set of lab exercises, you will find various RPG topical areas explained in detail when they are essential to understanding the logic of the program. If all RPG information, were inserted into this lab guide / tutorial, it would more than likely be greater in total pages than the almost 1000 pages in <u>The System i RPG and RPGIV Pocket Guide</u> (a book designed as a college textbook that often serves as a companion to the tutorial). So, if you do not have the Pocket Guide, be ready to look up a number of items in Google for clarification.

However, as you will find, RPG operations themselves are fairly self-explanatory once you get the rhythm.   Moreover, the technique to teach you how to write advanced programs assures your learning the most important parts of the language as reflected by the program solutions and shells. For example each lab contains the program solution with items XXed out. This means that you do not have to do a lot of typing and it means that you get to learn a bit of how to solve a programming problem by hearing the problem and getting a piece of the solution given to you.

*** End of Simple LAB03PY RPG Decoding Lesson ***

Exiting SEU and Saving Your Source

Figure 3-26 SEU Exit Panel

```
                                      Exit
   Type choices, press Enter.

      Change/create member  . . . . . . .    Y           Y=Yes, N=No
         Member   . . . . . . . . . . . .    LAB03PY     Name, F4 for list
         File  . . . . . . . . . . . . .     SOURCE      Name, F4 for list
            Library . . . . . . . . . . .      YOURLIB   Name
         Text  . . . . . . . . . . . . .     Lab 03

         Resequence member . . . . . . . .    Y           Y=Yes, N=No
            Start . . . . . . . . . . . .     0001.00     0000.01-9999.99
            Increment . . . . . . . . . .     01.00       00.01-99.99

      Print member  . . . . . . . . . . .     N           Y=Yes, N=No

      Return to editing . . . . . . . . .     N           Y=Yes, N=No

      Go to member list . . . . . . . . .     N           Y=Yes, N=No
   F3=Exit    F4=Prompt    F5=Refresh    F12=Cancel
```

35. Hit F3 to begin the Exit SEU process. Exit with the options shown in figure 3-24.

Assure that the change/create member option is set to Y or your work session changes will not update the LAB03PY source member in your library. If you see a "Y" in Return to editing," the SEU syntax checker knows that you have not removed all of the XX syntax errors from your program.. Thus, if you hit ENTER with a "Y" in this area, the SEU exit will re-invoke the SEU editor and reconnect you to your SEU workspace until you have corrected the program to SEU's satisfaction. When you have done so, again press F3 and the SEU Exit Panel in Figure 3-26 will appear again. This time, after assuring a "Y" in the Change / create member prompt, press ENTER and you will be back to the PDM panel as shown in Figure 3-27.

36. Type a 14 next to the LAB03PY source member which holds the source statements for the soon-to-be LAB03PY program object. This will translate the source into object code and

create an *PGM object type in your library (if you removed all of the XX's and replaced them with valid code. If you have not removed all of the errors, depending on severity, you will see a message at the bottom of the screen right where the message **"Member LAB03PY in file YOURLIB/SOURCE changed with 51 records"** is in the panel in Figure 3-27. The difference will be that it will be a different error such as the one listed below:

Compile stopped. Severity level 40 errors found in file.

Figure 3-27 Compile the LAB03PY program

```
                          Work with Members Using PDM              YOURSYS

File . . . . . .    SOURCE
  Library . . . .      YOURLIB                Position to . . . . .

Type options, press Enter.
  2=Edit          3=Copy   4=Delete 5=Display         6=Print      7=Rename
  8=Display description  9=Save  13=Change text  14=Compile  15=Create module...

Opt  Member     Type      Text
     LAB03PS    RPG       Code from Book - Internally Described 01
14   LAB03PY    RPG       Lab 03
     LANGUAGE   PF        LANGUAGE File For Hello World
     MAIN       RPGLE     Prototype Two- procs - All in one X
     MLHMAST    PF
     NAMEDCON   RPGLE
     NEW        DSPF
     PANEL      DSPF      Display File Panel For Advanced Hello World
                                                                 More...
Parameters or command
===>
F3=Exit          F4=Prompt          F5=Refresh          F6=Create
F9=Retrieve      F10=Command entry  F23=More options    F24=More keys
Member LAB03PY in file YOURLIB/SOURCE changed with 51 records.
```

37. If you get a bad guy message such as this, if you know what the error is intrinsically (magically) then go back to source and correct it and resubmit your compile. If you do not know what the error is then exit PDM (F3 twice) and you will return to the RPG Programming Menu.

Figure 3-28 RPG Programmer Menu - Pick Option 1

```
RPGMENU                      RPG Programming Menu

Select one of the following:

     1. Work with output queue
     2. Refresh Files After Creation
     3. Start PDM
     4. Start SQL
     5. Display Library List
     6. Run AS/400 Query
     7. Work With Submitted Jobs
     8. Start Screen Design Aid (SDA
     9.
    10. Run Some Programs
    11. Signoff

Selection or command
===> 1
F3=Exit    F4=Prompt    F9=Retrieve    F12=Cancel
F13=Information Assistant  F16=System main menu
```

38. From the RPG Programming Menu in Figure 3-28, pick option 1 to examine your output. The startup program has set your session up so that your output goes into your own output queue in your own library so your output is segregated from all other student's output. Take option 1 and press ENTER to see the contents of your Output Queue. It will be very similar to the panel shown in Figure 3-29 below:

Figure 3-27 Looking at your Output Queue

```
                        Work with Output Queue

Queue:    YOURQUEUE         Library:    YOURLIB          Status:    RLS

Type options, press Enter.
  1=Send    2=Change    3=Hold    4=Delete    5=Display    6=Release    7=Messages
  8=Attributes          9=Work with printing status

Opt  File         User         User Data    Sts    Pages    Copies  Form Type     Pty
 5   LAB03PY      YOURLIB                    RDY       9        1    *STD          5



                                                                      Bottom
Parameters for options 1, 2, 3 or command
===>
F3=Exit    F11=View 2    F12=Cancel    F20=Writers    F22=Printers
F24=More keys
```

39. Type 5 next to what may be the only entry in the queue and press ENTER. The next panel you see will show you the full contents of your RPG compile listing, including the errors that caused your program not to compile. It is good to have an error at this point so that you can examine how this process works. So, if your program compiles the first time, go back and intentionally make a mistake so you can follow through on the procedure to view errors.

When you type 5 as above and press ENTER, you will see a panel as shown in Figure 3-28 below:

Figure 3-30 -- First page of compile listing

```
                        Display Spooled File
File . . . . . :   LAB03PY                    Page/Line    1/1
Control . . . .                               Columns      1 - 78
Find . . . .
*...+....1....+....2....+....3....+....4....+....5....+....6....+....7....+...
 5722WDS V5R4M0   060210                    IBM RPG/400                  YOURLIB
 Compiler . . . . . . . . . . . . . :   IBM RPG/400
 Command Options:
   Program  . . . . . . . . . . . . :   YOURLIB/LAB03PY
   Source file  . . . . . . . . . . :   YOURLIB/SOURCE
   Source member  . . . . . . . . . :   LAB03PY
   Source listing options . . . . . :   *SOURCE       *XREF       *GEN        *N
   Generation options . . . . . . . :   *NOLIST       *NOXREF     *NOATR      *N
   Source listing indentation . . . :   *NONE
   Type conversion options  . . . . :   *NONE
   Sort sequence  . . . . . . . . . :   *HEX
   Language identifier  . . . . . . :   *JOBRUN
   SAA flagging . . . . . . . . . . :   *NOFLAG
   Generation severity level  . . . :   9
   Print file . . . . . . . . . . . :   *LIBL/QSYSPRT
   Replace program  . . . . . . . . :   *NO
                                                                     More...
F3=Exit    F12=Cancel    F19=Left    F20=Right    F24=More keys
```

40. Use the roll down key to find the RPG errors. Along the way, if you remove no XXs from your LAB03PY program, your first error panel will appear as follows in Figure 3-31.

Figure 3-31 -- RPG Errors in File Descriptions

```
                          Display Spooled File
File . . . . . :    LAB03PY                    Page/Line   2/1
Control . . . .                                Columns     1 - 78
Find . . . . . .    2054
*...+....1....+....2....+....3....+....4....+....5....+....6....+....7....+...
 5722WDS V5R4M0  060210                IBM RPG/400                    YOURLIB
 SEQUENCE
 NUMBER      *...1....+....2....+....3....+....4....+....5....+....6....+....7..
                          S o u r c e   L i s t i n g
       100  H* RPG HEADER (CONTROL) SPECIFICATION FORMS    LAB03PS
       200  H* SOLUTION FOR LAB03
       300  H
       400  F*
       500  F* RPG FILE DESCRIPTION SPECIFICATION FORMS
       600  F*
       700  FEMPMAST IXX X       XX              DISK
* 2054          2054-*.  .    .
* 2045          2045-* .      .
* 2006           2006-*    .
* 2007               2007-****
       800  FQPRINT  O   F      78      XX      PRINTER
                                                        More...

F3=Exit   F12=Cancel   F19=Left   F20=Right   F24=More keys
```

41. As you can see from the compile listing in Figure 3-31, the RPG compiler is calling out four errors near the bottom of the panel on the left. To see the description of these errors, either scroll to the bottom of the listing or type in one of the numbers such as 2054 as done in Figure 3-31 and hit F14 to search for the error message. After a few F14's you will see a panel similar to that shown in Figure 3-32. This panel has the RPG error message descriptions.

Figure 3-32 String Found -- RPG Error Message Descriptions

```
                        Display Spooled File
File . . . . . :    LAB03PY                    Page/Line   7/19
Control . . . . .                              Columns     1 - 78
Find . . . . . .    2054
*...+....1....+....2....+....3....+....4....+....5....+....6....+....7....+...
          blank.
* QRG2054 Severity:  20    Number:     1
          Message . . . . :    The file-designation entry is not valid.
* QRG4020 Severity:  30    Number:     1
          Message . . . . :    Record-identifying indicator entry is not
             valid. Entry is ignored.
* QRG4034 Severity:  20    Number:     4
          Message . . . . :    From-Field-Location entry is invalid. Entry
             defaults to 1.
* QRG4035 Severity:  20    Number:     4
          Message . . . . :    To-Field-Location entry is invalid. Entry
             defaults to From-Field-Location entry.
* QRG4045 Severity:  10    Number:     1
          Message . . . . :    Decimal-Positions entry not 0-9 or blank.
             Defaults to blank.
* QRG5038 Severity:  20    Number:     1
                                                        More...
F3=Exit    F12=Cancel    F19=Left    F20=Right    F24=More keys
String found in position 6.
```

42. To bring your program to a clean compile, work through your source and remove all of the errors, replacing the bad code with code that is correct. To help you do this SEU has some helpful tools as does the IBM i Access tool. From IBM i Access, for example, you can open up a second PC5250 display and window both displays so they do not take up the whole screen. Then, look for the errors in the one version and make correction in the other.

43. Another way to use this effectively is to exit the WRKOUTQ function and return to SEU. Edit the LAB03PY member and take the F15 option as shown in Figure 3-33 as repeated below for your convenience.

Figure 3-33 Browse / COPY Options to bring in LAB03P source

```
                     Browse/Copy Options

Type choices, press Enter.

   Selection . . . . . . . . . . . .    2            1=Member
                                                     2=Spool file
                                                     3=Output queue
   Copy all records  . . . . . . .    N            Y=Yes, N=No
   Browse/copy member  . . . . . .    LAB03P       Name, F4 for list
      File  . . . . . . . . . . . .      SOURCE     Name, F4 for list
        Library . . . . . . . . . .        YOURLIB  Name, *CURLIB, *LIBL

   Browse/copy spool file  . . . .    LAB03PY      Name, F4 for list
      Job . . . . . . . . . . . . .      LAB03PY    Name
        User  . . . . . . . . . . .        YOURLIB  Name, F4 for list
          Job number  . . . . . . .          *LAST  Number, *LAST
      Spool number  . . . . . . . .        *LAST    Number, *LAST, *ONLY

   Display output queue  . . . . .    QPRINT       Name, *ALL
      Library . . . . . . . . . . .      *LIBL      Name, *CURLIB, *LIBL

F3=Exit          F4=Prompt        F5=Refresh        F12=Cancel
F13=Change session defaults    F14=Find/Change options
```

44. Instead of copying source to the bottom of the screen as we did in Figure 3-33, pick the option that says the following:

Browse/copy spool file .... LAB03PY   Name, F4 for list

45. Make sure you have this area selected . Change the option at the top of Figure 3-33 to option 2, Spool file instead of Member. Make sure all the other parameters reflect your environment and press the ENTER key

Figure 3-34 Spool Panel on Bottom of SEU panel

```
Columns . . . :    1  71           Edit            YOURLIB/SOURCE
SEU==>                                             LAB03PY
FMT *    ..... *. 1 ...+... 2 ...+... 3 ...+... 4 ...+... 5 ...+... 6 ...+... 7
004.00      F*
005.00      F* RPG FILE DESCRIPTION SPECIFICATION FORMS
006.00      F*
007.00      FEMPMAST IXX X     XX          DISK
008.00      FQPRINT  O  F      78    XX    PRINTER
009.00      I*
010.00      I* RPG INPUT SPECIFICATION FORMS

Columns . . . :    1  71          Browse        Spool file . . :    LAB03PY
SEU==>    F 2054
001.92            blank.
001.93 * QRG2054 Severity:  20    Number:    1
001.94           Message . . . . :    The file-designation entry is not valid.
001.95 * QRG4020 Severity:  30    Number:    1
001.96           Message . . . . :    Record-identifying indicator entry is not
001.97           valid. Entry is ignored.
001.98 * QRG4034 Severity:  20    Number:    4

F3=Exit   F4=Prompt   F5=Refresh   F9=Retrieve   F11=Toggle   F12=Cancel
F16=Repeat find      F17=Repeat change           F24=More keys
String 2054 found.
```

46. When you get the panel on Figure 3-34, position yourself to the SEU==> prompt on the bottom and enter the FIND command along with 2054 to locate the 2054 error description or the 2054 error in source. Note the use of the F 2054 in the bottom panel. This SEU Find command goes out and locates the "2054" match records and then tells you when you get a hit as shown at the bottom of the bottom panel in Figure 3-34.

47. Use the spool list on the bottom to find the errors one at a time and then position the cursor to the top part of the panel to use the editor to make the necessary changes. Repast for as many errors as you find.

49. When you have seen enough of the spool file on the bottom and you want to go back to full screen mode, just hit F12 (CANCEL) and you will be back in the SEU full screen edit session as first shown in expanded form in Figure 3-19.

50. From here hit F3 to exit SEU and take option 14 again to compile the LAB03PY program.

51. Repeat the process of reviewing the compile listing and editing in split screen mode until you have no more compile errors -- i.e. you have a clean compile, which will be recognized by this message on the bottom of the screen:

Program LAB03PY is placed in library YOURLIB. 00 highest severity. Created

52. Once your program is compiled cleanly, you can run it.

53. On the PDM Work with members menu the RUN option does not exist. That's because members are non executable. Members contain source used to create objects. When you cleanly compiled the LAB03PY program, the PDM instructions to the compiler told it to place the **object** in your library. The member you supplied was the input to the compiler and now the object is the output and it is in your library. Thankfully, PDM offers a tool called Work with members that enables us to see the object in our library and to run (execute) it. To get to Work with Objects, hit F3 from Work with members panel and then take option 2 on the Main PDM menu to Work with Objects. You will see a panel similar to that shown in Figure 3-35

Figure 3-35 Work with Objects Options Panel

```
                     Specify Objects to Work With

Type choices, press Enter.

   Library  . . . . . . . . . .   YOURLIB      *CURLIB, name
   Object:
      Name . . . . . . . . . .    *ALL         *ALL, name, *generic*
      Type . . . . . . . . . .    *ALL         *ALL, *type
      Attribute  . . . . . . .    *ALL         *ALL, attribute, *generic*, *BLANK
F3=Exit        F5=Refresh       F12=Cancel
```

Figure 3-36 Work with Objects -- Hit F23 then take option 16 to run program

```
                     Work with Objects Using PDM                 YOURSYS

Library . . . . .    YOURLIB           Position to . . . . . . . .
                                       Position to type  . . . . .

Type options, press Enter.
   2=Change         3=Copy         4=Delete       5=Display      7=Rename
   8=Display description           9=Save        10=Restore     11=Move ...

Opt  Object     Type      Attribute    Text
     RPGRFSH    *PGM      CLP          Refresh Business Files
     GRNCLIENT1 *PGM      RPGLE        Download Inc Program
     HELLOAC001 *PGM      CBL          COBOL VERIFICATION PROGRAM
     HELLOAR001 *PGM      RPG          Advanced Hello World, RPG/400, Pgm1,
     LAB03ES    *PGM      RPG          Code from Book - Internally Described
 16  LAB03PY    *PGM      RPG          Lab 03
     RPGSTART   *PGM      CLP          Profile start program for RPG Course
     WORKQ      *PGM      CLP          Chnge work output queue display to st
                                                                     More...
Parameters or command
===>
F3=Exit           F4=Prompt          F5=Refresh          F6=Create
F9=Retrieve       F10=Command entry  F23=More options    F24=More keys
Have you tried the modern alternative to PDM? Press F1 for more details.
```

Figure 3-37 F23 First Panel Options

```
Type options, press Enter.
   12=Work with          13=Change text         15=Copy file
   16=Run               18=Change using DFU    25=Find string ...
```

54. When you arrive at Figure 3-36, it has the options as shown. However, RUN is not one of those options. To see more PDM Object options, press F23 and the insert shown in Figure 3-37 appears and replaces the options insert shown in Figure 3-36.

55. Now we are ready to run. Place the "16" option (RUN) next to LAB03PY and press Enter. You will see a panel similar to that shown in Figure 3-36 with the 3-37 insert -- but the 16 will no longer be there. . In other words, your 16 disappeared and that is it. That's all you get...

56. So, what happened? How do you even know what happened?

57. It ran. Well, one thing is for sure. You wrote the program so one way of figuring out what is supposed to happen is to go to the source that you typed and read it again. When you do this, you will reintroduce yourself to the notion of a P file (primary) for EMPMAST and you know that the RPG cycle will have read every record in that file until it ended. So, what did it do with the records? The answer to that lies in your output specifications. What did you tell it to do? Output in RPG always reflects what you tell the program to do with the data that is read. A quick look tells you that in this program, you would have said to print a report.

58. OK, where is the report? By typing in 16 and hitting enter the report program ran and it produced its output in your default output queue according to the RPG programmer menu. So, just as you looked at your compile listings with option 1 of the RPG programmer menu, take it again and see what is there. You will be taken to a panel that looks similar to that shown in Figure 3-38.

Figure 3-38 Work with Files in your output queue

```
                         Work with Output Queue

   Queue:    YOURQUEUE         Library:     YOURLIB         Status:     RLS


   Type options, press Enter.
     1=Send     2=Change    3=Hold    4=Delete    5=Display    6=Release    7=Messages
     8=Attributes           9=Work with printing status


   Opt   File          User          User Data     Sts    Pages    Copies   Form Type     Pty
         LAB03PY       YOURLIB                      RDY       9        1      *STD           5
         LAB03PY       YOURLIB                      RDY       9        1      *STD           5
         LAB03PY       YOURLIB                      RDY       6        1      *STD           5
    5    QPRINT        YOURLIB       LAB03PY        RDY       1        1      *STD           5

                                                                                Bottom
   Parameters for options 1, 2, 3 or command
   ===>
   F3=Exit    F11=View 2    F12=Cancel    F20=Writers    F22=Printers
   F24=More keys
```

59. As you can see in this snapshot, there are two LAB03PY printouts, each nine pages long, and there is one that is 6 pages. The ones that are nine pages are the two times that I compiled and there were syntax errors -- three pages worth. The final one is when I got a clean compile and there was no need for 3 whole pages of errors. The last item in the spooled output file list was produced via the QPRINT file. You may recall this standard printer file controlled the printing in your RPG program LAB03PY and therefore its name (QPRINT) shows up in the output queue.

In 3-38, you can see that I already placed a 5 in front of this printer output file so make sure you place a 5 next to this entry, then hit ENTER and see what you get. The panel in Figure 3-39 should appear if all was done correctly.

Figure 3-39 QPRINT output file produced by the LAB03PY program

```
                        Display Spooled File
File  . . . . . :     QPRINT                      Page/Line   1/6
Control . . . . .                                 Columns     1 - 78
Find  . . . . . .
*...+....1....+....2....+....3....+....4....+....5....+....6....+....7....+...
           THE DOWALLOBY COMPANY EMPLOYEE LIST        BY STATE          6/12/07
   ST     CITY                      ZIP     EMP#   EMPLOYEE NAME            RATE
   PA     WILKES-BARRE             18702    001    BIZZ NIZWONGER            7.80
   PA     WILKES-BARRE             18702    002    WARBLER JACOBY            7.90
   PA     SCRANTON                 18702    003    BING CROSSLEY            8.55
   AK     FAIRBANKS                99701    004    UPTAKE N. HIBITER         7.80
   AK     FAIRBANKS                99701    005    FENWORTH GRONT            9.30
   AK     FAIRBANKS                99701    007    BI NOMIAL                 8.80
   AK     JUNEAU                   99801    008    MILLY DEWITH              6.50
   AK     JUNEAU                   99801    009    SARAH BAYOU              10.45
   NJ     NEWARK                   07101    010    DIRT MCPUG                6.45
   NJ     NEWARK                   07101    011    BANDAID JONES             4.50
                    HASH TOTAL OF THE RATES                 78.05



                                                           Bottom
F3=Exit    F12=Cancel    F19=Left    F20=Right    F24=More keys
```

60. Not only did this produce a clean compile but the program actually ran without any errors at all. If the printing was not in the correct columns or if the program produced some other type of error when you ran it, your job would be to go into problem determination mode. This would involve looking at the printout -- either by printing the spool file or by the other methods (split screen and two terminals sessions) as discussed previously. You would go back to PDM and SEU and into the LAB03PY source and make the necessary changes and keep at it until your report is as clean as that shown in Figure 3-39.

Once you get to this point with a clean compile and a perfect printout, you have completed Lab 03. Congratulations...

Lecture E: Understanding the RPG Fixed Logic Cycle

Long before programmers learn their first language, they are introduced to computer concepts. Within the notion of basic computer concepts is the notion of INPUT > PROCESS >OUTPUT as shown in Figure C-1

Figure C-1 Input Process & Output

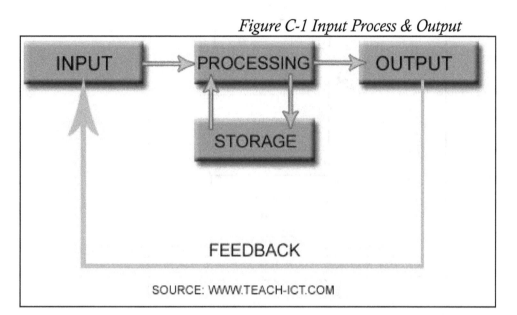

SOURCE: WWW.TEACH-ICT.COM

Just about any computer program that you will ever write accepts input, processes the input, and produces a report of some kind. The report may be a line on a screen or a full display panel or a real business report. Moreover, as you can see in Figure 3-1, in addition to producing output in the form of a report or display, a program also can store data in database files (storage) for future use.

So, whether you write the cycle yourself in every program or you choose to use the IBM RPG fixed logic cycle, which by the way is excellent for report-writing, your code will behave as if it is in a big INPUT> PROCESS> OUTPUT cycle for in fact, it is.

Report Headings

The RPG cycle is built so that report titles are a natural part of the language and they occur first. Thus as difficult as it may be to realize at first, output happens before input at the beginning of each RPG cycle from the first through the end of the program. Rather than start with input, it starts with output thereby giving the program the opportunity to get those titles on the report before the first data is read.

Let's take a look at the RPG cycle first shown in Figure C-2.

Figure C-2 The 7 Major Steps of the RPG Fixed Logic Cycle

The various work components of the RPG cycle as shown in Figure C-2 are as follows:

Step 1 – Write Heading and Detail Lines

1A. For reports, first page headings that you specify are printed.

1B. For reports, overflow headings that you specify are printed. Overflow headings are those headings that are repeated on each page after the prior page hits a bottom of the page overflow

1C. Detail output is printed. On the first cycle, since no data has been read, there is no detail data to print. Detail output consists of any output line that can be written or updated to any device – printer, disk, tape, etc. Data fields that are read during the input part of the cycle in Step 2 are held in memory as variables and are not made available to the program until Step 6.

Step 2-- Get Input Data

2. The first record is read from the primary file. Though the record has been read, RPG does not make the data available to the program until Step 6 of the cycle. In many ways, in addition to bringing the record into a buffer in memory, Step 2 finds RPG peeking ahead in the read buffer (where the record exists before being processed) to see what the next record really is. In this way, it "knows if" whether it should take totals or if it should keep reading records from the current group. This facility also comes in handy when doing matching records so that RPG can look ahead to see the sequence of the matches so that it knows which record to move in for processing.

Step 3 – Perform Total Calculations

3. Total calculations are then performed. Total calculations are totals that occur after major, intermediate, or minor control field breaks.

Step 4 -- Write Total Output

4. Total output is printed. Total output includes totals that have been accumulated, such as a field in which we might store a total for a city or a field in which we store the state total. When the city total changes, for example, we probably want to print the total on the report with the City name next to it. This type of output would occur during the Level 1 (aka L1) output cycle. If there were no control breaks during this cycle, then no output triggered by a control indicator (L1 or L2) would be produced.

If the L2 control field changes (say a state field such as PA) that automatically means that an L1 break also occurs. (If the state changes, by definition, you can bet the city changes). So for an L2 break, L2 totals are produced as well as L1 totals. Likewise if an L9 break occurs, all other total levels from L8 to L1, in addition to L9, are prepared to produce output. Likewise if a final total occurred, it would automatically create a level break at the highest level defined in the program – L9 at the highest but just L2 in our case with State and City.

Step 5 – LR On?

5. The program checks to see if it should end by checking the LR indicator. A special "indicator" called LR causes the program to end if it is set on when all of the files that are being processed are out of records or if this indicator "LR" it is set on in detail calculations

from the last cycle. When the program sees that LR is on at this point of the cycle, it ends the program gracefully and closes all of the files.

Step 6 Move Data from Input Area to Fields

6. Input is processed by moving input area buffer contents from Step 2 to the RPG fields that you defined to hold them. When RPG has completed performing level (control break) output the cycle moves to input processing time and it populates the fields with the data that is stored in the input buffer from Step 2..

Step 7 Perform Detail Calculations

7. Detail calculations are performed. What are detail calculations? They are calculations that get performed when records are processed. Detail calculations are permitted to occur for each record that passes through Step 6 of the RPG cycle as shown in Figure 3-2. If, for example, each record contains the order quantity and the price, each RPG cycle as coded in the C specifications, the programmer can write code to multiply the quantity ordered by the price and create a result field called the extended price.

RPG calculations have what are called conditioning indicators. In other words, the calculation statements are not necessarily performed each time that the program passes through the detail calculations part of the RPG fixed logic cycle. If, for example, the master and the time card records for payroll are being processed through one file, and, assuming that masters are sequenced before corresponding time card records, the programmer may wish to take action only when a time card record is read. In that way, the information from the master such as the pay rate can be stored until the time card is read. Then the rate can be used when the time record is read and the program can multiply the two numbers to get the gross pay amount. To set this up, the programmer would assign a switch called an indicator to the master and an indicator to the transaction file and those RPG cycles, in which a master record is read, based on its indicator, calculations can be conditioned not to occur. Likewise, for those RPG cycles in which a time card is read, based on its indicator, calculations can be conditioned to occur.

RPG Matching Records Processing

RPG can match records from two or more files. For example, you may have master payroll records specified as *File 1*. You may have time cards specified as *File 2*. To prepare for this computer run, which depends on both files being in sequence by say, employee number or a field called EMPNO, you would sort the both files by employee number so they are in the same sequence. Your program logic would want to be able to read the master payroll record for employee 1 and then the time card for employee 1 and then it would want to read employee 2's master and then employee 2's time card and so on until all employees were processed. Once the program reads the master and the time card for each employee, it has enough information to calculate the payroll.

During the input part of the cycle in Step 2, RPG provides for a period in which two or more files of records that are all in sequence by the fields specified for the match can be read and be declared a match. In this scenario that we are discussing, the time cards and the employee master file are in different files. This notion is referred to in RPG as "matching records" and it is a big plus for using the RPG cycle for report writing functions when two or more files are needed for processing. It is also handy when updating master files from transaction files.

Designating Record Types

RPG provides a designator that can be placed next to the field names in both files within the RPG Input Specifications. In other words, the programmer must place a designator in a field from each of the files to be matched. This can be referred to as a matching designator. If there is just one field to match, then the only matching designator required is known to RPG as "M1." However, unlike the present example, which needs just one field (EMPNO), if there is more than one field that must be matched (and up to nine fields), then RPG makes available other matching designators --- M2 through M9. When more than one matching designator (M2 to M9) is specified, all match fields that are specified must be matched from each file before the special "indicator" known as "MR" for match indicator is as we say, "turned on."

So, let's say in our simple example that we have two files. We mark the employee number fields (EMPNO) in both files in the RPG program input specs with the M1 designator. From here on, when this program runs, RPG itself makes sure that both files are in sequence and when there is a match, it turns on a special matching switch called the matching record indicator or MR. The programmer can then use the status of this switch (on or off) to cause desired events to occur in the program that otherwise would be difficult to achieve. Additionally, if by any chance the files are found by RPG to not be in sequence by the matching designators, the program will halt with an error condition.

Record Identifying Indicator Processing

There is another phenomenon in the RPG fixed cycle called the record identifying indicator. Each time RPG reads a master record with the cycle, for example, it tells the programmer from which file it read the record by turning on an indicator that the programmer associates with the file. If RPG turns indicator 01 on for example, that may mean a master record has been read and if RPG turns on indicator 02 that may mean that a time card record has been read. This powerful, yet simple communication gives RPG a simple way of telling programs what is happening so that the program can take the proper action.

What is an indicator?

The RPG language provides a programmer with a tool box of 99 indications to use for their own purposes. The indication that a particular record type has been read can be stored in a special type of "field" called an indicator. To make it easy to remember, most programmers use various indications to change the value of the indicator fields from 0 to 1. Moreover, because these are special fields that exist in no other programming language, RPG also permits just two values in the field – either a "0" or a "1." When the value is "0," RPG programmers say the indicator (numbered 1 through 99) is "off." Just like a light switch, when the value is one, RPG programmers say that the indicator is "on." So all 99 indicators in RPG can be tested to see if they contain values of "0" or "1" as well as being tested for "on" or "off."

With the notion of indicators and the RPG cycle, the compiler provides some additional facility. If, next to the input record on the RPG Input Specification, you choose to specify an indicator to turn on if a particular record ID is read, RPG will gladly turn on that indicator if it reads a record meeting the criteria you have specified. In the time card file and master file example, since we would only have one time card for one master, it would suffice to do no testing for record contents since it is reading the data from two different files. In this scenario, we already know that if a record is read from the primary it is a master and if it is read from the secondary, it is a time card. Thus, in this two-file example, there is no further need to define markings inside the records to identify them.

So, for the record that defines the master file on the RPG Input specifications in the RPG program, the programmer assigns an indicator. Let's say the programmer choose indicator 01. Now, for the record that defines the time card in the RPG program, let's say the programmer chooses 02.

Once the programmer has done this, independent of the matching status or the reading sequence of the program, whenever the program reads a master record, regardless of its EMPNO value, record identifying indicator "01" will be turned on and record identifying indicator "02" (time card) will be off. That is because only one record identifying indicator can be on at one time. RPG processes just one record each cycle. Likewise, whenever the program reads a record from the time card file, independent of the matching status or the reading sequence of the program, and regardless of its EMPNO value, record identifying indicator "02" will be turned on and record ID indicator 01 will be turned off.

Primary and Secondary Files

The second last phenomenon that we will discuss regarding matching records is the notion of primary and secondary files. The 407 Accounting Machine had just one hopper so it did not need anything on a wiring board to signal a match from two card readers. RPG is more sophisticated. It says that one file can be designated as primary and a second file can be designated as secondary for processing purposes within a program. If there are three card readers and/or many tape and many disk devices (files) in play, then theoretically, there can be as many – even twenty or more files defined in just one program. If these files are not defined as random or keyed-access files – in other words, they are to be processed sequentially, the programmer would need to designate all but one as secondary files in terms of matching records processing. Just one file in all cases can be defined as the primary file.

Internally, based on the order of specification (Line 1 vs. Line 2) defined in the program, RPG would designate these files as tertiary, quaternary, quinary, senary, septenary, octonary, nonary etc. based upon the order in which the programmer specified them in the File Description Specification section in RPG. In today's processing, I rarely if ever see a tertiary sequential file. Multiple files other than the primary and the designated secondary are most often defined to RPG as something other than secondary – such as keyed index files or random files. However, you may run into someone else's code in which they have chosen to use more than one secondary file for matching records purposes.

The MR Indicator

The last phenomenon in understanding the RPG cycle with matching records is that the MR indicator comes on at a certain times in the cycle as do the record identifying indicators. They are turned off by RPG at a designated time in the cycle. For the novice RPG programmer, this is really a big pain to understand. "Real programmers" and RPG purists like to be in control of the program. Great programmers however can take a powerful tool like "Matching Records," learn it inside and out, and be substantially more real and more productive than a "real programmer." More importantly, by understanding the cycle, as noted earlier in this book, programmers can get much more done in report programs than by having to write the code themselves. To be good at the cycle, however, you have to understand the cycle. You have to know when RPG does what it does. You have to understand when RPG turns on record IDs and matching indicators and when it turns them off.

For example, if the pay rate is in the master record, we know that when it is read, indicator 01, the designated master record identifying indicator, is turned on. If the next master record has the same EMPNO field value as the record just read, RPG will read another record from the master file (primary). Since we have a one to one relationship of master to time card, in this example this cannot happen – but if it does, it is an error condition.

In this example, we know that the next record that RPG will read will come from the time card file (secondary) one input cycle after the matching master was read. Right before RPG reads the record for the time card record; it cleans up its act and turns off the indicator (01) that recognized that a master had been read in the last cycle. Prior to the time card record being read then, there are no record identifying indicators in the "on" condition. When RPG goes ahead and reads the time card record from the secondary file, it turns on indicator 02.

It helps to know that RPG can actually peek ahead (Step 2 of the cycle) at the cards or sequential disk records or tape records to see what they contain even if it is not going to read them on this particular input cycle. No, I am not kidding. RPG knows for example when it reads the master record from file 1 for EMPNO # 1 that there is a matching time card record for employee 1. It already knows that because it has peeked ahead. So, even though it is processing the payroll master record from the primary file with indicator 01, it is smart enough to turn on this special indicator called "MR" to indicate that the next time card record what will be read from the secondary file will match this master that is now being processed. The fact is that when the master is read, RPG "sees" the matching time card record sitting over there in the other file's input buffer, even though it has yet to read it. Yes, that is neat!

If the pay rate is in the master and the hours are in the time card record, when the master is read and indicator 01 comes on, the hours are still not yet available for employee # 1. So, we cannot calculate gross pay at that time in the cycle. So a condition that we might call "MR" and "01," means that we have a master read and being processed and its *matching* time card has not yet been read. Notice the word matching in the prior sentence. When we eventually read the time card, RPG has already turned off the master indicator (01) and then it turns on indicator 02. So, if you are keeping score at home, you might say that when the record identifying indicator "02" and the "MR" indicator is on, the primary record just read matches the secondary record that is now being processed. That is great information for a programmer to gain without having to write the code for it. All you must do is be conversant with the RPG cycle.

RPG Fixed Logic Cycle Summary

If we go back to Step 6 and Step 7 of the cycle, once a given input record is read, the next step is that it is time again for detail calculations. This is the classic processing part of the RPG cycle that we have just described. The next step, of course is output at Step 1 and thus we have a complete cycle:

INPUT >> PROCESSING >> OUTPUT

We learned that detail calculations occur in that part of the RPG cycle after the detail input has been read. The word "detail" describes what happens in each normal RPG cycle as an individual record is processed (not counting total calculations or total output time). As noted above in the matching example, a detail record ID indicator of 02 means we have read in a time card. If we also have an MR match with the master record, then we know that the master record for that time card is also in memory.

If we are trying to assure that our output occurs after all of the information for one employee has been read, RPG helps again. We know that the detail time card record turns on indicator 02. We know that because this record matches a master, RPG is keeping indicator MR on for us. So, if indicator 02 is on and indicator MR is on, we know that RPG is processing a time card record and the time card record matches the master record that RPG read in the prior cycle. Thus, it is a logical time to condition some calculations that should occur when the time card is being processed for a matched master.

In other words, it would be quite appropriate to condition detail calculations to occur when both indicators 02 and MR are both on. In this case, we specify a calculation to multiply the rate times the hours to produce the first gross amount for the employee. Since the first gross amount per employee would not be an input field, the program would use RPG calculations to create this field for us within the detail calculation specifications.

So, as we wrap up this example in summary form, RPG will have read all of the data and performed the calculations and more than likely, because we have told it so, it will print an output line on a piece of paper that is in the printer. Once this happens, it is time to recycle – run the cycle again and again and again – until we run out of input.

So, the next generic cycle step is to skip back to the beginning of the RPG cycle to that spot that we designated above as the first step (1) in the cycle. Of course, we ignore the headings now since we are not on the 1st page headings since they occur just once in a program – to be able to print the first page information. They were done in cycle 1. Since RPG at this point is continuing to processing its first input record, it is highly unlikely that we printed enough detail records that the first page is full. Therefore, there will be no overflow processing on the second cycle and the next record can be brought in at Step 2 of the cycle. Then, we finish up total calculations from the prior input record in Step 3 in the cycle and the cycle keeps moving. In step 1, it helps to remember that RPG will print anything it can such as the contents of the last record read– not just headings as long as the output lines are either not conditioned or are conditioned with indicators that are on.

That actually about does it for our treatment of the generic RPG cycle in this book. To strengthen your knowledge of the RPG cycle, however, we provide a living example of the processing we have just explained in words. We defer this example to Chapter 5 in which we show the code to achieve what we have discussed regarding the cycle and as we fill them out, we describe the RPG specification forms so that you can get a better appreciate the form of this phenomenal language.

We just introduced the RPG cycle, a very powerful tool for report writing programs. At this point in this tutorial, you should know that the cycle begins by providing an opportunity to print headings, then it reads a data record, provides total calculations and total output, checks for end of job, makes fields available from the record just read, performs detail calculations and detail out put and gets ready for another round of output on the second cycle. The cycle cycles and cycles until all the input is processed.

RPG has a notion called an indicator that can be assigned to records in files. When particular records are read, RPG turns on indicators associated with them and turns off all of the other record identifying indicators. RPG also has a means of taking summary totals using various control levels from 1 to 9. Total calculations and total output occur when there is a change in a control record.

Matching records is another very powerful tool in RPG, especially when there are just two sequenced files in a program, though many files can be matched. By designating various fields in records to match with up to 9 designators (M1 to M9), when all of the matched fields in one file match those in another, RPG turns on the special MR indicator.

Because you can define multiple detail records for each input cycle, RPG has the ability of printing (outputting) multiple lines or records during one cycle or every cycle based on output record conditioning by using indicators to determine what gets output in what cycle. From output to input the cycle permits those specifications in RPG that invoke the various levels of the cycle to "do their thing." When you know the RPG cycle, you have mastered quite a bit since most report programs written by real RPG programmers use the cycle.

Lab 4 Using RPG Externally Described Files

Lab 4 Objectives:

Gives students opportunity to learn the differences between coding internally described files in RPG and coding externally described files.

Lab 4 – Exercise 1 External Master Listing

There are two approaches to this lab.

1. You may take the program LAB03PY that you just made work and use that to populate the program named LAB04EY that is the purpose of this lab.

2. You may use the shell program named LAB04E and work the lab by removing the XXs from the shell and making the code work.

In either case, you may look at the solution called LAB04ES when things aren't going well so that you know how your program solution is to be coded.

Purpose: gives students opportunity to change a program to make its main file use the externally described method of RPG coding. ..

Program Specifications

The program name when completed is to be LAB04EY. The "E" is for externally described files. The Y is because it is "Y"our program. Remember the solution is in LAB04ES and of course that "S" means "S"olution.

1. Look at the employee file and look at the report with its report and column headings

Figure 4-1 is a look at a record in the EMPMAST file with its default column headings. Use these headings for your report. Figure 4-1 shows a record in EMPMAST and its field contents. Figure 4-2 shows the data description specifications (DDS) that were used to define the EMPMAST database file. Figure 4-3 shows a query list of the data in the EMPMAST file that you will be using in your Labs. Figure 4-4 shows a Query listing of the data in the TIMCRD file that you will be using in your labs. Figure 4-5 is the report layout (without spacing) that you need to use to get your print positions correct in your program modifications.

Figure 4-1 EMPMAST Data Record

```
WORK WITH DATA IN A FILE              Mode . . . . :    CHANGE
Format . . . . :    EMPR              File . . . . :    EMPMAST


EMP NBR:           1
EMP NAME:          BIZZ NIZWONGER
EMP RATE:          780
EMPLOYEE CITY:     WILKES-BARRE
EMP STATE:         PA
EMP ZIP:           18702
SAL CODE:          N
DEPT CODE:         PING
```

Figure 4-2 Data Description for EMPMAST

```
Columns . . . :   1  71          Browse              YOURLIB/SOURCE
SEU==>                                               EMPMAST
FMT PF .....A..........T.Name++++++RLen++TDpB......Functions++++++++++++++++++
           *************** Beginning of data ****************************************
001.00      A         R EMPR
002.00      A           EMPNO      3S 0      COLHDG('EMP' 'NBR')
003.00      A           EMPNAM     30        COLHDG('EMP' 'NAME')
004.00      A           EMPRAT     5S 2      COLHDG('EMP' 'RATE')
005.00      A           EMPCTY     20        COLHDG('EMPLOYEE' 'CITY')
006.00      A           EMPSTA     2         COLHDG('EMP' 'STATE')
007.00      A           EMPZIP     5S 0      COLHDG('EMP' 'ZIP')
008.00      A           EMPSCD     1         COLHDG('SAL' 'CODE')
009.00      A           EMPDPT     4         COLHDG('DEPT' 'CODE')
010.00      A         K EMPNO
           ***************** End of data ****************************************
```

Figure 4-3 Query Listing of EMPMAST File Data

	EMP #	EMPNAM	EMP RAT	EMPCTY	EMP STA	EMP ZIP
000001	1	Bizz Nizwonger	7.80	Wilkes-Barre	PA	18702
000002	2	Warbler Jacoby	7.90	Wilkes-Barre	PA	18702
000003	3	Bing Crossley	8.55	Scranton	PA	18702
000004	4	Uptake N. Hibiter	7.80	Fairbanks	AK	99701
000005	5	Fenworth Gront	9.30	Fairbanks	AK	99701
000006	7	Bi Nomial	8.80	Fairbanks	AK	99701
000007	8	Milly Dewith	6.50	Juneau	AK	99801
000008	9	Sarah Bayou	10.45	Juneau	AK	99801
000009	10	Dirt McPug	6.45	Newark	NJ	07101

```
****** ********  End of report  ********
```

Figure 4-4 Query Listing of TIMCRD File Data

```
          EMPNO   EMPHRS
000001      1      35.00
000002      2      40.00
000003      3      65.00
000004      4      25.00
000005      5      33.00
000006      6      40.00
000007      7      39.00
000008      8      40.00
000009      9      40.00
000010     10      35.00
****** ********  End of report  ********
```

Figure 4-5 Spool File Look of Program Output

```
                    Display Spooled File
File  . . . . . :    QPRINT              Page/Line   1/6
Control . . . . .                        Columns     1 - 78
Find  . . . . . .
*...+....1....+....2....+....3....+....4....+....5....+....6....+....7....+...
         THE DOWALLOBY COMPANY EMPLOYEE LIST     BY STATE        6/09/07
  ST    CITY                 ZIP    EMP#   EMPLOYEE NAME          RATE
  PA    WILKES-BARRE        18702   001    BIZZ NIZWONGER         7.80
  PA    WILKES-BARRE        18702   002    WARBLER JACOBY         7.90
  PA    SCRANTON            18702   003    BING CROSSLEY          8.55
  AK    FAIRBANKS           99701   004    UPTAKE N. HIBITER      7.80
  AK    FAIRBANKS           99701   005    FENWORTH GRONT         9.30
  AK    FAIRBANKS           99701   007    BI NOMIAL              8.80
  AK    JUNEAU              99801   008    MILLY DEWITH           6.50
  AK    JUNEAU              99801   009    SARAH BAYOU           10.45
  NJ    NEWARK              07101   010    DIRT MCPUG             6.45
  NJ    NEWARK              07101   011    BANDAID JONES          4.50
              HASH TOTAL OF THE RATES               78.05
```

The written specifications for LAB03 are repeated below with the proper changes for LAB04 since this version of the program is to perform the same function. Read each of the specifications that are in bold since they are somewhat different to achieve the objectives of this lab. After the repeated information, additional instructions are given as to the approach to take to make this manual conversion from internally described files to externally described files happen correctly.

Space each field on the report so that it looks similar to the report shown above. Please note that the line spacing does not show in the spool file display but it does show on the actual printout.

1. Start your Lab exercise by signing on to the system and after a few panels you will see your RPG Programming Menu. This is the menu you will use for all of your RPG programming needs in all labs.

2. Continue this startup by taking option 3 and pressing Enter to start the program development manager (PDM).

3. From here (The PDM main panel), choose the Work with Members option # 3.

4. Type in SOURCE and your library name and press ENTER. When you get to the Work with members panel similar to the one shown in Figure 3-6, scroll until you find the LAB04E shell.

5. Make sure that in the report shown in Figure 4-5 (the objective output of this program) that you space each field on the report so that it looks similar to the report shown above in Figure 4-5.

6. Your mission again is to modify the existing LAB04E program in your SOURCE file to be an Externally Described program. It is to print the employee list as shown above just as the LAB03PY program did. We recommend that you copy the LAB04E shell rather than the LAB03PY program for this exercise.

7. The input is the EMPMAST file shown above and the output is a printer file. Use QPRINT for the file name.

8. The existing LAB04E program is similar to a copy of the LAB03PY solution. It helps to recall that Externally Described Data Files in RPG/400 do not need a record length in File Descriptions and they require no input specifications at all. So, your mission is to change the internal designator (F) in File Description of EMPMAST to E to make it externally described and to delete or comment (* in column 7) all of the input specs. You need no input specs for EMPMAST in program LAB04EY.

9. The record length for the QPRINT file should be 78.

10. Figure out how to make the report print using this record length. Hint (no end position can be past column 78)—just as was done with LAB03PY

11. Use the RPG cycle - make EMPMAST a primary file - Externally described

12. Do not bother with an indicator in input. Do not use indicator for LAB04EY.   There are no input specs so let's make this easy and not use a record identifying indicator -- (1 or 02 are not needed.) Basically the specs are the same as LAB03PY other than internal to external description change.

13. Skip to line 6 before printing the report title.

14. Space two spaces after printing the report title

15. Print the report title on the first page and on any overflow lines

16. Condition a line of column headings as shown in Figure 3-5 above spacing 3 after each heading... Note again that in the sample printout above, you do not see the proper line spacing

17. Space 1 before each detail line

18. Each record that is read turns on no indicator (01 is not necessary) Do not condition the calculation of the EMPRAT field to be totaled in an accumulator field called TOTRAT that is size 7 with 2 decimal places. No record ID indicator is needed and consequently no input specs at all are needed and no calc conditioning indicator is needed. .

19. Define this field, TOTRAT as a new field in RPG calcs.

20. There is a shell program named LAB04E (E = program described) for your use. This member in your source file contains the program that you are to modify -- namely LAB04E. It is in a state in which it reflects internally described data and your mission is to convert it to externally described. Thus, there is no need for the shell. It also has a number of XXs placed where things need to change.

The Y designator means that you created the program LAB04EY

The next set of steps outlined show you how to accomplish this SEU copy

21. The steps to get you actually moving again in this Lab are shown below beginning with this step. You have already started PDM and you are looking at the members list.

22. Hit F6 in PDM to create a new member Use LAB04EY as its name in your SOURCE file in YOUR library. Source type should be RPG

23. You will then be taken to the main SEU entry panel

24. Notice there is no source in the LAB04EY source member.

25. You need to hit F15 and begin the CC copy as you did in Lab 03. You need to copy this shell statements in LAB04E to the new source member LAB04EY.

26. You now have the program LAB04EY in your SEU Edit panel. Begin the edit process to solve the programming problem as defined at the beginning of this lab.

Figure 4-6 shows the entire program as it exists in your source file. As you can see on your own machine, however, just one page of this program is in your edit window. To see the rest of the program on your machine, scroll to the end.

When you finish editing the XXs and are reasonably assured that the program will run, end your SEU session by pressing F3..   The initial things that you need to eliminate or modify in LAB04EY are shown in Figure 4-6 as underlined. Additionally, you will have to change the xx conditioning indicator on the calculation line.

Figure 4-6 SEU Edit Panel with some required changes highlighted

```
 Columns . . . :    1  71              Edit                    YOURLIB/SOURCE
  SEU==>                                                       LAB04EY
 FMT *     ..... *. 1 ...+... 2 ...+... 3 ...+... 4 ...+... 5 ...+... 6 ...+... 7
           ************** Beginning of data **********************************
0001.00     H* RPG HEADER (CONTROL) SPECIFICATION FORMS    LAB03PS
0002.00     H* SOLUTION FOR LAB03
0003.00     H
0004.00     F*
0005.00     F* RPG FILE DESCRIPTION SPECIFICATION FORMS
0006.00     F*
0007.00     FEMPMAST IXX X       XX                DISK
0008.00     FQPRINT  O   F       78     XX         PRINTER
0009.00     I*
0010.00     I* RPG INPUT SPECIFICATION FORMS
0011.00     I*
0012.00     IEMPMAST AA   XX
0013.00     I                                      1     30EMPNO
0014.00     I                                      4     33 EMPNAM
0015.00     I                                      34    382EMPROT
0016.00     I                                      39    58 EMPCTY
0017.00     I                                      XX    XX EMPSTA
0018.00     I                                      XX    XXXEMPZPP
0019.00     I                                      XX    XX SALCOD
0020.00     I                                      XX    XX DEPT
0042.00     O        D 1      XX

 F3=Exit    F4=Prompt    F5=Refresh    F9=Retrieve    F10=Cursor   F11=Toggle
 F16=Repeat find         F17=Repeat change           F24=More keys
                                       (C) COPYRIGHT IBM CORP. 1981, 2005.
```

There are no steps 27 to 32 required.

33. Take the LAB04EY simple RPG programming lesson that begins immediately below and ends at Step 35. Then, you will have learned enough to modify the program to make it work and to produce the output in Figure 4-5.

34. Now, before you end anything since you have not changed anything, let's talk about this simple program as it should be in externally described form as it exercises the RPG cycle. Before this Lab, there is a short tutorial on the RPG cycle. It is important for you to read this if you have not done so in Lab 3—even before you take this Lab 4 simple programming lesson.

Because this is your first Externally Described Data Program, we have included the code below without the input specs and without the conditioning indicator on the calc spec and with. Note there is really only one decision for you as you look at the program below. This is the big one in File Description. Hint: Internally described files use an F for fixed format in column 19 and externally described files use an E-- for externally described. The program below marked in Figure 4-7 is almost ready to compile but the one change. Your program, however in your source file -- called LAB04EY is not in this good a shape and needs work to get it to this good a shape and then it needs you to make the decision as to what gets put in the one X shown in Figure 4-7.

Figure 4-7 The Whole LAB04EY Program with XXed out areas.

```
 Columns . . . :     1  71              Browse              RPGOBJ/SOURCE
 SEU==>                                                          LAB04E
 FMT *      ....*... 1 ...+... 2 ..+... 3 ...+... 4 ...+... 5 ...+... 6 ...+... 7
           *************** Beginning of data *********************************
0001.00        H* RPG HEADER (CONTROL) SPECIFICATION FORMS    LAB03PS
0002.00        H* SOLUTION FOR LAB03
0003.00        H
0004.00        F*
0005.00        F* RPG FILE DESCRIPTION SPECIFICATION FORMS
0006.00        F*
0007.00        FEMPMAST IPE X                      DISK
0008.00        FQPRINT  O  F      78      OF       PRINTER
0009.00        I*
0010.00        I* RPG INPUT SPECIFICATION FORMS
0011.00        I*
0012.00        C*
0013.00        C* RPG CALCULATION SPECIFICATION FORMS
0014.00        C*
0015.00        C                    ADD  EMPRAT    TOTRAT  72
0016.00        O*
0017.00        O* RPG OUTPUT SPECIFICATION FORMS
0018.00        O*
0019.00        OQPRINT  H  206    1P
0020.00        O       OR  206    OF
0021.00        O                               32 'THE DOWALLOBY COMPANY'
0022.00        O                               55 'EMPLOYEE LIST       BY '
0023.00        O                               60 'STATE'
0024.00        O                      UDATE Y  77
0025.00        OQPRINT  H  3      1P
0026.00        O       OR  3      OF
0027.00        O                                4 'ST'
0028.00        O                               13 'CITY'
0029.00        O                               37 'ZIP'
0030.00        O                               46 'EMP#'
0031.00        O                               61 'EMPLOYEE NAME'
0032.00        O                               77 'RATE'
0033.00        O       D  1
0034.00        O                      EMPSTA    4
0035.00        O                      EMPCTY   29
0036.00        O                      EMPZIP   39
0037.00        O                      EMPNO    45
0038.00        O                      EMPNAM   78
0039.00        O                      EMPRAT1  77
0040.00        O       T  22     LR
0041.00        O                               51 'HASH TOTAL OF THE RATES '
0042.00        O                      TOTRAT1  72
```

The LAB04EY Simple RPG Programming Lesson

RPG OUTPUT is First

From the RPG lecture immediately preceding this Lab 4, you may recall that output is done before input. The RPG cycle does all of the record reads without the programmer needing a READ or CHAIN statement. However, even before the first read, so that the program can print report titles and column headings, RPG first produces output. When RPG is ready to produce output, it will write to the device specified all of the lines defined that are unconditioned or those conditioned lines whose conditions are met. This is true whether the file is externally described or internally described.

The operative file that changes in this program from Lab 03 is the EMPMAST file. In this program (LAB04EY) it is defined as externally described. The QPRINT print file remains as internally described and therefore is almost exactly the same as it was in Lab 3.

The only real difference in how the output is treated is because we chose not to use an indicator for the Master input file in LAB04EY. In Lab 3, you may recall we suggested the use of indicator 01 since the examples were built to fit that. However, you could have used any numeric indicator as long as you used it consistently on input and output. Since in this program it is easier to merely permit the detail record to print unconditionally, thereby eliminating the requirement for input specs totally that is the change that is made. So, as you look at LAB04E, you will find the output detail line that had been conditioned with 01 to now be the following:

```
0033.00          O          D 1
```

To repeat, in Lab 3, you may recall that this line was conditioned by indicator 01.

The EMPMAST file is the input file for the LAB04EY program, just as it was for LAB03PY. We know that because, as shown in Figure 4-7, it is designated in column 15 with an I. Since it is now externally described, however, there are no input specifications required or defined for this file.

Primary File Description

After RPG does its heading work on the very first cycle, when indicator 1P is on, it goes to step 2 of the cycle to read in a record from the files defined either as primary or secondary in column 16 of file description. It reads the contents of the record into the input buffer. When a programmer uses a P or an S in column 16 of a file used for input (I) or update (U), that is how RPG becomes aware to use the cycle. Therefore, since LAB04EY requires the cycle to control input, you need to code EMPMAST in this program using the same P for primary designation that you used in Lab 3.

Column 17 in EMPMAST's file description entry should have an E in it to tell the program not to end until at least all the records from this file are read. This obviously has more meaning in programs that have more than one file and it is the same as in LAB03PY.

Input Happens in INPUT

There should be no input specifications defined for this file at all and none are needed. If we insisted on using the indicator 01 to condition the detailed output, however, we would have required a few input specifications that used file's format ID as NAME rather than its file name. In later labs we will show this technique for you to use then. For now, it is a fact that no input specifications are needed since you have no need in LAB04EY for record identifying indicators, matching records entries or control totals.

You probably have guessed that the big mystery in this program and what changes it from LAB03PY is the entry in column 19. This column in the description specification needs to say external and not be coded with an F for Fixed format (internal). If it is not an F, then it must be an E. If it is an E, then the input specifications will be fetched into the program from the EMPMAST database file at compile time and there is no reason for the programmer to have to type them in as in LAB03PY.

Getting Processing Done

Line 15 in calculations as depicted below shows that there is no Factor 1 needed in the statement but there is an entry in the Op-code, Factor2, and the Result field. No conditioning indicator is needed meaning that this code will be executed for each record read -- unconditionally.

```
0012.00    C*
0013.00    C* RPG CALCULATION SPECIFICATION FORMS
0014.00    C*
0015.00    C              ADD  EMPRAT   TOTRAT 72
```

This is exactly the same coding as we used in LAB03PY and thus there is no further explanation required in this Lab

*** End of Simple LAB04EY RPG Lesson ***

35. Hit F3 to begin the Exit SEU process.

36. Type a 14 next to the LAB04EY source member which holds the source statements for the soon-to-be LAB04EY program object. This will translate the source into object code and create an *PGM object type in your library (if you removed all of the XX's and replaced them with valid code. If you have not removed all of the errors, depending on severity, you will see a an error message:

`Compile stopped. Severity level 40 errors found in file.`

37. If you get a bad guy message such as this, if you know what the error is intrinsically (magically) then go back to source and correct it and resubmit your compile.

38. From the RPG Programming Menu , pick option 1 to examine your output. Take option 1 and press ENTER to see the contents of your Output Queue.

39. Type 5 next to what may be the only entry in the queue and press ENTER.

40. Use the roll down key to find the RPG errors.

41. If things don't go right, the RPG compiler calls out errors near the bottom of the panel on the left.

42. To bring your program to a clean compile, work through your source and remove all of the errors, replacing the bad code with code that is correct.

43. Another way to use this effectively is to exit WRKOUTQ and return to SEU. Edit the LAB04EY member and take the F15 option to copy the printout to the bottom of the screen panel.

44. Instead of copying source to the bottom of the screen this time, pick the option that says the following:

```
Browse/copy spool file .... LAB03EY   Name, F4 for list
```

45. Change the option to option 2, Spool file instead of Member. Make sure all the other parameters reflect your environment and press the ENTER key

46. When you get the next panel, position yourself to the SEU==> prompt on the bottom and enter the FIND command along with your error #, such as 2054 to locate the 2054 error description or the 2054 error in source.

47. Use the spool list on the bottom to find the errors one at a time and then position the cursor to the top part of the panel to use the editor to make the necessary changes. Repeat for as many errors as you find.

49. When you have seen enough of the spool file on the bottom and you want to go back to full screen mode, just hit F12 (CANCEL) and you will be back in the SEU full screen edit session.

50. From here hit F3 to exit SEU and take option 14 again to compile the LAB04EY program.

51. Repeat the process of reviewing the compile listing and editing in split screen mode until you have no more compile errors -- i.e. you have a clean compile, which will be recognized by this message on the bottom of the screen:

```
Program LAB04EY is placed in library YOURLIB. 00 highest
severity. Created
```

52. Once your program is compiled cleanly, you can run it.

53. Hit F3 from Work with members panel and then take option 2 on the Main PDM menu to Work with Objects

54. When you arrive at the panel it does not show all the options. RUN is not shown. To see RUN, press F23.

55. Now you are ready to run. Place the "16" option (RUN) next to LAB04EY and press Enter.

56. So, what happened? How do you even know what happened.?

57. It ran. Check out the report with option 1 of the RPG programming menu.

58. Just as you looked at your compile listings with option 1 of the RPG programmer menu, take it again and see what is there.

59. There may be two or more LAB04EY or LAB03PY printouts with varying amounts of pages depending on how often you tried to compile unsuccessfully. Look for the last item in the spooled output file list (QPRINT file). You may recall this standard printer file controlled the printing in your RPG program LAB03PY and therefore its name (QPRINT) shows up in the output queue. F18 gets you to the last printout.

60. Place a 5 next to the right QPRINT to see your report. If the program produced some other type of error when you ran it, your job would be to go into problem determination mode. This would involve looking at the printout -- either by printing the spool file or by the other methods (split screen and two terminals sessions) as discussed previously. You would go back to PDM and SEU and into the LAB03EY source and make the necessary changes and keep at it until your report is as clean as that shown in Figure 4-5.

Once you get to this point with a clean compile and a perfect printout, you have completed Lab 04. Congratulations...

Lab 5 RPG to RPGIV

Lab 5 Objectives:

Gives students opportunity to learn simple differences between coding RPG programs and RPGIV programs. Students will gain practical experience in converting RPG programs to RPGIV programs and seeing the functions work in the RPGIV environment.

Lab 5 Exercise 1

If you were doing this manually, without the command, you would copy both the internal and external versions (LAB03PY and LAB04EY) of the past programs and then start making the changes in much the same way as the last lab. First you would copy the internal version. The program name when copied would be LAB05P4Y. Then you would copy the external version to LAB05E4Y. The "E" is for externally described files. The 4 is for RPGIV. The P is for internal version. Because there is a program to do this for you, hold on for now on the copy.

Program Specifications

The LAB05P4Y and LAB05E4Y programs both list the employee file with report and column headings by converting the LAB03PY program to LAB05P4Y using the IBM CVTRPGSRC utility and by converting the LAB04EY program to LAB05E4Y. Once converted, compile and run the converted program.

Lab steps:

1. Use the PDM option on your RPG programming menu.

2. Take work with members (option 3) and press Enter. You will see a panel similar to that shown in Figure 5-1. This is merely to assure that the original programs are there and that the new programs are not there.

Figure 5-1 Preparing to run CVTRPGSRC

```
                      Work with Members Using PDM              YOURSYS

File . . . . .        SOURCE
  Library . . . .     YOURLIB               Position to . . . . .

Type options, press Enter.
 2=Edit          3=Copy   4=Delete 5=Display      6=Print      7=Rename
 8=Display description  9=Save  13=Change text  14=Compile  15=Create module...

Opt  Member       Type        Text
     INSTRUCT     TXT         MWOOD Installation Instructions
     LAB03ES      RPG         Code from Book - Internally Described 01
     LAB03P       RPG         Code from Book - Internally Described 01
     LAB03PS      RPG         Code from Book - Internally Described 01
     LAB03PY      RPG         Lab 03
     LAB04EY      RPG         Lab 03
     LANGUAGE     PF          LANGUAGE File For Hello World
     MAIN         RPGLE       Prototype Two- procs - All in one X
                                                              More...
Parameters or command
===> CVTRPGSRC
F3=Exit           F4=Prompt              F5=Refresh           F6=Create
F9=Retrieve       F10=Command entry      F23=More options     F24=More keys
```

3. Type CVTRPGSRC on the command line and press ENTER. You will see a panel that is not quite as complete as that shown in Figure 5-2.

Figure 5-2 CVTRPGSRC Parameter Panel for LAB03PY to LAB05P4Y

```
                      Convert RPG Source (CVTRPGSRC)

  Type choices, press Enter.

  From file  . . . . . . . . . .  > SOURCE        Name
    Library  . . . . . . . . . .  >   YOURLIB     Name, *LIBL, *CURLIB
  From member  . . . . . . . . .  > LAB03PY       Name, generic*, *ALL
  To file  . . . . . . . . . . .  > SOURCE        Name, *NONE, QRPGLESRC
    Library  . . . . . . . . . .  >   YOURLIB     Name, *LIBL, *CURLIB
  To member  . . . . . . . . . .  > LAB05P4Y      Name, *FROMMBR




                                                 Bottom
  F3=Exit    F4=Prompt   F5=Refresh F10=Additional parameters F12=Cancel
  F13=How to use this display        F24=More keys
```

4. Fill in the panel as shown in Figure 5-2 and press ENTER to convert your internal RPG code to RPGIV. FYI, your SOURCE file has already been expanded to work with 112 character records as required by RPGIV. Since 112 is bigger than 92, the size needed to work with RPG/400 programs, both types of programs fit fine inside of the one SOURCE file.

5. Fill up Figure 5-2 again by typing in CVTRPGSRC. This is shown in Figure 5-3. This time the from member needs to be LAB04EY and the to member needs to be LAB05E4Y. Run the conversion program.

Figure 5-3 CVTRPGSRC Parameter Panel for LAB04EY to LAB05E4Y

```
                    Convert RPG Source (CVTRPGSRC)

Type choices, press Enter.

From file  . . . . . . . . . . . > SOURCE        Name
  Library  . . . . . . . . . . >    YOURLIB      Name, *LIBL, *CURLIB
From member  . . . . . . . . . > LAB04EY         Name, generic*, *ALL
To file  . . . . . . . . . . . > SOURCE          Name, *NONE, QRPGLESRC
  Library  . . . . . . . . . . >    YOURLIB      Name, *LIBL, *CURLIB
To member  . . . . . . . . . . > LAB05E4Y        Name, *FROMMBR




                                         Bottom
F3=Exit    F4=Prompt    F5=Refresh F10=Additional parameters F12=Cancel
F13=How to use this display        F24=More keys
```

Figure 5-4 The program LAB05P4Y and LAB05E4Y have been converted to RPGIV

```
                    Work with Members Using PDM              YOURSYS

File  . . . . . .      SOURCE
  Library . . . .        YOURLIB            Position to  . . . . .

Type options, press Enter.
 2=Edit          3=Copy  4=Delete 5=Display        6=Print      7=Rename
 8=Display descr  9=Save  13=Change text  14=Compile  15=Create module...

Opt  Member      Type        Text
     INSTRUCT    TXT         MWOOD Installation Instructions
     LAB03ES     RPG         Code from Book - Internally Described 01
     LAB03P      RPG         Code from Book - Internally Described 01
     LAB03PS     RPG         Code from Book - Internally Described 01
     LAB03PY     RPG         Lab 03
     LAB04EY     RPG         Lab 04
2    LAB05P4Y    RPGLE       Lab 05.1 Internal RPG IV Converted Code
     LAB05E4Y    RPGLE       Lab 05.2 External RPG IV Converted Code
     LANGUAGE    PF          LANGUAGE File For Hello World
     MAIN        RPGLE       Prototype Two- procs - All in one X
                                                            More...
Parameters or command
===>
F3=Exit          F4=Prompt          F5=Refresh          F6=Create
F9=Retrieve      F10=Command entry  F23=More options    F24=More keys
Member LAB05E4Y added to file SOURCE, library YOURLIB.
```

One after the other as the two programs are converted the system provides a message at the bottom of the panel as shown in Figure 5-4 for LAB05E4Y.

Member LAB05P4Y added to file SOURCE, library YOURLIB
Member LAB05E4Y added to file SOURCE, library YOURLIB

5. Notice that LAB05P4Y has been added to your source file in YOURLIB. When you run the CVTRPGSRC against LAB04EY as directed above, LAB05E4Y will also appear in the Work with Members list (shown in Figure 5-4 above). Now, so you can get a look at what the conversion to RPGIV did, take option 2 to edit the LAB05P4Y program. You can also take option 5 because we will not be changing anything. Take note that the TYPE is now RPGLE (RPGIV) and the program is different though as you will see in Figure 5-4, it is not substantially different since the conversion program merely took what was in the RPG/400 program and reformatted it for the RPGIV column structure.

After you convert LAB05E4Y, bring it up with SEU in the same fashion so that you can see its differences also

Figure 5-5 AN SEU Look at the CONVERTED RPG Internal Data Description Code

```
  Columns . . . :    6  76            Browse                YOURLIB/SOURCE
  SEU==>                                                    LAB05P4Y
  FMT H     HKeywords+++++++++++++++++++++++++++++++++++++++++++++++++++++++++++++++++++
            *************** Beginning of data *************************************
  0001.00 H* RPG HEADER (CONTROL) SPECIFICATION FORMS    LAB05P4Y
  0002.00 H* SOLUTION FOR LAB03
  0003.00 H
  0004.00 F*
  0005.00 F* RPG FILE DESCRIPTION SPECIFICATION FORMS
  0006.00 F*
  0007.00 FEMPMAST    IPE  F   70           DISK
  0008.00 FQPRINT     O    F   78           PRINTER OFLIND(*INOF)
  0009.00 I*
  0010.00 I* RPG INPUT SPECIFICATION FORMS
  0011.00 I*
  0012.00 IEMPMAST    AA   01
  0013.00 I                                 1     3 0EMPNO
  0014.00 I                                 4    33  EMPNAM
  0015.00 I                                34    38 2EMPRAT
  0016.00 I                                39    58  EMPCTY

   F3=Exit    F5=Refresh    F9=Retrieve   F10=Cursor    F11=Toggle    F12=Cancel
   F16=Repeat find          F24=More keys
                                  (C) COPYRIGHT IBM CORP. 1981, 2005.
```

6. Take note of this first page of the converted code. The most major change is the keyword used in line 8. RPGIV uses keywords to perform functions that took columns in RPG/400. Hit F3 when you have analyzed this program enough and go back to PDM Work with members. Scroll through the program to notice that for the most part, the rest of the program looks very similar.

7. . Now, since your program compiled as LAB03PY, in LAB 03, take option 14 against its RPGIV version LAB05P4Y and press ENTER. Do the same for LAB05E4Y

8. You should see at the bottom of your panel

Program LAB05P4Y placed in library YOURLIB 00 highest severity. Created on

Program LAB05E4Y placed in library YOURLIB 00 highest severity. Created on

9. The compile listing for LAB05EY is shown below. Note that the files that were externally described are expanded and shown in the compile listing, just as with RPG/400.

Figure 5-6 Compile Listing of LAB05E4Y (RPGIV External) Converted Program

```
...
  Preprocessor options . . . . . . :    *NONE
  5761WDS V6R1M0  080215 RN       IBM ILE RPG          RPGOBJ/LAB05E4S
Line   <-------------------- Source Specifications ----------------------
Number ....1....+....2....+....3....+....4....+....5....+....6....+....7....+.
                          S o u r c e   L i s t i n g
     1 H* RPG HEADER (CONTROL) SPECIFICATION FORMS   LAB05
     2 H* SOLUTION FOR LAB03
     3 H
     4 F*
     5 F* RPG FILE DESCRIPTION SPECIFICATION FORMS
     6 F*
     7 FEMPMAST    IPE  E            DISK
        *-----------------------------------------------------------------
        *                            RPG name          External name
        * File name. . . . . . . . :  EMPMAST          RPGOBJ/EMPMAST
        * Record format(s) . . . . :  EMPR             EMPR
        *-----------------------------------------------------------------
     8 FQPRINT    O   F  78          PRINTER OFLIND(*INOF)
     9 C*
    10 C* RPG CALCULATION SPECIFICATION FORMS
    11 C*
    12=IEMPR
        *-----------------------------------------------------------------
        * RPG record format  . . . . :  EMPR
        * External format  . . . . . :  EMPR : RPGOBJ/EMPMAST
        *-----------------------------------------------------------------
    13=I                              S    1    3 0EMPNO
    14=I                              A    4   33  EMPNAM
    15=I                              S   34   38 2EMPRAT
    16=I                              A   39   58  EMPCTY
    17=I                              A   59   60  EMPSTA
    18=I                              S   61   65 0EMPZIP
    19=I                              A   66   66  EMPSCD
    20=I                              A   67   70  EMPDPT
    21 C                 ADD     EMPRAT        TOTRAT           7 2
    22 O*
    23 O* RPG OUTPUT SPECIFICATION FORMS
    24 O*
    25 OQPRINT    H    1P                       2 06
    26 O            OR    OF                    2 06
    27 O                                              32 'THE DOWALLOBY COMPANY'
    28 O                                              55 'EMPLOYEE LIST       BY '
    29 O                                              60 'STATE'
    30 O                    UDATE           Y   77
    31 OQPRINT    H    1P                       3
    32 O            OR    OF                    3
    33 O                                               4 'ST'
    34 O                                              13 'CITY'
    35 O                                              37 'ZIP'
    36 O                                              46 'EMP#'
  5761WDS V6R1M0  080215 RN       IBM ILE RPG          RPGOBJ/LAB05E4S
Line   <-------------------- Source Specifications ----------------------
```

```
Number ....1....+....2....+....3....+....4....+....5....+....6....+....7....+.
      37 O                                               61 'EMPLOYEE NAME'
      38 O                                               77 'RATE'
      39 O              D                       1
      40 O                        EMPSTA                  4
      41 O                        EMPCTY                 29
      42 O                        EMPZIP                 39
      43 O                        EMPNO                  45
      44 O                        EMPNAM                 78
      45 O                        EMPRAT         1       77
      46 O          T   LR                    2 2
      47 O                                               51 'HASH TOTAL OF THE RATES
      48 O                        TOTRAT         1       72
          * * * * *   E N D   O F   S O U R C E   * * * * *
```

```
5761WDS V6R1M0  080215 RN        IBM ILE RPG           RPGOBJ/LAB05E4S
          A d d i t i o n a l   D i a g n o s t i c   M e s s a g e s
   Msg id  Sv Number  Seq      Message text
  *RNF7086 00      7 000700    RPG handles blocking for file EMPMAST. INFDS is upd
                              only when blocks of data are transferred.
   * * * * *   E N D   O F   A D D I T I O N A L   D I A G N O S T I C   M E S S
          O u t p u t   B u f f e r   P o s i t i o n s
   Line   Start End    Field or Constant
   Number Pos   Pos
      27   12    32   'THE DOWALLOBY COMPANY'
      28   34    55   'EMPLOYEE LIST        BY '
      29   56    60   'STATE'
      30   70    77   UDATE
      33    3     4   'ST'
      34   10    13   'CITY'
      35   35    37   'ZIP'
      36   43    46   'EMP#'
      37   49    61   'EMPLOYEE NAME'
      38   74    77   'RATE'
      40    3     4   EMPSTA
      41   10    29   EMPCTY
      42   35    39   EMPZIP
      43   43    45   EMPNO
      44   49    78   EMPNAM
      45   72    77   EMPRAT
      47   28    51   'HASH TOTAL OF THE RATES '
      48   64    72   TOTRAT
   * * * * *   E N D   O F   O U T P U T   B U F F E R   P O S I T I O N   * *
```

```
5761WDS V6R1M0  080215 RN        IBM ILE RPG           RPGOBJ/LAB05E4S
                    C r o s s   R e f e r e n c e
      File and Record References:
          File               Device          References (D=Defined)
           Record
          EMPMAST            DISK                7D
           EMPR                                  7D      12
           QPRINT            PRINTER             8D      25        31
      Global Field References:
          Field              Attributes       References (D=Defined M=Modified
          *INOF              N(1)                8D
          EMPCTY             A(20)              16D      41
  *RNF7031 EMPDPT            A(4)               20D
          EMPNAM             A(30)              14D      44
          EMPNO              P(3,0)             13D      43
          EMPRAT             P(5,2)             15D      21        45
  *RNF7031 EMPSCD            A(1)               19D
          EMPSTA             A(2)               17D      40
          EMPZIP             P(5,0)             18D      42
          TOTRAT             P(7,2)             21D      48
          UDATE              S(6,0)             30
      Indicator References:
          Indicator                           References (D=Defined M=Modified
          LR                                   46
          OF                                    8D      26        32
          1P                                   25       31
          * * * * *   E N D   O F   C R O S S   R E F E R E N C E   * * * * *
```

```
5761WDS V6R1M0  080215 RN        IBM ILE RPG           RPGOBJ/LAB05E4S
                 E x t e r n a l   R e f e r e n c e s
      Statically bound procedures:
          Procedure                           References
          No references in the source.
```

```
        Imported fields:
            Field              Attributes         Defined
            No references in the source.
        Exported fields:
            Field              Attributes         Defined
            No references in the source.
     * * * * *  E N D   O F   E X T E R N A L   R E F E R E N C E S   * * * * *
     5761WDS V6R1M0  080215 RN      IBM ILE RPG          RPGOBJ/LAB05E4S
                            M e s s a g e   S u m m a r y
     Msg id  Sv Number Message text
     *RNF7031 00       2 The name or indicator is not referenced.
     *RNF7086 00       1 RPG handles blocking for the file. INFDS is updated only wh
                         blocks of data are transferred.
                                                                        More...
          * * * * *  E N D   O F   M E S S A G E   S U M M A R Y  * * * * *
     5761WDS V6R1M0  080215 RN      IBM ILE RPG          RPGOBJ/LAB05E4S
                            F i n a l   S u m m a r y
      Message Totals:
        Information   (00) . . . . . . . . :          3
        Warning       (10) . . . . . . . . :          0
        Error         (20) . . . . . . . . :          0
        Severe Error (30+) . . . . . . . . :          0
        -----------------------------------  -------
        Total . . . . . . . . . . . . . . :          3
      Source Totals:
        Records . . . . . . . . . . . . . :         48
        Specifications . . . . . . . . . :         37
        Data records . . . . . . . . . . :          0
        Comments . . . . . . . . . . . . :         11
            * * * * *  E N D   O F   F I N A L   S U M M A R Y   * * * * *
                                                                        More...
     Program LAB05E4S placed in library RPGOBJ. 00 highest severity. Created on
     07/24/09 at 06:30:32.
```

Figure 5-7 Reading an RPGIV Compiler Listing

Section/ Description

1.   Compile Options e.g. Preprocessor options . . . . :   *

2.   Source Listing e.g. S o u r c e   L i s t i n g
   Note the expansion of the EMPMAST file format EMPR in line 12

3.   Additional Diagnostic Messages e.g.
   A d d i t i o n a l   D i a g n o s t i c   M e s s a g e s
   Msg id   Sv Number Seq   Message text
   *RNF7086 00   7 000700 RPG handles blocking for file EMPMAST. INFDS is upd
   only when blocks of data are transferred.
   Note that this is severity zero -- ignore

4.   Program Field Definitions / Buffer Positions e.g.
   O u t p u t   B u f f e r   P o s i t i o n

5.   Cross References -- for finding things e.g.
   C r o s s   R e f e r e n c **e s**

6.   External References e.g.
   Exported fields:

7.   Message Summary -- Look here first for error messages e.g.
   *RNF7031 00   2 The name or indicator is not referenced
   Note such errors occur frequently -- fields in files not always used.

8.   Final Summary Summation

9.   Program compiled and Saved messages e.g.
   Program LAB05E4S placed in library RPGOBJ. 00 highest severity.
   Created on 07/24/09 at 06:30:32.

10. Make sure that you have performed steps 1 through 9 for both programs LAB03PY and LAB04EY. In other words, convert, compile, and run the programs after they are stored as LAB05P4Y and LAB05E4Y respectively. When you are finished the conversion and the clean compilation, you should see , you are just about done with lab 5.

Using the command line, type in the following to execute these programs.

```
CALL LAB05P4Y
CALL LAB05E4Y
```

Use your RPG menu to display your output queue and look for the two printouts. They should not only be identical but they should also be identical to the printouts for LAB03PY and LAB04EY.

*** You have now successfully completed Lab 5.

Lab 6:   Create a Payroll Register Report with RPG, Two Input Files Internally Described

Lab 6 Objectives:

Students learn how to use the report writing productivity features of the RPG language including matching records and control level processing. This program is very similar to the PAREG program defined withing the RPG Pocket Text Book that is often used with this Lab Book.

Lab 6 – Exercise 1

Method 1: *More Difficult Approach - Not Recommended* -- Copy your Lab 3 result using PDM COPY to create the beginnings of an internally described version of a new program called LAB06PY. To this, you will have to add all of the code to support the new requirements that are listed for Method 2. The Payroll Master Definition and some of the output is valid and gives the student a small head start to getting the mission accomplished.

Method 2: *Recommended* -- USE PDM COPY (option 3) to copy the LAB06P shell into your source file and rename the copy as LAB06PY. Do not use the SEU COPY. The Y stands for you. To this, you will have to add certain codes that have been omitted and you will have to change the XXs in the code to the proper entries. Method 2 should be the easier method and is recommended for beginners. This Lab offers more of an opportunity to perform the function on the machine without everything being given in the instructions. Since you have already written a few successful RPG programs, this exercise builds on the skills you have already gained and does not attempt to re-teach all of them.

Whichever method is used, the program is to produce a gross pay register in sequence city within state. It should provide city totals, state totals, and final totals as shown in Figure 6-1.

Program Specifications

Assume the data is in sequence city within state. By design (an this is admittedly a learning contrivance), it is also in EMPNO sequence. Thus both the level totals on city and state and the matching records on employee number both work effectively. However, most real life situations will not have data so nicely organized.

The final report should look like the report shown in Figure 6-1 with one exception. There will be one record in your report for Bandaid Jones that is not shown in the below report.

Figure 6-1 Gross Pay Register by State -- Report Model

```
THE DOWALLOBY COMPANY GROSS PAY REGISTER BY STATE        2/21/06

ST     CITY          EMP#    EMPLOYEE NAME        RATE     HOURS      CHECK

PA     Wilkes-Barre  001     Bizz Nizwonger       7.80     35.00     273.00
PA     Wilkes-Barre  002     Warbler Jacoby       7.90     40.00     316.00

                             TOTAL CITY  PAY FOR Wilkes-Barre         589.00

PA     Scranton      003     Bing Crossley        8.55     65.00     555.75

                             TOTAL CITY  PAY FOR Scranton             555.75

                             TOTAL STATE PAY FOR PA                 1,144.75

AK     Fairbanks     004     Uptake N. Hibiter    7.80     25.00     195.00
AK     Fairbanks     005     Fenworth Gront       9.30     33.00     306.90
                     006 NO MATCHING MASTER                40.00
AK     Fairbanks     007     Bi Nomial            8.80     39.00     343.20

                             TOTAL CITY  PAY FOR Fairbanks           845.10

AK     Juneau        008     Milly Dewith         6.50     40.00     260.00
AK     Juneau        009     Sarah Bayou         10.45     40.00     418.00

                             TOTAL CITY  PAY FOR Juneau              678.00

                             TOTAL STATE PAY FOR AK                 1,523.10

NJ     Newark        010     Dirt McPug           6.45     35.00     225.75

                             TOTAL CITY  PAY FOR Newark              225.75

                             TOTAL STATE PAY FOR NJ                  225.75

                             FINAL TOTAL PAY                       2,893.60
```

Figure 6-2 is the same look at a single record in the EMPMAST file with its default column headings as we saw in Lab 3. Use these headings for your report. Figure 6-3 shows the data description specifications (DDS) that were used to define the EMPMAST database file. Figure 6-4 is a picture of all the Employee data in the file from a spooled query printout. Figure 6-5 is a look at a record in the TIMCRD (payroll time cards) file with default column headings. Use these headings as necessary for the register report. Figure 6-6 shows the data description specifications (DDS) that were used to define the TIMCRD database file. Figure 6-7 is a picture of all the time card data in the TIMCRD file from a spooled printout.

Figure 6-2 EMPMAST Data Record

```
WORK WITH DATA IN A FILE                      Mode . . . . :     CHANGE
Format . . . . :     EMPR                      File . . . . :     EMPMAST


EMP NBR:              1
EMP NAME:            BIZZ NIZWONGER
EMP RATE:            780
EMPLOYEE CITY:      WILKES-BARRE
EMP STATE:          PA
EMP ZIP:            18702
SAL CODE:           N
DEPT CODE:          PING
```

Figure 6-3 Data Description for EMPMAST

```
Columns . . . :    1  71         Browse              YOURLIB/SOURCE
SEU==>                                                EMPMAST
FMT PF .....A.........T.Name+++++RLen++TDpB.....Functions++++++++++++++++++
       *************** Beginning of data ********************************
001.00      A       R EMPR
002.00      A         EMPNO      3S 0       COLHDG('EMP' 'NBR')
003.00      A         EMPNAM     30         COLHDG('EMP' 'NAME')
004.00      A         EMPRAT     5S 2       COLHDG('EMP' 'RATE')
005.00      A         EMPCTY     20         COLHDG('EMPLOYEE' 'CITY')
006.00      A         EMPSTA     2          COLHDG('EMP' 'STATE')
007.00      A         EMPZIP     5S 0       COLHDG('EMP' 'ZIP')
008.00      A         EMPSCD     1          COLHDG('SAL' 'CODE')
009.00      A         EMPDPT     4          COLHDG('DEPT' 'CODE')
010.00      A       K EMPNO
       ***************** End of data ********************************
```

Figure 6-4 Query Report of EMPMAST Data

```
                           Display Report
                                     Report width . . . . . :        66
Position to line . . . . .        Shift to column . . . . . .
Line      ....+....1....+....2....+....3....+....4....+....5....+....6....+.
       EMP EMP                 EMP   EMPLOYEE        EMP   EMP SAL DEPT
       NBR NAME                RATE  CITY            STATE ZIP COD CODE
000001   1 BIZZ NIZWONGER      7.80  WILKES-BARRE    PA    18702 N  PING
000002   2 WARBLER JACOBY      7.90  WILKES-BARRE    PA    18702 N  MILL
000003   3 BING CROSSLEY       8.55  SCRANTON        PA    18702 Y  GRND
000004   4 UPTAKE N. HIBITER   7.80  FAIRBANKS       AK    99701 Y  GRND
000005   5 FENWORTH GRONT      9.30  FAIRBANKS       AK    99701 N  MILL
000006   7 BI NOMIAL           8.80  FAIRBANKS       AK    99701 N  PING
000007   8 MILLY DEWITH        6.50  JUNEAU          AK    99801 N  SAND
000008   9 SARAH BAYOU        10.45  JUNEAU          AK    99801 N  SAND
000009  10 DIRT MCPUG          6.45  NEWARK          NJ    07101 N  MILL
000010  11 BANDAID JONES       4.50  NEWARK          NJ    07101 N  PING
****** ******** End of report  ********
```

Figure 6-5 TIMCRD Data Record

```
WORK WITH DATA IN A FILE                    Mode . . . . :    CHANGE
Format . . . . :     TIMR                    File . . . . :    TIMCRD


EMP NBR:      1
EMP HOURS: 3500






F3=Exit                F5=Refresh           F6=Select format
F9=Insert              F10=Entry            F11=Change
```

Figure 6-6 Data Description for EMPMAST

```
 Columns . . . :    1  71          Browse              YOURLIB/SOURCE
  SEU==>                                                    TIMCRD
 FMT PF .....A.........T.Name+++++++RLen++TDpB......Functions++++++++++++++++++
        *************** Beginning of data **********************************
0001.00    A          R TIMR
0002.00    A            EMPNO        3S 0        COLHDG('EMP' 'NBR')
0003.00    A            EMPHRS       4S 2        COLHDG('EMP' 'HOURS')
0004.00    A          K EMPNO
        ***************** End of data ************************************
```

Figure 6-7 Query Listing of TIMCRD File Data

```
        EMPNO   EMPHRS
000001     1     35.00
000002     2     40.00
000003     3     65.00
000004     4     25.00
000005     5     33.00
000006     6     40.00
000007     7     39.00
000008     8     40.00
000009     9     40.00
000010    10     35.00
****** ******** End of report ********
```

If you choose to use Method 1, the above specifications are still adequate. You need to read the specifications for method 2 and extrapolate for Method 1. The specifications for LAB 06 Exercise 1 for Method 2 are shown below:

Space each field on the report so that it looks similar to the report shown in Figure 6-1. The final arbiter of whether you have done the job is if your report, when run, looks like the report as shown in Figure 6-1. Please note that the line spacing does not show in the spool file display but it does show on the actual printout presented in Figure 6-1. .

Since we have already discussed the rudiments of RPG specification sheets in Lab 4 and we have described the most basic operations in terms of the spec sheets, this information is not repeated in Lab 6. The RPG Text book has chapters on each of the RPG specifications if you need to learn more or if you need a refresher. Additionally, the instructions for building PAREG program, introduced in Chapter 6 of the RPG text book and used as the sample program to describe all of the RPG forms in subsequent chapters may be helpful in this exercise. As noted previously, the LAB06 program set in this Lab book is very similar if not identical to PAREG from the RPG text book. The names have been changed in the Lab book to accommodate the Lab naming structure. .

Detailed Lab 06 Instructions

1. Write the LAB06PY internally described program to print the Gross Pay Register as shown above

2. The input is the EMPMAST and the TIMCRD files shown above.

3. The output is a printer file. Use QPRINT for the file name for the report shown in Figure 6-1.
.

4. Record length for EMPMAST is 70, TIMCRD is 7.

5. The record length for the QPRINT file should be 77.

6. Figure out how to make the report print using this record length - check out figure 6-1.

7. Use the RPG cycle - make EMPMAST a primary file - program described

8. Use indicator 01 to recognize a master record read on the input cycle

9. Use the RPG cycle, make TIMCRD a secondary file - program described.

10. Use indicator 02 to recognize a time card record read on the input cycle

11. Set up two control levels -- City within state -- EMPMAST input record -- not necessary on time card.

12. Set up matching records so that the match field is EMPNO. File sequence is contrived to be in EMPNO sequence and in CITY within state to make this program work.

13. Skip to line 6 before printing the report title.

14. Space two spaces after printing the report title

15. Print the report title on the first page or on any overflow lines.

16. Condition a line of column headings as in Figure 6-1 spacing 3 after each heading. In the sample printout above in Figure 6-1, the line spacing is correct.

17. Space 1 before each detail line

18. Rehash the rules of matching records from the System i Pocket RPG & RPGIV Guide or from the IBM RPG Reference Manual or Lecture E. Take note specifically the relationship of the record ID indicator with the matching record indicator For example, in order to write this program properly, you need to know what causes the following indicator conditions to occur -- given that we are using matching records and indicator 01 for a master (EMPMAST) record read and indicator 02 for a transaction (TIMCRD) record read. You must understand what causes these conditions to occur to condition output properly:

	01	02	MR	RPG Coding	Meaning
1.	ON	OFF	ON	01 MR	Match and EMPMAST is read
2.	OFF	ON	ON	02 MR	Match and TIMCRD is read
3.	ON	OFF	OFF	01 NMR	No Match and EMPMAST
4.	OFF	ON	OFF	02 NMR	No Match and TIMCRD

When listed condition 2 occurs, that is the time that detail calculations should be performed followed by detailed output. When condition 1 occurs, the master is read and there is a match but the time card data (the rate) has not been read yet so that is not a good condition upon which to base calculations or output.

19. It is OK to have a master without a time card since some weeks some people do not work. Therefore the condition (3) known as 01 NMR is OK.

20. It is not OK to have a time card without a master. Therefore, an error condition must be printed on the report when a time card record is being processed (record ID indicator 02) that does not match a master record (NMR) Therefore, for the condition coded as 02 NMR, the error message NO MATCHING MASTER needs to be printed on the report as shown in Figure 6-1. for employee # 6.

21. For a matched master, 01 MR, no calculations or output needs to be done.

22. When a matched secondary arrives, it means the master for that secondary has already been processed and its information is in the master fields. The field "rate" is the important field for calculations. Therefore, for the condition of 02 MR (secondary matched), the pay rate from the master should be multiplied by the number of hours in the time card record..

23. Also, for the condition of a matched secondary, 02 MR, the extension (rate X hours) needs to be added to the CITY total.

24. Also, for the condition of a matched secondary, 02 MR, the detail line for the Gross Register should be printed.

25. Define the city total field in an RPG calculations spec as 9 places, 2 decimals..

26. Code all other information so that the report occurs as noted in Figure 6-1.

27, When the City field changes during the secondary cycle (L1 condition), add the city total to the state total. Skip the proper amount of spaces and print the city total field. along with the prompt as shown in Figure 6-1. You would have previously assigned the L1 indicator to the city control field.

28. Also, when the city field changes, during the secondary cycle, clear out the city total so the next city's total can begin to accumulate. An effective way to do this is to use the blank after facility in output (put a B in column 39), rather then trying to do this in calculations.

29. When the State field changes during the secondary cycle, add the state total to the final total. Skip the proper amount of spaces and print the State total field. along with the prompt as shown in Figure 6-1. You would have previously assigned the L2 indicator to the state control field.

30. Also, when the state field changes, during the secondary cycle, clear out the state total so the next state's total can begin to accumulate. An effective way to do this is to use the blank after facility in output (B in 39), rather then trying to do this in calculations.

31. When LR is on, print the final totals. since there are no more totals to process, you do not have to blank out this field.

32. Your program will end

Operational Instructions

33. To prepare for this logic, when you start PDM, copy the LAB06P shell into a new member that you will call LAB03PY as follows as shown in Figure 6-9. Start the process by going back to your RPG Programming menu as shown in Figure 6-8.

Figure 6-8 RPG Programming Menu with Option 3 selected to start PDM

```
RPGMENU                         RPG Programming Menu

 Select one of the following:

         1. Work with output queue
         2. Refresh Files After Creation
         3. Start PDM
         4. Start SQL
         5. Display Library List
         6. Run AS/400 Query
         7. Display Submitted Jobs
         8. Start Screen Design Aid (SDA
         9.
        10. Run Some Programs
        11. Signoff




 Selection or command
 ===> 3

 F3=Exit    F4=Prompt    F9=Retrieve    F12=Cancel
```

34. From your main RPG Programming Menu, take option 3 to start PDM.

Figure 6-9 Work With Members -- Select the LAB06P Shell

```
                    Work with Members Using PDM          YOURSYS

 File . . . . . .   SOURCE
   Library . . . .   YOURLIB              Position to . . . . .

 Type options, press Enter.
  2=Edit          3=Copy  4=Delete 5=Display       6=Print     7=Rename
  8=Display description  9=Save  13=Change text  14=Compile  15=Create module...

 Opt  Member      Type        Text
      INSTRUCT    TXT         MWOOD Installation Instructions
      LAB03ES     RPG         Code from Book - Internally Described Solution
      LAB03P      RPG         Code from Book - Internally Described Problem
      LAB03PS     RPG         Solution for Lab 03 program described
      LAB03PY     RPG         Lab 03 RPG Internally Described
      LAB04EY     RPG         Lab 04 RPG Externally Described
      LAB05E4Y    RPGLE       LAB 05 RPGIV Externally Described
  3   LAB06P      RPG         LAB 06 Internally Described Problem
                                                           More...
 Parameters or command
 ===>
 F3=Exit          F4=Prompt           F5=Refresh           F6=Create
 F9=Retrieve      F10=Command entry   F23=More options     F24=More keys
```

35. Place a 3 next to the LAB06P shell as above and hit ENTER.

Figure 6-10 Copy Members to create LAB06PY

```
                            Copy Members

  From file . . . . . . . . :       SOURCE
    From library . . . . :         YOURLIB


  Type the file name and library name to receive the copied members.

    To file . . . . . . . .      SOURCE         Name, F4 for list
      To library . . . . .         YOURLIB


  To rename copied member, type New Name, press Enter.


  Member              New Name
  LAB06P              LAB06PY




                                                           Bottom

  F3=Exit              F4=Prompt       F5=Refresh      F12=Cancel
  F19=Submit to batch
```

36. When you see this happy panel, type in LAB06PY and hit ENTER to get to the next panel:

Figure 6-11 Source Member LAB06PY appears in your members panel after COPY

```
                    Work with Members Using PDM              YOURSYS

  File . . . . . .      SOURCE
    Library . . . .       YOURLIB           Position to . . . . .

  Type options, press Enter.
    2=Edit          3=Copy  4=Delete 5=Display       6=Print      7=Rename
    8=Display description  9=Save  13=Change text  14=Compile  15=Create module...

  Opt  Member        Type        Text
       LAB06PS       RPG         LAB 06 Internally Described Solution
    2  LAB06PY       RPG         LAB 06 Internally Described Problem
       LANGUAGE      PF          LANGUAGE File For Hello World
       MAIN          RPGLE       Prototype Two- procs - All in one X
       MLHMAST       PF
       NAMEDCON      RPGLE
       NEW           DSPF
       PANEL         DSPF        Display File Panel For Advanced Hello World
                                                                   More...
  Parameters or command
  ===>
  F3=Exit           F4=Prompt           F5=Refresh           F6=Create
  F9=Retrieve       F10=Command entry   F23=More options     F24=More keys
```

37. Scroll down until you see LAB06PY and take option 2 to edit the source program

Figure 6-12 SEU Edit Panel for LAB06PY

```
 Columns . . . :      1  71            Browse              YOURLIB/SOURCE
  SEU==>                                                        LAB06PY
 FMT *   ..... *. 1 ...+... 2 ...+... 3 ...+... 4 ...+... 5 ...+... 6 ...+..
         *************** Beginning of data **********************************
0001.00       H* RPG HEADER (CONTROL) SPECIFICATION FORMS
0002.00       H
0003.00       F*
0004.00       F* RPG FILE DESCRIPTION SPECIFICATION FORMS
0005.00       F*
0006.00       FEMPMAST IPEAF      70            DISK
0007.00       FTIMCRD  IXXXX       7            XXXXXXX
0008.00       FQPRINT  O  F       77     OF     PRINTER
0009.00       I*
0010.00       I* RPG INPUT SPECIFICATION FORMS
0011.00       I*
0012.00       IEMPMAST AA   01
0013.00       I                                    1    30EMPNO    XX
0014.00       I                                    4   33 EMPNAM
0015.00       I                                   34  382EMPRAT
0016.00       I                                   39  58 EMPCTYXX

 F3=Exit     F5=Refresh     F9=Retrieve   F10=Cursor   F11=Toggle   F12=Cancel
 F16=Repeat find           F24=More keys
                                  (C) COPYRIGHT IBM CORP. 1981, 2005.
```

38. Notice the XX on line 13 of LAB06PY in Figure 6-12. . This spot is for some type of matching record indication. Throughout the LAB06PY source program so that you do not have to type the whole thing, XXs are provided in which you need to select the appropriate response. Additionally, there are some areas that have no entries or perhaps the wrong entries so this is a thinking exercise. From 6-12, perform all your editing, scrolling through the source member to achieve this while making necessary changes.

39. Once all the editing changes are completed, pick F3 and end the SEU program and choose to save your source in member LAB06PY (the default at this point).

40. Now that you have saved the source member, compile it by placing a 14 next to LAB06PY in the PDM member list. When the compile finishes cleanly, you will receive a message at the bottom of your PDM panel that looks like the following:

Program LAB06PY is placed in library YOURLIB. 00 highest severity. Created

41. Now you have compiled the contents of a source member named LAB06PY in file SOURCE in YOURLIB. The result of the compilation using PDM is to place the compiled **OBJECT** into the same library in which your source member is located. (You can change this when you place F14 next to the member to compile by hitting F4 and getting a prompted compile with all of the parameters available for modification.). However, the PDM defaults that place the object in YOURLIB are fine for these Lab Exercises.

Your next step is to run or execute (synonyms in this case) the LAB06PY program that is now resident as an object in your library. The first step in this process is to exit the Work with members display of PDM and go to the PDM main menu. Take F3 to do this and you will be taken to a panel similar to Figure 6-13 below:

Figure 6-13 PDM Main Menu -- Moving to the Work with Objects Panel

```
                    Programming Development Manager (PDM)

Select one of the following:

     1. Work with libraries
     2. Work with objects
     3. Work with members

     9. Work with user-defined options




     Information about new tools - press F1 for details




Selection or command
===> 2

F3=Exit        F4=Prompt        F9=Retrieve        F10=Command entry
F12=Cancel     F18=Change defaults
```

42. We had been operating with option 3 Work with members. Our source statements collectively named LAB06PY are stored in a file object named SOURCE within a member named LAB06PY. The file SOURCE is an object in your library (We use YOURLIB to refer to your library) When you pick option 2 above and hit ENTER, if you choose to scroll down far enough in the *OBJECT* list, you will come to SOURCE, the file object. You may recall that you can place a 12 (work with members in source) next to this object and it will take you back to the Work with members panel inside the SOURCE file object. Since we have already done our editing and have in fact compiled the program (Created the program object), there is no need to take option 12.. We provide this information as a reminder to help differentiate the notion of source and members and objects.

So, to continue, place a 2 as shown in Figure 6-13 and press the ENTER key. This will take you to the Specify Objects to Work With objects panel as shown in Figure 6-14.

Figure 6-14 Specify Objects to Work With (not members)

```
                    Specify Objects to Work With

Type choices, press Enter.

  Library  . . . . . . . . . .      YOURLIB   *CURLIB, name

  Object:
    Name . . . . . . . . . .        *ALL      *ALL, name, *generic*
    Type . . . . . . . . . .        *ALL      *ALL, *type
    Attribute  . . . . . . . .      *ALL      *ALL, attribute, *generic*,
                                              *BLANK


F3=Exit      F5=Refresh      F12=Cancel
```

43. Press ENTER to advance to the PDM Objects panel

Figure 6-15 Work with objects -- find LAB06PY to run

```
                 Work with Objects Using PDM            YOURSYS

Library . . . . .   YOURLIB          Position to . . . . . . . .
                                     Position to type  . . . . .

Type options, press Enter.
  2=Change         3=Copy         4=Delete      5=Display       7=Rename
  8=Display description           9=Save       10=Restore      11=Move ...

Opt  Object      Type      Attribute   Text
16   LAB06PY     *PGM      RPG         LAB 06 Internally Described Solution
     PAREGP      *PGM      RPG         Code from Book - Internally Described
     RPGSTART    *PGM      CLP         Profile start program for RPG Course
     WORKQ       *PGM      CLP         Chnge work output queue display to st
     RPGGUY01    *OUTQ
     CUSTAUTH    *FILE     PF-DTA      Customer Download Authentication File
     CUSTOMER    *FILE     PF-DTA      Customer physical file (used to compi
     CUSTOMER1   *FILE     PF-DTA      Customer physical file (used to compi
                                                                      More...
Parameters or command
===> CALL YOURLIB/LAB06PY
F3=Exit            F4=Prompt             F5=Refresh         F6=Create
F9=Retrieve        F10=Command entry     F23=More options   F24=More keys
```

44. Take option 16 to run the program object.   However, before you do that look at the command line at the bottom:

CALL YOURLIB/LAB06PY

First of all, this is invalid. If you hit the ENTER key now, you will get the following message:

Positional value cannot follow keyword parameter.

PDM does not permit you to pick a command option and also type in a command. That's why this error occurs. However, either option will perform the same thing if the other is taken away. For example, if you remove the 16 or you remove the CALL statement, and you press F4 to get a prompt for the command, both options will render to you the following panel in Figure 6-16..

Figure 6-16 Call Program under prompt

```
                          Call Program (CALL)

  Type choices, press Enter.


  Program  . . . . . . . . . . . . > LAB06PY        Name
    Library  . . . . . . . . . . . >   YOURLIB      Name, *LIBL, *CURLIB
  Parameters . . . . . . . . . . .

                     + for more values



                                                              Bottom
  F3=Exit F4=Prompt F5=Refresh F12=Cancel    F13=How to use this display
  F24=More keys
```

45. From PDM, we know that option 16 runs a program. Well in IBM i/OS this translates to a command language (CL) call statement and the prompt is as shown in Figure 6-16. PDM pre-prompts with the current library as you can see and the command that we entered includes the library so both will give the same thing. Press enter now to run the program. After the program runs, you will return to PDM as shown in Figure 6-17.

Figure 6-17 After the program runs (almost instantaneously)

```
                   Work with Objects Using PDM              YOURSYS

   Library . . . . .    YOURLIB        Position to . . . . . . . .
                                       Position to type  . . . . .


   Type options, press Enter.
     2=Change        3=Copy        4=Delete      5=Display      7=Rename
     8=Display description         9=Save        10=Restore     11=Move ...

   Opt  Object     Type     Attribute   Text
        LAB06PY    *PGM     RPG         LAB 06 Internally Described Solution
        PAREGP     *PGM     RPG         Code from Book - Internally Described
        RPGSTART   *PGM     CLP         Profile start program for RPG Course
        WORKQ      *PGM     CLP         Chnge work output queue display to st
        RPGGUY01   *OUTQ
        CUSTAUTH   *FILE    PF-DTA      Customer Download Authentication File
        CUSTOMER   *FILE    PF-DTA      Customer physical file (used to compi
        CUSTOMER1  *FILE    PF-DTA      Customer physical file (used to compi
                                                                    More...
   Parameters or command
   ===>
   F3=Exit          F4=Prompt        F5=Refresh        F6=Create
   F9=Retrieve      F10=Command entry F23=More options F24=More keys
```

46. Notice that you get no messages. The program runs in an instant and places its output in your output queue. Go back to your RPG Programming Menu to check out the spool file produced for this report.   Hit F3 twice to go back to your RPG Programmer Menu

Figure 6-18 Preparing to see the printed output

```
RPGMENU                         RPG Programming Menu

Select one of the following:

       1. Work with output queue
       2. Refresh Files After Creation
       3. Start PDM
       4. Start SQL
       5. Display Library List
       6. Run AS/400 Query
       7. Work With Submitted Jobs
       8. Start Screen Design Aid (SDA).
       9.
      10. Run Some Programs
      11. Signoff


Selection or command
===> 1


F3=Exit    F4=Prompt    F9=Retrieve    F12=Cancel
F13=Information Assistant  F16=System main menu
```

47. Take Option 1 from your menu to go to your output queue to look for the printout.

Figure 6-19 The Expanding Output Queue in YOURLIB

```
                      Work with Output Queue

Queue:   YOURQ          Library:   YOURLIB       Status:   RLS

Type options, press Enter.
  1=Send    2=Change    3=Hold    4=Delete    5=Display    6=Release    7=Messages
  8=Attributes         9=Work with printing status

Opt   File        User         User Data     Sts   Pages   Copies   Form Type   Pty
      LAB03PY     RPGGUY01                   RDY     9       1      *STD         5
      LAB03PY     RPGGUY01                   RDY     9       1      *STD         5
      LAB03PS     RPGGUY01                   RDY     6       1      *STD         5
      QPRINT      RPGGUY01     LAB03PS       RDY     1       1      *STD         5
      LAB06PY     RPGGUY01                   RDY     6       1      *STD         5
5     QPRINT      RPGGUY01     LAB06PY       RDY     1       1      *STD         5


                                                            Bottom
Parameters for options 1, 2, 3 or command
===>
F3=Exit    F11=View 2    F12=Cancel    F20=Writers    F22=Printers
F24=More keys
```

48. Notice QPRINT is in the list. The print file in your program LAB06PY is QPRINT so one of these two QPRINT files is the one you are looking for. With no other information, you would pick the last one in the queue since they are displayed in the queue FIFO and the last one is the last thing you printed. Type a 5 on the last QPRINT while you notice that its USER DATA is the name of the program that ran to produce the output - LAB06PY. This is another way to ID your stuff in an Output Queue.

Figure 6-20 The Printed Report Solution from LAB06PY with poetic license

```
                         Display Spooled File
File  .  .  .  .  .  :    QPRINT                  Page/Line    1/6
Control  .  .  .  .  .                            Columns      1 - 78
Find  .  .  .  .  .  .
*...+....1....+....2....+....3....+....4....+....5....+....6....+....7....+...
          THE DOWALLOBY COMPANY GROSS PAY REGISTER BY STATE          6/15/07
   ST      CITY         EMP#      EMPLOYEE NAME       RATE   HOURS     CHECK
   PA    WILKES-BARRE  BIZZ NIZWONGER               7.80    35.00    273.00
   PA    WILKES-BARRE  WARBLER JACOBY               7.90    40.00    316.00
                          TOTAL CITY   PAY FOR WILKES-BARRE         589.00
   PA    SCRANTON      BING CROSSLEY                8.55    65.00    555.75
                          TOTAL CITY   PAY FOR SCRANTON            555.75
                          TOTAL STATE PAY FOR PA                 1,144.75
   AK    FAIRBANKS     UPTAKE N. HIBITER            7.80    25.00    195.00
   AK    FAIRBANKS     FENWORTH GRONT               9.30    33.00    306.90
                       006 NO MATCHING MASTER               40.00
   AK    FAIRBANKS     BI NOMIAL                    8.80    39.00    343.20
                          TOTAL CITY   PAY FOR FAIRBANKS           845.10
   AK    JUNEAU        MILLY DEWITH                 6.50    40.00    260.00
   AK    JUNEAU        SARAH BAYOU                 10.45    40.00    418.00
                          TOTAL CITY   PAY FOR JUNEAU             678.00
                                                              More...
                          TOTAL STATE PAY FOR AK               1,523.10
   NJ    NEWARK        DIRT MCPUG                   6.45    35.50    228.97
                          TOTAL CITY   PAY FOR NEWARK            228.97
                          TOTAL STATE PAY FOR NJ                 228.97
                             FINAL TOTAL PAY                   2,896.82
```

49. Examine the output in the queue. It should be very similar to that shown in Figure 6-20. When your program produces results like this, you have succeeded. It may not look exactly like Figure 6-1 which is a real printout but if it looks like Figure 6-20, it has done its job. If anything is wrong with your printout, go back and edit the program, make the fixes and repeat this process until this is exactly correct.

When you are sure this work is exactly correct, then you have successfully completed Lab 6.

Lab 7:   Create a Payroll Register Report with RPG, Two Input Files Externally Described

Lab 7 Objectives:

Students learn how to write a report writing program (Payroll Register) using productivity features of the RPG language including matching records and control level processing as created in Lab 6 Exercise 1 while changing the DB files to externally described. The program, LAB07EY is very similar if not identical to the externally described version of PAREG in the RPG text book.

Lab 7 – Exercise 1

Method 1: Copy your Lab 4 result to create another externally described version of a new program called LAB07EY. To this, you will have to add all of the code to support the new requirements as described for LAB 06 and then apply the external DB changes required for LAB 07. This is the more difficult method and I do not recommend this approach -- at least your first time through.

Method 2: Use PDM to copy the LAB06PY completed program from Lab 6 into your source file and rename the copy as LAB07EY. Check the task list outlined in Lab 4 to help get you through this lab. LAB04 was the lab in which you first converted an internally described RPG program to an externally described version. The Y as you have learned stands for "_Y_our" program. In Lab 6, you already completed the program by added codes that had been omitted and you changed the XXs in the code to the proper entries. Method 2 again is the easier method and I recommend that you use this method. .

Whichever method is used, just as LAB06PY, the LAB07EY program is to produce a gross pay register in sequence of city within state. It should provide city totals, state totals, and final totals as per the sample report shown in Figure 7-1. You are to assume the data is in sequence city within state and though admittedly this arrangement is contrived for teaching purposes. The data is also in EMPNO sequence and this too is part of the contrivance. The final report should look like the report shown in Figure 7-1 with one exception. There will be one record in your report for Bandaid Jones that is not shown in the below report.

The essence of this Lab 7 Exercise 1 then is to take the work completed in LAB 6, a program called LAB06PY, that you built as internally described and convert it manually to a program that uses externally described files for both the EMPMAST and TIMCRD payroll files. Then in their external format, the files provide input to the PAY07EY program as they did in PAY06PY and the program produces the Gross Pay Register as shown in Figure 7-1 below:

Figure 7-1 Gross Pay Register by State -- Report Model

```
        THE DOWALLOBY COMPANY GROSS PAY REGISTER BY STATE        2/21/06

ST      CITY            EMP#    EMPLOYEE NAME         RATE    HOURS     CHECK

PA      Wilkes-Barre    001     Bizz Nizwonger        7.80    35.00    273.00
PA      Wilkes-Barre    002     Warbler Jacoby        7.90    40.00    316.00

                                TOTAL CITY PAY FOR Wilkes-Barre        589.00

PA      Scranton        003     Bing Crossley         8.55    65.00    555.75

                                TOTAL CITY PAY FOR Scranton           555.75

                                TOTAL STATE PAY FOR PA             1,144.75

AK      Fairbanks       004     Uptake N. Hibiter     7.80    25.00    195.00
AK      Fairbanks       005     Fenworth Gront        9.30    33.00    306.90
                        006 NO MATCHING MASTER                40.00
AK      Fairbanks       007     Bi Nomial             8.80    39.00    343.20

                                TOTAL CITY PAY FOR Fairbanks          845.10

AK      Juneau          008     Milly Dewith          6.50    40.00    260.00
AK      Juneau          009     Sarah Bayou          10.45    40.00    418.00

                                TOTAL CITY PAY FOR Juneau            678.00

                                TOTAL STATE PAY FOR AK            1,523.10

NJ      Newark          010     Dirt McPug            6.45    35.00    225.75

                                TOTAL CITY PAY FOR Newark            225.75

                                TOTAL STATE PAY FOR NJ              225.75

                                FINAL TOTAL PAY                   2,893.60
```

Program Specifications

The overall program specifications are the same as those for LAB06PY. The difference in this program will be that the File Descriptions must change to show the files as externally described. Unlike LAB04EY, which required no input specifications since the externally described file EMPMAST in the program relieved the programmer of coding any input specifications at all, this program needs a few input specifications. Since program LAB06PY uses matching records and it uses control totals (level breaks) input specifications need to be provided to cause these facilities to be activated. Otherwise, there would be no way to specify the M1 and L1 facilities required by the program. However, any input fields other than these and a record format input line are not required.

Let me repeat this again for effect. One of the major advantages of defining files in an external fashion in RPG and RPGIV is that input and output coding is not required. However, one of the biggest advantages of the RPG cycle, which is used in the internal and external versions of this program, is that it handles matching records processing and control level processing very efficiently.

This program uses two matched files with EMPNO as the matched fields, and it produces final, state (report total level 2) and city (report total level 1) totals in the report. It is impossible to get L1 and L2 totals without input fields as that is where the L1 and L2 are specified. Likewise it is impossible to use MR logic without specifying M1 on an input spec. Thus, input is required for the two DB files but the input records required is just for those fields requiring the L1, L2, and M1 specifications. The other DB fields do not need to be specified.

Thus, this program should be structured very much like LAB06PY in the description of the input specifications. You are to change the input record format to be external and include the field definitions only for those fields needing M1, L1, L2 as coded in PAY06PY. The best way to do this is to keep all the input fields from LAB06PY that have either an L1, L2, or M1 on them. Delete all the other input specifications since you will be changing the file descriptions for EMPMAST and TIMCRD to an "E" format for externally described. The deleted input specs will be brought back into the program by the compiler from the database at compile time. Thus, they will display even though you did not have to code them in the program.

For your convenience, the EMPMAST data record is presented as is the TIMCRD record. Figure 7-2 is the same look at a record in the EMPMAST file with its default column headings as we saw in Lab 6. Use these headings for your report. Figure 7-3 shows the data description specifications (DDS) that were used to define the EMPMAST database file. Figure 7-4 is a picture of all the Employee data in the file from a spooled printout. Figure 7-5 is a look at a record in the TIMCRD (payroll time cards) file with default column headings. Use these headings as necessary for the register report. Figure 7-6 shows the data description specifications (DDS) that were used to define the TIMCRD database file. Figure 7-7 is a picture of all the time card data in the TIMCRD file from a spooled printout.

Figure 7-2 EMPMAST Data Record

```
WORK WITH DATA IN A FILE              Mode . . . . :    CHANGE
Format . . . . :    EMPR              File . . . . :    EMPMAST


EMP NBR:            1
EMP NAME:          BIZZ NIZWONGER
EMP RATE:            780
EMPLOYEE CITY: WILKES-BARRE
EMP STATE:         PA
EMP ZIP:           18702
SAL CODE:          N
DEPT CODE:         PING
```

Figure 7-3 Data Description for EMPMAST

```
Columns . . . :    1  71        Browse              YOURLIB/SOURCE
SEU==>                                                     EMPMAST
FMT PF  .....A..........T.Name+++++RLen++TDpB......Functions++++++++++++++++++
       *************** Beginning of data ***************************************
001.00    A          R EMPR
002.00    A            EMPNO         3S 0      COLHDG('EMP' 'NBR')
003.00    A            EMPNAM       30         COLHDG('EMP' 'NAME')
004.00    A            EMPRAT        5S 2      COLHDG('EMP' 'RATE')
005.00    A            EMPCTY       20         COLHDG('EMPLOYEE' 'CITY')
006.00    A            EMPSTA        2         COLHDG('EMP' 'STATE')
007.00    A            EMPZIP        5S 0      COLHDG('EMP' 'ZIP')
008.00    A            EMPSCD        1         COLHDG('SAL' 'CODE')
009.00    A            EMPDPT        4         COLHDG('DEPT' 'CODE')
010.00    A          K EMPNO
       ***************** End of data *****************************************
```

Figure 7-4 Query Report of EMPMAST Data

```
                              Display Report
                                   Report width . . . . . :      66
Position to line  . . . . .        Shift to column . . . . . .
Line      ....+....1....+....2....+....3....+....4....+....5....+....6....+.
         EMP EMP               EMP  EMPLOYEE       EMP      EMP SAL DEPT
         NBR NAME              RATE CITY           STATE    ZIP COD CODE
000001    1 BIZZ NIZWONGER     7.80 WILKES-BARRE    PA    18702  N  PING
000002    2 WARBLER JACOBY     7.90 WILKES-BARRE    PA    18702  N  MILL
000003    3 BING CROSSLEY      8.55 SCRANTON        PA    18702  Y  GRND
000004    4 UPTAKE N. HIBITER  7.80 FAIRBANKS       AK    99701  Y  GRND
000005    5 FENWORTH GRONT     9.30 FAIRBANKS       AK    99701  N  MILL
000006    7 BI NOMIAL          8.80 FAIRBANKS       AK    99701  N  PING
000007    8 MILLY DEWITH       6.50 JUNEAU          AK    99801  N  SAND
000008    9 SARAH BAYOU       10.45 JUNEAU          AK    99801  N  SAND
000009   10 DIRT MCPUG         6.45 NEWARK          NJ    07101  N  MILL
000010   11 BANDAID JONES      4.50 NEWARK          NJ    07101  N  PING
****** ********  End of report  ********
```

Figure 7-5 TIMCRD Data Record

```
WORK WITH DATA IN A FILE                Mode . . . . :    CHANGE
Format . . . . :    TIMR                File . . . . :    TIMCRD


EMP NBR:      1
EMP HOURS: 3500




F3=Exit              F5=Refresh              F6=Select format
F9=Insert            F10=Entry               F11=Change
```

Figure 7-6 Data Description for EMPMAST

```
 Columns . . . :     1  71              Browse                YOURLIB/SOURCE
  SEU==>                                                             TIMCRD
  FMT PF .....A..........T.Name++++++RLen++TDpB......Functions+++++++++++++++++++
         *************** Beginning of data **********************************
0001.00       A         R TIMR
0002.00       A           EMPNO           3S 0        COLHDG('EMP' 'NBR')
0003.00       A           EMPHRS          4S 2        COLHDG('EMP' 'HOURS')
0004.00       A         K EMPNO
         ***************** End of data ***********************************
```

Figure 7-7 Query Listing of TIMCRD File Data

```
        EMPNO   EMPHRS
000001    1     35.00
000002    2     40.00
000003    3     65.00
000004    4     25.00
000005    5     33.00
000006    6     40.00
000007    7     39.00
000008    8     40.00
000009    9     40.00
000010   10     35.00
****** ******** End of report ********
```

If you choose to use Method 1, the above specifications are adequate. You may gain by reading the specifications for method 2, but do not follow them specifically. The specifications for LAB 07 Exercise 1 for Method 2 are shown below:

Space each field on the report so that it looks similar to the report shown above. Please note that the line spacing does not show in the spool file display but it does show on the actual printout.

Just as LAB04EY, this set of lab instructions will show those steps which need to be performed to make this internally described program into an externally described program.

Detailed Lab 07 Instructions

1. Convert the LAB06PY internally described program to be externally described named LAB07EY. Print the Gross Pay Register as shown above

2. The input is the EMPMAST and the TIMCRD files shown above.

3. The output is a printer file. Use QPRINT for the file name.

4. Record length for EMPMAST is 70, TIMCRD is 7. (Remove the record length from the files. NO record length required for external files. The compiler learns the record length by examining the metadata in the DB file objects.)

5. The record length for the QPRINT file should be 77.

6. Figure out how to make the report print using this record length - check out figure 7-1.

7. Use the RPG cycle - make EMPMAST a primary file - program described

8. Use indicator 01 to recognize an external master record read on the input cycle, Use the record format name rather than the file name as the input name in the RPG program. When using internally described data in INPUT, the file name is appropriate. So, you need to know the DB record format name to use here.

Note: to find out the record format name in a database file object, you may use the display file description command. This command goes into the file and displays all important attributes, including the record format name. So, type DSPFD EMPMAST and press Enter. Then, scroll down a number of times until you see the following information on one of the screen panel:


```
Record Format List

                       Record   Format Level
   Format      Fields  Length   Identifier
   EMPR             8      70    3AA650ABA83F4
```


In your input record specification, since this is externally described and yet still needs input because of MR and L1/L2, you must specify the record format name of the EMPMAST file. As you can see immediately above as the result of the DSPFD, the name to use is "EMPR." So, make sure you put EMPR in the input name for the EMPMAST input specifications.

Use DSPFD again for the TIMCRD file, scroll and find its record format name so that in the input specs for the TIMCRD file, you can use this record format name discovered by executing the DSPFD command. FYI, the name is TIMR

9. Use the RPG cycle, make TIMCRD a secondary file - externally described.

10. Use indicator 02 to recognize an external time card record read on the input cycle Specify the format names not the file names.

11. Set up two control levels -- City (L1) within state (L2) --using EMPR input record format - external form and TIMR input record format

12. Set up matching records so that the match field is EMPNO. Specify M1 on both the EMPMAST (EMPR) input field EMPNO and the TIMCRD (TIMR) field EMPNO. File sequence is contrived to be in EMPNO sequence and in CITY within state to make this program work. Use A for ascending in column 18 of file descriptions for each file.

13. Skip to line 6 before printing the report title.

14. Space two spaces after printing the report title.

15. Print the report title on the first page or on any overflow lines.

16. Condition a line of column headings as above spacing 3 after each heading

17. Space 1 before each detail line

18. Rehash the rules of matching records from the System i Pocket RPG & RPGIV Guide, Lecture E, or the IBM manuals available on the Web -- or all three. Take note specifically the relationship of the record ID indicator with the matching record indicator For example, in order to write this program properly, you need to know what causes the following indicator conditions to occur -- given that we are using matching records and indicator 01 for a master (EMPMAST) record read and indicator 02 for a transaction (TIMCRD) record read. You must understand what causes these conditions to occur to condition output properly:

```
        01   02   MR      RPG Coding   Meaning
1.      ON   OFF  ON      01   MR      Match and EMPMAST is read
2.      OFF  ON   ON      02   MR      Match and TIMCRD is read
3.      ON   OFF  OFF     01   NMR     No Match and EMPMAST read
4.      OFF  ON   OFF     02   NMR     No Match and TIMCRD read
```

When listed condition 2 occurs, that is the time that detail calculations should be performed followed by detailed output. (02 MR) When condition 1 occurs, the master is read and there is a match but the time card data (the rate) has not been read yet so that is not a good condition upon which to base calculations or output processing. When 02 and MR is there, the time card and the master data for a particular employee is available and ready to process.

19. It is OK to have a master without a time card since in some pay some weeks some people do not work. Therefore the condition known as 01 NMR is OK.

20. It is not OK to have a time card without a master. Therefore, an error condition must be printed on the report when a time card record is being processed (record ID indicator 02) that does not match a master record (NMR) Therefore, for the condition coded as 02 NMR, the error message NO MATCHING MASTER needs to be printed on the report as shown in Figure 6-1. for employee # 6. Do not code anything specifically for employee # 6. If you code the 02 NMR on a detail line by itself, it will take care of this condition.

21. For a matched master, 01 MR, no calculations or output needs to be done.

22. When a matched secondary arrives, it means the master for that secondary has already been processed and its information is in the master fields. The field rate is the important field for calculations. Therefore, for the condition of 02 MR (secondary matched), the pay rate from the master should be multiplied by the number of hours in the time card record..

23. Also, for the condition of a matched secondary, the extension (rate X hours) needs to be added to the CITY total.

24. Also, for the condition of a matched secondary, the detail line for the Gross Register should be printed.

25. Define the city total field in RPG calcs as 9 places, 2 decimals..

26. Code all other information so that the report occurs as noted.

27, When the City field changes during the secondary cycle, add the city total to the state total. Skip the proper amount of spaces and print the city total field. along with the prompt as shown in Figure 6-1. You would have previously assigned the L1 indicator to the city control field. Use Group indication the next cycle for the City.

28. Also, when the city field changes, during the secondary cycle, clear out the city total so the next city's total can begin to accumulate. An effective way to do this is to use the blank after facility in output, rather then trying to do this in calculations.

29, When the State field changes during the secondary cycle, add the state total to the final total. Skip the proper amount of spaces and print the State total field. along with the prompt as shown in Figure 6-1. You would have previously assigned the L2 indicator to the state control field.

30. Also, when the state field changes, during the secondary cycle, clear out the state total so the next state's total can begin to accumulate. An effective way to do this is to use the blank after facility in output, rather then trying to do this in calculations.

31. Since there are no more totals to process, you do not have to blank out this field.

32. Your program will end

33. To prepare for this logic, when you start PDM, copy the LAB06PY program into a new member that you will call LAB07EY as follows as shown in Figure 7-9. Start the process by going back to your RPG Programming menu as shown in Figure 7-8.

Figure 7-8 RPG Programming Menu with Option 3 selected to start PDM

```
RPGMENU                         RPG Programming Menu

  Select one of the following:


         1.  Work with output queue
         2.  Refresh Files After Creation
         3.  Start PDM
         4.  Start SQL
         5.  Display Library List
         6.  Run AS/400 Query
         7.  Display Submitted Jobs
         8.  Start Screen Design Aid (SDA
         9.
        10.  Run Some Programs
        11.  Signoff




  Selection or command
  ===> 3


  F3=Exit    F4=Prompt    F9=Retrieve    F12=Cancel
```

34. From your main RPG Programming Menu, take option 3 to start PDM.

Figure 7-9 Work With Members -- Select the LAB06PY source program

```
                    Work with Members Using PDM            YOURSYS

  File . . . . . .    SOURCE
    Library . . . .   YOURLIB               Position to  . . . . .

  Type options, press Enter.
    2=Edit          3=Copy   4=Delete 5=Display       6=Print      7=Rename
    8=Display description  9=Save  13=Change text  14=Compile  15=Create module...

  Opt  Member       Type        Text
       INSTRUCT     TXT         MWOOD Installation Instructions
       LAB03ES      RPG         Code from Book - Internally Described Solution
       LAB03P       RPG         Code from Book - Internally Described Problem
       LAB03PS      RPG         Solution for Lab 03 program described
       LAB03PY      RPG         Lab 03 RPG Internally Described
       LAB04EY      RPG         Lab 04 RPG Externally Described
       LAB05E4Y     RPGLE       LAB 05 RPGIV Externally Described
  3    LAB06PY      RPG         LAB 06 Internally Described Problem
                                                                      More...
  Parameters or command
  ===>
  F3=Exit          F4=Prompt            F5=Refresh           F6=Create
  F9=Retrieve      F10=Command entry    F23=More options     F24=More keys
```

35. Place a 3 next to the LAB06PY as above and hit ENTER.

Figure 7-10 Copy Members to create LAB07EY

```
                           Copy Members

  From file . . . . . . . . :    SOURCE
    From library  . . . . :        YOURLIB

  Type the file name and library name to receive the copied members.

     To file . . . . . . .      SOURCE       Name, F4 for list
        To library . . . . .     YOURLIB

  To rename copied member, type New Name, press Enter.


  Member            New Name
  LAB06PY            LAB07EY


                                                        Bottom
  F3=Exit                F4=Prompt       F5=Refresh      F12=Cancel
  F19=Submit to batch
```

36. When you see this happy panel, type in LAB07EY and hit ENTER to get to the next panel:

Figure 7-11 Source Member LAB07EY appears in your members panel after COPY

```
                  Work with Members Using PDM            YOURSYS

  File . . . . . .    SOURCE
    Library . . . .    YOURLIB            Position to . . . . .

  Type options, press Enter.
   2=Edit         3=Copy  4=Delete 5=Display      6=Print     7=Rename
   8=Display description  9=Save  13=Change text  14=Compile  15=Create module...

  Opt  Member      Type      Text
       LAB06PS     RPG       LAB 06 Internally Described Solution
   2   LAB07EY     RPG       LAB 07 Externally Described Problem
       LANGUAGE    PF        LANGUAGE File For Hello World
       MAIN        RPGLE     Prototype Two- procs - All in one X
       MLHMAST     PF
       NAMEDCON    RPGLE
       NEW         DSPF
       PANEL       DSPF      Display File Panel For Advanced Hello World
                                                              More...
  Parameters or command
  ===>
  F3=Exit         F4=Prompt             F5=Refresh          F6=Create
  F9=Retrieve     F10=Command entry     F23=More options    F24=More keys
```

37. Scroll down until you see LAB07EY and take option 2 to edit the source program

Figure 7-12 SEU Edit Panel for LAB07EY

```
 Columns . . . :    1  71            Edit              YOURLIB/SOURCE
 SEU==>                                                LAB07EY
 FMT *   ..... *. 1 ...+... 2 ...+... 3 ...+... 4 ...+... 5 ...+... 6 ...+... 7
         *************** Beginning of data ***************************************
0001.00      H* RPG HEADER (CONTROL) SPECIFICATION FORMS
0002.00      H
0003.00      F*
0004.00      F* RPG FILE DESCRIPTION SPECIFICATION FORMS
0005.00      F*
0006.00      FEMPMAST IPEAF       70           DISK
0007.00      FTIMCRD  ISEAF        7           XXXX
0008.00      FQPRINT  O   F       77    OF     PRINTER
0009.00      I*
0010.00      I* RPG INPUT SPECIFICATION FORMS
0011.00      I*
0012.00      IEMPMAST AA   01
0013.00      I                                  1    30EMPNO    XX
0014.00      I                                  4    33 EMPNAM
0015.00      I                                 34    382EMPRAT
0016.00      I                                 39    58 EMPCTY


 F3=Exit   F4=Prompt   F5=Refresh   F9=Retrieve   F10=Cursor   F11=Toggle
 F16=Repeat find       F17=Repeat change          F24=More keys
                                  (C) COPYRIGHT IBM CORP. 1981, 2005.
```

38. Make the changes as required in the program specs. Replace the F with an E in EMPMAST & TIMCRD File Descriptions. Also remove record length. Make sure TIMCRD has a valid device. Use SEU format FX for file description - external. For input, use SEU format IX for input record external. Change EMPMAST to EMPR and place the letters PIX on the line (over the line #s on the left) and that will help you get the input formatting correct for the externally described input specs for both TIMCRD (TIMR) and EMPMAST (EMPR). Use PJX (prompt input fields external) on the fields that will be changed, assuring that the M1 and L1, L2 notations are done in the correct columns. Then, remove the input specs that do not have an M1, L1, or L2 designator required.

39. Once all the editing changes are completed, and you have no more syntax errors, pick F3 to end the SEU program and choose to save your source in member LAB07EY (the default at this point).

40. Now that you have saved the source member, compile it by placing a 14 next to LAB07EY in the member list. When the compile finishes cleanly, you will receive a message at the bottom of your PDM panel that looks like the following:

Program LAB07EY is placed in library YOURLIB. 00 highest severity. Created

--- if your program does not compile, repeat the SEU and compile process until all errors are corrected. Remember that member name LAB07ES is the solution and you may gain from looking at this while making your program operational.

41. Now you have compiled the contents of a source member named LAB07EY in file SOURCE in YOURLIB. The result of the compilation using PDM is to place the compiled OBJECT into the same library in which your source member is located. (You can change

this when you place F14 next to the member to compile by hitting F4 and getting a prompted compile with all of the parameters available for modification.). However, the PDM defaults that place the object in YOURLIB are fine for these Lab Exercises.

Your next step is to run or execute (synonyms in this case) the LAB07EY program that is now resident as an object in your library. The first step in this process is to exit the Work with members display of PDM and go to the PDM main menu. Take F3 to do this and you will be taken to the PDM Main panel.

42. We had been operating with option 3 Work with members. Our source statements collectively named LAB07EY are stored in a file object named SOURCE within a member named LAB07EY. The file SOURCE is an object in your library (We use YOURLIB to refer to your library -- always change this to be the actual name of your library) When you pick option 2, Work with Objects, hit ENTER. Scroll down far enough in the OBJECT list, and you will come to SOURCE, the file object. You may recall that you can place a 12 (work with members in source) next to this object and it will take you back to the Work with members panel inside the SOURCE file object. Since we have already done our editing and have in fact compiled the program (Created the program object), there is no need to take option 12.. We provide this information as another reminder to help differentiate the notion of source and members and objects.

So, to continue, select Work with Objects and press the ENTER key. You will first see the Specify Objects to Work With panel.

43. Press ENTER to advance to the Work with objects panel

44. Scroll to LAB07EY and take option 16 to run the program object

45. Notice that you get no messages on the PDM screens. The program runs in an instant and places its output in your output queue. Go back to your RPG Programming Menu to check out the spool file produced for this report.   Hit F3 twice to go back to your RPG Programming Menu

46. Take Option 1 from your RPG Programming Menu to go to your output queue to look for the printout.

47. Notice another QPRINT is in the list. The print file in your program LAB07EY is QPRINT so one of these three QPRINT files is the one you are looking for. With no other information, you would pick the last one in the queue since they are displayed in the queue FIFO and the last one is the last thing you printed. Type a 5 on the last QPRINT while you notice that its USER DATA is the name of the program that ran to produce the output - LAB07EY. This is another way to ID your stuff in an Output Queue.

Figure 7-13 The Printed Report Solution from LAB07PY (poetic license formatting)

```
                      Display Spooled File
File  . . . . . :   QPRINT              Page/Line   1/6
Control . . . . .                       Columns     1 - 78
Find  . . . . . .
*...+....1....+....2....+....3....+....4....+....5....+....6....+....7....+...
         THE DOWALLOBY COMPANY GROSS PAY REGISTER BY STATE            6/15/07
  ST    CITY          EMP#      EMPLOYEE NAME         RATE   HOURS    CHECK
  PA    WILKES-BARRE BIZZ NIZWONGER                   7.80   35.00   273.00
  PA    WILKES-BARRE WARBLER JACOBY                   7.90   40.00   316.00
                         TOTAL CITY   PAY FOR WILKES-BARRE          589.00
  PA    SCRANTON     BING CROSSLEY                    8.55   65.00   555.75
                         TOTAL CITY   PAY FOR SCRANTON             555.75
                         TOTAL STATE  PAY FOR PA                 1,144.75
  AK    FAIRBANKS    UPTAKE N. HIBITER                7.80   25.00   195.00
  AK    FAIRBANKS    FENWORTH GRONT                   9.30   33.00   306.90
                     006 NO MATCHING MASTER                  40.00
  AK    FAIRBANKS    BI NOMIAL                        8.80   39.00   343.20
                         TOTAL CITY   PAY FOR FAIRBANKS            845.10
  AK    JUNEAU       MILLY DEWITH                     6.50   40.00   260.00
  AK    JUNEAU       SARAH BAYOU                     10.45   40.00   418.00
                         TOTAL CITY   PAY FOR JUNEAU              678.00
                                                                  More...
                         TOTAL STATE  PAY FOR AK                 1,523.10
  NJ    NEWARK       DIRT MCPUG                       6.45   35.50   228.97
                         TOTAL CITY   PAY FOR NEWARK              228.97
                         TOTAL STATE  PAY FOR NJ                  228.97
                         FINAL TOTAL PAY                        2,896.82
```

48. Examine the output in the queue. It should be very similar to that shown in Figure 7-13 When your program produces results like this, you have succeeded. If anything is wrong with your printout, go back and edit the program, make the fixes and repeat this process until this is exactly correct.

When you are sure this work is exactly correct, then you have successfully completed Lab 7.

Lab 8 Payroll Register -- Internally Described and Externally Described Converted to RPGIV

Lab 8 Objectives:

Provides students the opportunity to learn simple differences between coding RPG matching records and control level programs and performing the same function with RPGIV programs. Students will gain additional practical experience in converting RPG programs to RPGIV programs and seeing these popular RPG functions work in the RPGIV environment.

Lab 8 Exercise 1 Convert Code to RPGIV

Both the internal RPG (LAB06PY) and external RPG versions (LAB07EY) need to be converted to RPGIV using the CVTRPGSRC command. The program names when converted are to be LAB08P4Y for the internal version and LAB08E4Y for the external version. The "P" is for program described files". The "E" is for externally described files. The 4 is for RPGIV. The Y is for Your code. In your Lab Package, there are two files ending in "S" that contain the solution.

Program Specifications

Just as the prior two labs, (LAB06PY and LAB07EY), the specs for this program are the same. List the employee file with Report and column headings by converting the LAB06PY program to LAB08P4Y using the IBM CVTRPGSRC utility. Compile and run the converted program.

Detailed Lab Instructions:

1. Use the PDM option on your RPG programming menu.

2. Take work with members (option 3) and press Enter. You will see a panel similar to that shown in Figure 8-1

Figure 8-1 Preparing to run CVTRPGSRC

```
                   Work with Members Using PDM              YOURSYS

File  . . . . . .     SOURCE
  Library . . . .       YOURLIB              Position to . . . . .

Type options, press Enter.
 2=Edit          3=Copy  4=Delete 5=Display      6=Print      7=Rename
 8=Display description  9=Save 13=Change text  14=Compile  15=Create module...

Opt  Member      Type        Text
     LAB03P      RPG         Code from Book - Internally Described Problem
     LAB03PS     RPG         Solution for Lab 03 program described
     LAB03PY     RPG         Lab 03 RPG Internally Described
     LAB04EY     RPG         Lab 04 RPG Externally Described
     LAB05E4Y    RPGLE       LAB 05 RPGIV Externally Described
     LAB06P      RPG         LAB 06 Internally Described Problem
     LAB06PS     RPG         LAB 06 Internally Described Solution
     LAB06PY     RPG         LAB 06 Internally Described Problem
                                                             More...
Parameters or command
===>  CVTRPGSRC_____
F3=Exit          F4=Prompt          F5=Refresh          F6=Create
F9=Retrieve      F10=Command entry  F23=More options    F24=More keys
```

3. Type CVTRPGSRC on the command line and press ENTER or F4. You will see a panel that is not quite as complete as that shown in Figure 5-2.

Figure 5-2 CVTRPGSRC Parameter Panel

```
                    Convert RPG Source (CVTRPGSRC)

 Type choices, press Enter.

 From file  . . . . . . . . . . . > SOURCE       Name
   Library  . . . . . . . . . . > YOURLIB        Name, *LIBL, *CURLIB
 From member  . . . . . . . . . . > LAB06PY       Name, generic*, *ALL
 To file  . . . . . . . . . . . . > SOURCE       Name, *NONE, QRPGLESRC
   Library  . . . . . . . . . . > YOURLIB        Name, *LIBL, *CURLIB
 To member  . . . . . . . . . . . > LAB08P4Y      Name, *FROMMBR




                                                           Bottom
 F3=Exit    F4=Prompt    F5=Refresh    F10=Additional parameters  F12=Cancel
 F13=How to use this display      F24=More keys
```

4. Fill in the panel as shown in Figure 8-2 and press ENTER to convert your internally described RPG code to RPGIV. FYI, the source file has already been expanded to work with 112 character records as required by RPGIV. Since 112 is bigger than 92, the size needed to work with RPG/400 programs, both fit fine.

Figure 8-3 The program LAB08P4Y has been converted to RPGIV

```
                    Work with Members Using PDM              YOURSYS

File  . . . . . .      SOURCE
  Library . . . .      YOURLIB            Position to  . . . . .

Type options, press Enter.
 2=Edit          3=Copy  4=Delete 5=Display      6=Print     7=Rename
 8=Display description   9=Save  13=Change text  14=Compile  15=Create module...

Opt  Member      Type         Text
     INSTRUCT    TXT          MWOOD Installation Instructions
     LAB03ES     RPG          Code from Book - Internally Described 01
     LAB03P      RPG          Code from Book - Internally Described 01
     LAB03PS     RPG          Code from Book - Internally Described 01
     LAB03PY     RPG          Lab 03
     LAB04EY     RPG          Lab 04
2    LAB08P4Y    RPGLE        Lab 08 RPGIV internally described
     LANGUAGE    PF           LANGUAGE File For Hello World
     MAIN        RPGLE        Prototype Two- procs - All in one X
                                                            More...
Parameters or command
===>
F3=Exit          F4=Prompt           F5=Refresh          F6=Create
F9=Retrieve      F10=Command entry   F23=More options    F24=More keys
Member LAB08P4Y added to file SOURCE, library YOURLIB..
```

5. Notice in Figure 8-3 that LAB08P4Y has been added to your source file in YOURLIB. Now, take option 2 to edit the LAB08P4Y program. You can also take option 5 because we will not be changing anything. Take note that the TYPE is now RPGLE (RPGIV) and the program is different though as you will see in Figure 8-4, it is not substantially different since the conversion program merely took what was in the RPG/400 program and reformatted it for the RPGIV column structure.

Figure 8-4 AN SEU Look at the CONVERTED RPG code

```
Columns . . . :    6  76               Edit                 YOURLIB/SOURCE
 SEU==>                                                          LAB08P4Y
 FMT H    HKeywords++++++++++++++++++++++++++++++++++++++++++++++++++++++++++++
          *************** Beginning of data *********************************
0001.00 H* RPG HEADER (CONTROL) SPECIFICATION FORMS
0002.00 H
0003.00 F*
0004.00 F* RPG FILE DESCRIPTION SPECIFICATION FORMS
0005.00 F*
0006.00 FEMPMAST    IPE AF    70          DISK
0007.00 FTIMCRD            7
0008.00 FQPRINT     O   F   77          PRINTER OFLIND(*INOF)
0009.00 I*
0010.00 I* RPG INPUT SPECIFICATION FORMS
0011.00 I*
0012.00 IEMPMAST    AA  01
0013.00 I                              1    3 0EMPNO            M1
0014.00 I                              4   33  EMPNAM
0015.00 I                             34   38 2EMPRAT
0016.00 I                             39   58  EMPCTY

 F3=Exit     F4=Prompt    F5=Refresh    F9=Retrieve   F10=Cursor   F11=Toggle
 F16=Repeat find          F17=Repeat change           F24=More keys
                                              (C) COPYRIGHT IBM CORP. 1981, 2005.
(C) COPYRIGHT IBM CORP. 1981, 2005.
```

6. Take note of the converted code. The next Lab will use only an RPGIV example and not RPG/400. However, when we pick up the interactive programming in Lab 10 & 11, we go back to RPG. Then, we return to RPGIV only in Lab 12. The most major visible change in RPGIV in this program, is the keyword used in line 8 as shown in Figure 8-4. RPGIV uses keywords to perform functions that took columns in RPG/400.   Hit F3 when you have analyzed this program enough and go back to PDM's Work with members.

7. . Now, since your program compiled as LAB06PY, in LAB 06, take option 14 against its RPGIV version LAB08P4Y and press ENTER.

8. You should see at the bottom of your panel

```
Program LAB08P4Y placed in library YOURLIB 00 highest severity. Created on
```

9. Repeat steps 1 through 8 for program LAB07EY. In other words, convert, compile, and run program LAB07EY as LAB08E4Y when converted. When you are finished the conversion and the compilation, you should see a message as follows:

```
Program LAB08E4Y placed in library YOURLIB 00 highest severity. Created on
```

*** You have now successfully completed Lab 8. ***

Lab 9 Multi-File Processing Using READ and CHAIN Operations

Lab 9 Objectives:

In this Lab, Students learn how to use the report writing productivity features of the RPG language without the assistance of the RPG Cycle. The same Payroll Register is the ultimate goal but this time the student is to write the program without using the RPG cycle. Moving from the RPG cycle as in prior labs, this lab uses sequential and random database access and control total facilities without the use of the RPG cycle to accomplish the same reporting objectives as the prior Lab sets (Labs 6, 7, 8). Thus the objectives continue to be familiar but the means of attaining the objectives (no RPG cycle) are completely different. This brings an opportunity for significant learning to the student engaging this lab successfully.

This is the last internally described lab in this course. If you choose, of course, this lab and the next lab can both be coded in RPG/400 using external or internal descriptions. Professors wishing to teach this may add their own labs to this set of exercises.

Lab 9 – Exercise 1 No Cycle -- Internally and Externally Described Versions

Method 1: Copy your Lab 8 results, LAB08P4Y and LAB08E4Y that you converted in Lab 8 into your source file using LAB09 as a prefix. Name the new (Copied) programs LAB09P4Y and LAB09E4Y respectively. This will give you an internally described and externally described starter set of RPGIV programs called LAB09P4Y and LAB09E4Y respectively. To complete the lab using this method, you will have to add all of the code to support the new requirements that are described in detail in the Method 2 write-up. Chapter 23 of the RPG Text shows how to perform this task in detail. If you want to try method 1 and think you may need to actually use method 2, then copy the versions designed for method 2 with XXs called LAB09E4Y and LAB09P4Y as, LAB09E4YBU and LAB09P4YBU. The BU is stands for backup.

This method (Method 1) offers greater learning opportunities and greater creative opportunities for the student since the student must conceive of the solution when the sample code is not structured to assist in the endeavor. The solution is in the Lab material as LAB09P4S and LAB09E4S respectively. However, the operations to replace the cycle and to accommodate the addition of the SAFILE have yet to be used in prior Labs. Therefore, I do not recommend beginning with Method 1 for this Lab. After you complete the Lab using Method 2, you may want to go back and do it with less guidance as in Method 1.

Method 2: Use just the RPGIV prebuilt program shells, LAB09E4 and LAB09P4 to create LAB09P4Y and LAB09E4Y. PDM Copy will work fine for this. There is no requirement for RPG/400 versions in this lab. The Y, of course stands for you and the 4 stands for RPGIV and the "S" version in your Lab library stands for the solutions. . To these programs, just as in the other labs, you will have to add certain codes that have been omitted and you will have to change the XXs in the code to the proper entries. Method 2 is by far the easier method and the method which I recommend.

Two programs are in play here, LAB09E4Y and LAB09P4Y. Use the instructions to create and modify LAB09P4Y first since it is the longer of the two. Then modify LAB09E4Y and get it cleanly compiled and executed.

This program requires multiple files and control level type totals without using RPGIV Level indicators. Since the RPG cycle is not to be used, there are no handy M1 through M9 entries or L1 through L9 entries that can be used. All database file reading is to be program controlled -- not cycle controlled. Think of how to get the job done from Labs 6 through 8 without the internal RPG cycle and that is what we are about to do. You will find a new set of file description entries required as well as new calculations to mimic the actions once provided in past labs by the RPG cycle.

The RPG cycle is by far the easiest approach and should be used in practice instead of the approach shown in this lab. There are many newer RPG programmers, however, who would disagree with your author. They believe the cycle is passé. As noted, there is just a small amount of new function in this program to support the SALFILE but other than that, the function is the same and the purpose is to produce the report that we had already created four times even before in Labs 6, 7, and 8. In the final analysis, you will be the judge of which method is easier, -- the cycle or using procedural code.

Program Specifications

Whichever method is used, the program is to produce a gross pay register in sequence of city within state -- just as the prior set of labs. It should provide city totals, state totals, and final totals. Assume the data is in sequence city within state. The final report should look like the report shown in Figure 9-1.

There will be no record identifying RPG indicators, no primary or secondary files, no level breaks, and no matching records. RPG/400 and RPGIV are both excellent procedural languages. The additional forms as well as the free format RPGIV as well as the Built-In Functions make RPGIV the finest language built for any platform.

Figure 9-2 is the same look at a record in the EMPMAST file with its default column headings as we saw in prior labs. Use these headings for this lab's report. Figure 9-3 shows the data description specifications (DDS) that were used to define the EMPMAST database file. Figure 9-4 is a picture of all the Employee data in the file from a spooled printout. Figure 9-5 is a look at a record in the TIMCRD (payroll time cards) file with default column headings. Use these headings as necessary for the register report. Figure 9-6 shows the data description specifications (DDS) that were used to define the TIMCRD database file. Figure 9-7 is a picture of all the time card data in the TIMCRD file from a spooled printout.

Figure 9-1 Gross Pay Register by State -- Report Model

```
        THE DOWALLOBY COMPANY GROSS PAY REGISTER BY STATE          2/21/06

ST      CITY            EMP#    EMPLOYEE NAME          RATE    HOURS    CHECK

PA      Wilkes-Barre    001     Bizz Nizwonger         7.80    35.00   273.00
PA      Wilkes-Barre    002     Warbler Jacoby         7.90    40.00   316.00

                                TOTAL CITY PAY FOR Wilkes-Barre          589.00

PA      Scranton        003     Bing Crossley          8.55    65.00   555.75

                                TOTAL CITY PAY FOR Scranton              555.75

                                TOTAL STATE PAY FOR PA                 1,144.75

AK      Fairbanks       004     Uptake N. Hibiter      7.80    25.00   195.00
AK      Fairbanks       005     Fenworth Gront         9.30    33.00   306.90
                        006 NO MATCHING MASTER                 40.00
AK      Fairbanks       007     Bi Nomial              8.80    39.00   343.20

                                TOTAL CITY PAY FOR Fairbanks            845.10

AK      Juneau          008     Milly Dewith           6.50    40.00   260.00
AK      Juneau          009     Sarah Bayou           10.45    40.00   418.00

                                TOTAL CITY PAY FOR Juneau               678.00

                                TOTAL STATE PAY FOR AK                 1,523.10

NJ      Newark          010     Dirt McPug             6.45    35.00   225.75

                                TOTAL CITY PAY FOR Newark               225.75

                                TOTAL STATE PAY FOR NJ                  225.75

                                FINAL TOTAL PAY                       2,893.60
```

Figure 9-2 EMPMAST Data Record

```
WORK WITH DATA IN A FILE                  Mode . . . . :     CHANGE
Format . . . . :     EMPR                 File . . . . :     EMPMAST


EMP NBR:            1
EMP NAME:          BIZZ NIZWONGER
EMP RATE:           780
EMPLOYEE CITY: WILKES-BARRE
EMP STATE:         PA
EMP ZIP:           18702
SAL CODE:          N
DEPT CODE:         PING
```

Figure 9-3 Data Description for EMPMAST

```
Columns . . . :    1  71          Browse              YOURLIB/SOURCE
SEU==>                                                 EMPMAST
FMT PF ....A..........T.Name+++++RLen++TDpB......Functions++++++++++++++++++++
       ************** Beginning of data *************************************
001.00     A         R EMPR
002.00     A           EMPNO        3S 0      COLHDG('EMP' 'NBR')
003.00     A           EMPNAM       30        COLHDG('EMP' 'NAME')
004.00     A           EMPRAT       5S 2      COLHDG('EMP' 'RATE')
005.00     A           EMPCTY       20        COLHDG('EMPLOYEE' 'CITY')
006.00     A           EMPSTA       2         COLHDG('EMP' 'STATE')
007.00     A           EMPZIP       5S 0      COLHDG('EMP' 'ZIP')
008.00     A           EMPSCD       1         COLHDG('SAL' 'CODE')
009.00     A           EMPDPT       4         COLHDG('DEPT' 'CODE')
010.00     A         K EMPNO
       ***************** End of data *******************************************
```

Figure 9-4 Query Report of EMPMAST Data

```
                            Display Report
                                 Report width . . . . . :      66
Position to line  . . . . .        Shift to column  . . . . . .
Line     ...+....1....+....2....+....3....+....4....+....5....+....6....+.
         EMP EMP                  EMP  EMPLOYEE       EMP   EMP SAL DEPT
         NBR NAME                 RATE CITY           STATE ZIP COD CODE
000001    1 BIZZ NIZWONGER        7.80 WILKES-BARRE    PA  18702  N  PING
000002    2 WARBLER JACOBY        7.90 WILKES-BARRE    PA  18702  N  MILL
000003    3 BING CROSSLEY         8.55 SCRANTON        PA  18702  Y  GRND
000004    4 UPTAKE N. HIBITER     7.80 FAIRBANKS       AK  99701  Y  GRND
000005    5 FENWORTH GRONT        9.30 FAIRBANKS       AK  99701  N  MILL
000006    7 BI NOMIAL             8.80 FAIRBANKS       AK  99701  N  PING
000007    8 MILLY DEWITH          6.50 JUNEAU          AK  99801  N  SAND
000008    9 SARAH BAYOU          10.45 JUNEAU          AK  99801  N  SAND
000009   10 DIRT MCPUG            6.45 NEWARK          NJ  07101  N  MILL
000010   11 BANDAID JONES         4.50 NEWARK          NJ  07101  N  PING
****** ********  End of report  ********
```

Figure 9-5 TIMCRD Data Record

```
WORK WITH DATA IN A FILE              Mode . . . . :     CHANGE
Format . . . . :   TIMR               File . . . . :     TIMCRD


EMP NBR:     1
EMP HOURS: 3500




F3=Exit              F5=Refresh          F6=Select format
F9=Insert            F10=Entry           F11=Change
```

Figure 9-6 Data Description for EMPMAST

```
Columns . . . :    1   71              Browse                  YOURLIB/SOURCE
SEU==>                                                                TIMCRD
FMT PF .....A.........T.Name++++++RLen++TDpB.....Functions+++++++++++++++++++
         *************** Beginning of data ************************************
0001.00     A          R TIMR
0002.00     A            EMPNO          3S 0        COLHDG('EMP'  'NBR')
0003.00     A            EMPHRS         4S 2        COLHDG('EMP'  'HOURS')
0004.00     A          K EMPNO
         **************** End of data ****************************************
```

Figure 9-7 Query Listing of TIMCRD File Data

```
        EMPNO   EMPHRS
000001    1     35.00
000002    2     40.00
000003    3     65.00
000004    4     25.00
000005    5     33.00
000006    6     40.00
000007    7     39.00
000008    8     40.00
000009    9     40.00
000010   10     35.00
****** ********   End of report   ********
```

Figure 9-8 Data Description of Salary File (SALFILE)

```
   A          R SALR
   A            SALENO         3S 0        COLHDG('EMP'  ' #')
   A            SALYR          6S 0        COLHDG('YEARLY' 'SALARY')
   A          K SALENO
```

Figure 9-9 Query Listing of SALFILE Data (Just two employees are salaried)

```
        EMP     YEARLY
         #      SALARY
000001    3     23,000
000002    4     29,000
****** ********   End of report   ********
```

Yes, we did add a little bit of new function. The EMPNO in each employee master that is read is used to chain to the SALFILE. The SALFILE logic is simple. If there is a hit on the chain (salary record exists for the employee), the employee is salaried. If there is no hit, then the employee is considered to be hourly. The TIMCRD file provides the hours each pay period for employees and so for those non-salaried employees, the time card file will provide the # of hours for the pay period. The EMPMAST file will provide the pay rate, and the RPGIV calculations will calculate the gross pay.

The new file, SALFILE will need additional functions to process this file. Rather than extend the Payroll master, we stole a technique from the days of old when disk space was expensive. Since some programs in IBM i shops may go back that far, this technique should prove useful in your future programming endeavors.

To use the new salary file, we placed a salary payroll option in its own file (SALFILE). Thus, to calculate pay with a salaried employee, we must access this file using a random read (CHAIN). Once read in, the salary value will become the gross pay for the employee for this pay period. In other words, you will not take rate and multiply it by hours if there is a record for the employee in the salary file (SALFILE).

We also added an ERROR file in this program that is not in prior labs. This is not really additional function but it sure is implemented lots differently. The purpose of this file is capture the errors that occur when we have no time card. The Error file is not a disk file.. It is a printer file. You will not create this file as that is already done for you. Its inclusion in this exercise demonstrates how an externally described PRINTER file is used in an RPG program. The errors caught by this routine and printed using this special file were far easier to catch using the RPG cycle.

For this exercise, each employee, whether hourly or salary, is to submit a time card each and every pay. When there is no time card, there is an error. So, to capture the error, the program is to turn on an error indicator similarly to the example immediately below. This indicator will then be used in the next statement to send out the error message using the ERROR PRINTER file.

```
C...        HLDNO   CHAIN TIMCRD...        92
C... 92             EXCEPTNOTIME
```

An additional "** No Time Card **' message – also conditioned by indicator 92 -- is to appear appears on the normal employee print line for the report. Check figure 9-1 to see the example in which no master record is present.

The operations to access the SALFILE and the operations to prepare the SALARY to replace the PAY calculation are necessary for this program to be able to handle salaried and hourly employees.

The EMPMAST file needs to be the "primary file" for this program though the word, "primary" here means "most important" as contrasted with primary in the cycle method. The EMPMAST file therefore is to be the driver for this program's function. Using the master as the driver creates a situation for you that you need to resolve via an additional coding routine. Since your program will read a master and then chain for the time card, using this method, it is impossible to know if you have a time card in the file that does not have a master record.

Since a time card without a master is a major mistake, you need to code for this.   If by chance you chose to drive the program via the time card file (another option) when you chained to the master from the time card file, if there were no master, you would know immediately. However, the opposite problem would be in effect. You would not know if you had missing time cards. So whichever file drives the program action (in our case it is the employee master) you have the problem of finding an error condition for a missing transaction or master.   Thus, the routine to determine this must be included in the program.

The operation to read the employee master file as the driver for this program is shown below:

```
C...        READ   EMPMAST...              91
```

This READ operation is simple enough. Indicator 91 comes on when there are no more records in the EMPMAST file. When there are no more master records to crocess, it is OK for the program to end after providing all of what might be called "the last record" processing functions. The READ statement literally "reads" the EMPMAST file using the RPG READ consecutive operation and brings the data from the record directly into the input area of the program.

Since the file is defined to be processed by key in File Descriptions, (look for a K in file descriptions), when a READ is issued against EMPMAST, the index, which is always maintained in sequence, just as the index in the back of a book, is read first under the covers before the data is read. In fact, the index tells the system where the data is stored. Then RPG uses the address of the record found in the index to bring the Payroll Master data record into RPG program's memory.

For the next read, the next sequential index record is read and its data record is brought into program memory. From RPG's perspective the data is being processed in city within state sequence and thus for this program, it is always read in EMPNO sequence by key. This is a contrivance and it would not be how you would design your reporting programs. However, it permits me to demonstrate lots of key RPG facilities without your having to worry about issues with data. These will need to be dealt with in your own shop on another day but on that day, you will be more prepared.

The EMPMAST database index in this program assures that the data will be presented in EMPNO sequence. Without having made the EMPMAST file an indexed file, however, there would have been lots more work involved.

Missing Time Card Logic

Since you access a time card record directly by key only after first reading an EMPMAST record, the program does not necessarily process each of the time card records in the file. If there were a situation in which ther were not a time card for each master, by definition, this would indicate an error condition in the data. Having a time card record with no matching master for it is also an error condition.

In our earlier labs and in the PAREG programs for those following along in the IBM i RPG and RPGIV Pocket Guide, using real RPG Cycle Matching Record Logic, this was not a problem. You were able to print a message that there was no matching master merely by using the NMR (no matched record) status and the record ID of the time card file (02). There was no special routine needed to find a missing master. The RPG cycle provided this status with the NMR 02 indication. That was very easy. It is not that easy doing it manually with a random (indexed) file but we will accomplish it in this program.

If we read all fields sequentially/consecutively, instead of some randomly via CHAIN operations, the NMR conditions would be easier to spot but the code to process all files sequentially with no MR cycle assistance by RPG would be even more difficult. So, we opted for the easier way since most programmers would use the chain mechanism v. sequential processing as it is so straight forward. And thus, in this program, you get to learn how to use the CHAIN operation. The following information on the CHAIN operation should be helpful -- then we will return to the discussion of Lab 9:

The CHAIN Operation:

CHAIN provides random retrieval of records from a database File.

The CHAIN is a very powerful operation in RPG and is used in most programs for record retrieval by relative record # or by key. The operation retrieves a record from a full procedural file (F in position RPG/400 position 16) of the file description specifications), and places the data from the record into the input fields.

The search argument is provided in Factor 1. It must contain the key or the relative record number used to retrieve the record.

Factor 2 specifies the file or record format name if it is an externally described file that is to be read

There is no result field for a CHAIN operation but indicators are important.

Files specified as input, read all records without locks and position 53 of the Chain's calc spec format. in RPG/400 must be blank. To lock all records, the file must be specified as update and RPG/400 position 53 is blank.

Specify an "N" in RPG/400 53 so that no lock should be placed on a record when it is read.

RPGIV handles this with the OP Code Extender.

The HI positions 54 and 55 in RPG/400 and 71 and 72 in RPGIV must contain an indicator that is set on if no record in the file matches the search argument. The LO positions can contain an indicator that is on if the CHAIN operation is not completed successfully Error). The EQ positions must be blank.

A successful chain repositions the file cursor such that if it is followed by a READ operation the next sequential record following the retrieved record is read. If an update (on the calculation or output specifications) is done on the retrieved record after a successful CHAIN operation and before other access to that file, the last record retrieved is updated.

There are other ways to handle errors (not found) in RPG and RPGIV not discussed in this snippet.

Returning from the CHAIN Operation, how do you find missing masters for our time card records? The answer actually is simple. You must read each time card record and check each master to see if it exists for that particular employee time card record. So, you must create a routine right in the beginning of the program to test for this error condition. Some programmers might write this code in a prior program that forces all data to be correct when entering this program. Either way, it works. The EXSR (Execute Subroutine Operation) valid in both RPG/400 and RPGIV executes a group of statements known as a subroutine and then returns to the statement immediately following the EXSR. In our version of the program, this master checking code is initiated using the following subroutine call.

```
C* Check to see if there is a missing master
C             EXSR CHKMST
```

Figure 9-10 ERROR Externally Defined Printer File

```
FMTP   TName+RLen+TDpBLPosFunctions+++++++++++++++++++++++++++
03 A***************************************************
04 A...RHDR
05 A***************************************************
06 A***************************************************
07 A...                    SKIPB(001)
08 A...                    SPACEA(002)
09 A...              14
10 A...                 'This Error Report is a result of r-
11 A...                 eading the Time'
12 A...              14
13 A...                 'Card file completely and finding a-
14 A...                  missing employee '
15 A...                    SPACEB(001)
16 A...              14
17 A...                 'master record. The time card recor-
18 A...                  d was either       '
19 A...            SPACEB(001)
20 A...              14
21 A...                 'keyed wrong or the master has been-
22 A...                  inadvertently   '
23 A...                    SPACEB(001)
24 A...              14
25 A...                 'deleted.  Check payroll input data-
26 A...                 .            '
27 A...                    SPACEB(001)
28 A***************************************************
29 A***************************************************
30 A...RDTL
31 A***************************************************
32 A***************************************************
33 A...                    SPACEB(001)
34 A...              18
35 A...                 'Employee Number & HRS entered :'
36 A... EMPN      3S 00  +1
37 A... EMPHRS    4S 20  +3EDTCDE(1)
38 A***************************************************
```

This LAB09E4Y and LAB09P4Y programs includes a new print file called ERROR, defined in the program using the following RPGIV coding.

FERROR   O   E...   PRINTER

The E in column 19 differentiates this printer file from the QPRINT file defined in Line 9.

The DDS for the ERROR file coding is shown in Figure 9-10 for your convenience

It is not the intention in this lab to teach you how to create printer files, however, having the DDS as shown in Figure 9-10 is better than half the battle. As you can see in Figure 9-10, there are two record formats. One is called HDR for header line (Statement 4) and one is called DTL for detail line (Statement 30) and these are used in the CHKMST subroutine which is initiated / executed above. This file member (ERROR) is included in your IBM i SOURCE file. If it is not already created as an object in your library, take option 14 on the ERROR source for the PRTF object type and PDM will compile your version of the ERROR print file and store it it for your use in this program.

In the sample data for this program, there is just one missing master. There is a time card record for EMPNO 6 but there is no master. When your program encounters this, it needs to take the compiled formats in the ERROR DDS shown in Figure 9-10 and print out a message that in the System i spool queue shows as the message in Figure 9-11

Figure 9-11 ERROR Report – No Master for Time Card

```
*...+....1....+....2....+....3....+....4....+....5....+....6....+
            This Error Report is a result of reading the Time
            Card file completely and finding a missing employee
            master record. The time card record was either
            keyed wrong or the master has been inadvertently
            deleted.  Check payroll input data.
               Employee Number & HRS entered : 006   40.00
```

When you examine the program source for the LAB09 RPGIV programs, you will see that the CHKMST routine accomplishes this for you.

Control Level Breaks – No RPG Cycle

What causes a control level break? You have answered that a few times in the book and you have coded how to achieve this in the RPG cycle in prior labs. Now, you need to do this without an RPG cycle. The bottom line is that a control break occurs when the control field (EMPNO) in the next record to be processed is different from the record currently being processed. How do you know what the next record is? How do you read ahead to know how to do this. This is the trick to this program. Obviously, the L1 to L9 capabilities in the cycle provide this powerful function with little coding. This lab problem without using cycle level breaks will require some thinking.

Since you need to read the EMPMAST file, the first thing you do to assure two records in memory is to read in the first record at point label ("POINT 1") as shown in Figure 9-12. This READ statement is executed once and only once in the program.   Nine statements later, there is another READ statement that controls all other Reads to the EMPMAST file.

Since the "POINT 1" READ statement below in Figure 9-10 is executed just once and there will always be more than one record in EMPMAST file, the program does not have to do any work with the end of file indicator 91 from this initial READ statement. Instead, since this is the first record read for the Payroll Register, the next statement performs exception output to lines marked header as shown in the next executable statement in Figure 9-12.

Figure 9-12 Level Calculations

```
C*  First read ahead to check for Levels
POINT 1
C...                 READ    EMPMAST...          91
C* Send out headers
C...                 EXCEPTHEADER
C* Process this record (tuck it away for next cycle)
C* Move data into the hold field set in data structure (HLD)
C...                 EXSR    PROCES
C*  Run register until end of file
C...    *IN91        DOUEQ*ON
C*  SECOND READ UNTIL EOF - FOR LEVEL CHECK
C...                 READ    EMPMAST...          91
C...91...            LEAVE...
C*  Replaces L1 coding
C*  LEVEL1 TEST-- See if current city different
C...    EMPCTY       IFNE   HLDCTY
C...    EMPSTA       ORNE   HLDSTA
C...                 SETON...              L1
C...                 EXSR LEVEL1
C...                 ENDIF...
C*  Level 2 test -- See if state changed
C...    EMPSTA       IFNE HLDSTA
C* If State changes, city is automatically different
C...                 SETON...              L2
C...                 EXSR   LEVEL2
C...                 ENDIF
C...                 SETOF...              L1L2
C...                 EXSR   PROCES
C...                 ENDDO
C...                 EXSR   LEVEL1
C...                 EXSR   LEVEL2
C...                 EXCEPTLROUT
C...                 ENDSR
```

**** See Lab code for exact code

The two header output lines are almost identical to the header lines in the earlier labs except that there is an E (Exception output done in calcs) instead of an H (normal RPG Headings -- cycle oriented) in column 15 as shown below:

```
OQPRINT   E   206            HEADER
O         E   3              HEADER
```

As shown in Figure 9-12, the next operation is to execute the PROCES subroutine. In your LAB09P4Y and LAB09E4Y programs, the PROCES subroutine should call the following subroutines and then come back to the RUNREG subroutine.

MOVMS1
PAYCLC
PRNTLN

The MOVMS1 Subroutine – First Record

The MOVMS1 subroutine shown in the sample code in the source file starts at line 176 in LAB09P4Y and on line 122 in LAB09E4Y. This subroutine sets up the program for keeping two records in memory. After this first READ statement in RUNREG and the execution of the MOVMS1 subroutine, the fields of EMPMAST exist in two locations – the EMPMAST record itself and a data structure named HLDMST. Through several Z-ADD statements and a number of MOVE statements the individual fields in the EMPMAST record are moved to the individual fields of the HLDMST data structure. At this time in the program the contents of the current record (in process) as stored in the HLDMST data structure is exactly the same as the contents of the last EMPMAST record read.

For a detailed explanation of any of the RPG operations used in this code, please refer to the RPG Textbook or the ILE RPG Reference Manual that can be downloaded for free at **www.ibm.com**.

Before you continue, examine the question, what is a data structure? Chapter 17 of the RPG Pocket Guide goes over structures in detail. You can also type RPG data structure in Google for additional information. For now, consider a data structure as a means of defining one record in memory that has no necessary association with a database file. Once the MOVMS1 subroutine finishes its job and returns to the PROCES subroutine, that one record structure is populated with the data from the first EMPMAST record, and that is the data that will be processed in the subsequent subroutines in PROCES, namely, PAYCLC and PRNTLN.

Figure 9-13 RPGIV HLDMST Data Structure to Hold Current Record

```
    IHLDMST          DS
    I...                    1    30HLDNO
    I...                    1    70 HREC
    I...                    4    33 HLDNAM
    I...                    4    23 HLDNM
    I...                   34   382HLDRAT
    I...                   39   58 HLDCTY
    I...                   59   60 HLDSTA
    I...                   61   650HLDZIP
    I...                   66   66 HLDSCD
    I...                   66   66 HLDDPT
```

Let's take a quick break here from the program and look more deeply at the notion of a data structure:

What is a Data Structure?

A data structure is simply a packaging of data elements as in a record. In fact, a record is a data structure. In programming for computer science applications and business alike, a data structure is a way of storing data in a computer so that it can be used efficiently. In computer science, a carefully chosen data structure will allow a more efficient algorithm to be used. In business programming careful design of data structures can provide an ease of understanding and application standardization. A well-designed data structure allows a variety of critical operations to be performed using as little resources, including programmer coding time, as well as both execution time and memory space, as possible.

In this chapter you learn how write programs using both program-described and externally described data structures. A program described data structure is identified by a blank in position 17 of the data structure statement. The subfield specifications for a program-described data structure must immediately follow the data structure statement. An externally described data structure is identified by an E in position 17 of the data structure statement. The subfield descriptions for this are contained in an externally described file with one record format. The file merely serves as a means of grabbing the data definition.

The data contents of the file are irrelevant to the data structure. To bring the data structure definition from the external file into the program, at compile time, the RPG/400 program uses the external name to locate and extract the external description of the data structure subfields. An external subfield name can be renamed in the program, and additional subfields can be added to an externally described data structure in the program.

In RPG, Data structures are very powerful data configurations that have a number of purposes. For example, a data structure can be used to:

Allow the division of a field into subfields without using the MOVE or MOVEL operations.
Operate on a subfield and change the contents of a subfield.
Redefine the same internal area more than once using different data formats.

Data Structure Record ID Entries

Data structures are defined on the input specifications in RPG/400 and in the 'D' spec in RPGIV. In RPG/400, they are defined the same way records are defined. The record specification line contains the data structure statement (DS in positions 19 and 20) and the data structure name is optional. The field specification lines contain the subfield specifications for the data structure.

Though Data Structures (DS) use the Input specification, programmers must use care when arranging the structures so that they appear in the program after the normal input specifications for records. All entries describing a data structure and its subfields must appear together

In RPGIV, the data structure is defined on the new 'D' type specification. A hypothetical example of a data structure is shown below. It is similar to our EMPMAST file but it is not exactly the same. It also has more fields defined.

Sample Employee Data Structure

```
IEMPDS1       DS...     100
I...                      1    50EMPNO
I...                      6    30 EMPNAM
I...                     31    60 EMPAD1
I...                     61    90 EMPAD2
I...                     91   110 EMPCTY
I...                    111   112 EMPSTA
I...                    113  1170EMPZIP
I...                    118  1252EMPPAY
I...                    126  1310EMPHIR hiredate
I...                    126  1270EMPYR
I...                    128  1290EMPMO
I...                    130  1310EMPDA
```

This data structure (above) is internal. It is named EMPDS1. It has 100 occurrences of a record layout that has 12 fields. One field, EMPHIR (Employee date of hire) is subdivided by the structure into separate YEAR, MONTH and DAY fields. See how convenient it is to redefine a structure within RPG/400 with a data structure. Using the RPGIV "D" spec, this DS would look very similar.

The DS for this program is shown in Figure 9-13

The PAYCLC Subroutine - First Record

The PAYCLC subroutine as shown in the sample source code in your library calculates the Gross Pay by multiplying the hours from the time card by the rate from the employee master unless there is a salary record. To check to see if there is a salary record, the routine CHAINs to the SALFILE. If there is a salary record the routine uses the SALARY as the pay and stores it in the HLDPAY field which is defined within the PAYCLC routine itself. In addition to this the subroutine adds the HLDPAY amount to the City Level 1 total bucket, CITPAY. The PAYCLC routine then returns to the PROCES subroutine at line 160..

In the PROCES subroutine, you can see an EXSR PRNTLN statement. You may have to look at both the internal and external versions to see exactly where in the code the PROCES and other subroutines are located and also where they are called (EXSR.) So, at this point control is passed to the PRNTLN routine at statement 165. The PRNTLN routine as shown in the sample code also It asks that Headers be printed via the EXCPT HEADER statement at line 166 if the program senses that OVERFLOW has occurred on the printer. Additionally it sets off OF if it is in.

If OF is not on, the routine prints a detail line via the EXCEPT PRTLN1 statement of the PRNTLN subroutine. The PRNTLN's ENDSR causes the program to branch back to the line following the EXSR PRNTLN line in the PROCES subroutine. This happens to be an ENDSR for the PROCES subroutine. From here the ENDSR causes the program to branch back to a statement in the RUNREG subroutine.

At this point your program has (1) read the EMPMAST first record, (2) stored it in HLDMST, and (3) calculated gross pay and stored that in HLDPAY, and (4) printed the headings and the first detail line. Now you are finished with the unique things that must be done with the first record read when checking for control breaks. Right now, the same record resides in both the EMPMAST memory area the HLDMST data structure in memory -- and it has been processed.

Looking back at the code in Figure 9-12 code, you see the DO until statement. It is waiting for indicator 91 to turn on before it will end the DO loop. From Figure 9-12, you can see that this DOUEQ loop extends to where there is an ENDDO statement. So all of the statements in between the Do and ENDDO if properly conditioned will execute as often as the loop permits. Indicator 91 comes on when the last EMPMAST record has been processed and the program is trying to read a record after the last record that is not there. This ends the loop. Now, let's see what else happens in this very important loop.

There is also a READ statement very early in the loop. This means that for every iteration of the DO loop, a record will be read from the EMPMAST file. When the end of file indicator (91) is turned on with no record returned the next line tests to see if the last loop iteration should continue. As you can see in Figure 9-12, if end of file has been reached and thus no record has been read into EMPMAST, the loop is over and for that matter the program is almost over.

The LEAVE operation takes the program to statement 108 which causes the Level 1 subroutine, Level 2 subroutine and Last record subroutine to execute. Following this, in Figure 9-12, the ENDSR for RUNREG is encountered. This takes the program to the statement following the EXSR RUNREG. Here the LR is turned on and the program falls to the end of detail calculations. Since LR is on the program ends.

If there are records to process however, indicator 91 does not turn on. Therefore, the LEAVE operation should not be taken and the loop in Figure 9-3 would continue.

The next five lines get repeatedly executed until the test is satisfied.

Figure 9-14 Level 1 Test

```
C*    Replaces L1 coding
C*    LEVEL1 TEST- city different?
C...      EMPCTY      IFNE  HLDCTY
C...      EMPSTA      ORNE  HLDSTA
C...                  SETON...              L1
C...                  EXSR  LEVEL1
C...                  ENDIF...
```

Control Break Level 1 Processing

Since a state change by definition means that a city has also changed, the code tests to see if the current record being processed (stored in the HLDMST data structure) has a city or state change. The chances of a Wilkes-Barre, Alaska and a Wilkes-Barre Pennsylvania following each other in a payroll application are remote indeed but this code solves the problem if need be for other applications as well as this one.

What is an IF statement? The routine contains an IF not equal operation (IFNE). It tests to see if the contents of the EMPCTY field which comes from the record just read but is not yet in process is not equal (different) to the contents of the HLDCTY field in the record being processed.

What is an OR statement? An OR operation extends and IF statement by adding another set of circumstances for the test to be true. So, if by chance the two cities were equal making it false but the state comparison in the ORNE (or not equal) statement is true (states are different, the result of the IF would be true and the lines between the IF and OR statements would therefore be executed. On the other hand, if both conditions are false, meaning no city change and no state change, then the operations preceding the ENDIF statement would not be executed. Additional information on the IF statement is included in the insert below:

The IFxx Statement

If a condition labeled in the statement above as xx is true, then the IF statement permits those other RPG statements that sit between the respective IF and its corresponding IF-Group-Ending ENDIF statement to be executed.

Other than the requisite RPG columnar formatting, the RPG standard IFxx operation is similar in function to the "IF" statement varieties in other languages. As such it allows a group of calculations to be processed if a certain relationship, specified by xx, exists between RPG Factors 1 and Factor 2.

The "ENDIF" statement is the last statement in an "IF Group." The If tests can be made more complex by adding the "ANDxx" and "ORxx." operations. The If statement itself can have conditioning indicators but it does not use resulting indicators. Factor 1 and Factor 2 are compared just like the RPG COMP (compare) operation. If the relationship specified by the IFxx and any associated ANDxx or ORxx operations exists, the statements are true and therefore are executed.

If the relationship does not exist, control passes to the calculation operation immediately following the associated ENDIF operation. If an "ELSE" is also specified as described in available Google documentation under RPG ELSE, then the operations following the ELSE operation and before the ENDIF can be executed..

The conditions that are tested follow:

XX	Meaning
GT	Factor 1 is greater than factor 2.
LT	Factor 1 is less than factor 2.
EQ	Factor 1 is equal to factor 2.
NE	Factor 1 is not equal to factor 2.
GE	Factor 1 is greater than or equal to factor 2.
LE	Factor 1 is less than or equal to factor 2.

Blanks -Unconditional processing in appropriate operations -- Blank not valid for IF

If you got comfortable with level logic while decoding the cycle oriented programs, then this logic makes sense to you because it mimics the control break logic that RPG uses in the cycle. If you have not gotten comfortable with the L1 part of the cycle, this type of coding probably makes more sense to you.

So, if there is no control break, nothing happens in between records, but if there is a level 1 control break, the program turns on the L1 indicator since it is handy and available. It is a marker which then executes the L1 processing subroutine named LEVEL1. The ENDIF statement ends the IF statement. Each IF statement that you use in a program must be end with an ENDIF. If the either, any or all conditions in an ORed IF statement are true, the statements in between execute. If none are true they do not execute. If all conditions in an

ANDed IF operation are true, the statements in between execute. If any condition in an ANDed IF is not true, the statements do not execute.

Level 1 Subroutine

Before you come back for the L2 tests, look at the LEVEL1 subroutine that gets called when there is a control break. You can imagine what must happen. The calculations done at L1 detail time would be needed to be done in this LEVEL 1 subroutine. In other words, the CTYPAY would be added to STAPAY Additionally the functions done at L1 output time in the sample code would need to be done to print the City totals. As you can see in the code snippet below the LEVEL 1 subroutine does exactly this.

Figure 9-15 Level 1 Subroutine

```
C*    Level 1 Subroutine City Control break
C*
C...     LEVEL1     BEGSR
C...     CTYPAY     ADD     STAPAY     STAPAY   92
C...                EXCEPTL1OUT
C...                ENDSR
```

Control Break Level 2 Processing

So now that you have processed L1 totals without the RPG cycle, so now move on to Level 2 totals. By the way, similar logic works as you extend the number of total levels to three and four and so on. In Figure 9-3, the RUNREG code dealing with Level 2 processing is as follows:

Figure 9-16 Level 2 Test for Control Break

```
C*    Level 2 test Has state changed?
C... EMPSTA     IFNE   HLDSTA
C...            SETON...            L2
C...            EXSR   LEVEL2
C...            ENDIF
```

The Level 2 test is even easier than the Level 1 test. In this case, you already know that there is an L1 break. You just don't know if it was caused by a state change or not. So you have to test to see if the state has changed. Again, the current record is in the HLDMST data structure and the next record to be processed is the record that was just read from EMPMAST. The two state fields EMPSTA and HLDSTA are compared to see if there is a state change. If there is no state change then none of the statements get executed but if the IFNE statement is evaluated as true and the states have changed, then the two statements are executed.

The SETON L2 code creates a marker to set on the L2 indicator in case you need it someplace in the program. The L1 and L2 indicators can be used as regular indicators if you choose as in this program. Once L2 is turned on, the LEVEL 2 subroutine is executed via EXSR as shown above.

Before you check out the LR tests, let's look at the LEVEL2 subroutine that gets called when there is a control break. You can imagine what must happen. Just as with the cycle programs, the calculations done at L2 detail time would be need to be done in this LEVEL 1 subroutine. In other words, the STAPAY field value would be added to TOTPAY field. Additionally the functions done at L2 output time would need to be done to print the State totals from State total exception output lines. As you can see in the code snippet below the LEVEL 2 subroutine does exactly this.

Figure 9-17 Level 2 Subroutine for State Control break

```
C*   Level 2 Subroutine State break
C*
C...  LEVEL2     BEGSR
C...  STAPAY     ADD    TOTPAY     TOTPAY  92
C...             EXCEPTL2OUT
C...             ENDSR
```

Process the Record Just Read

The last few statements in the RUNREG subroutine are repeated below for convenience in referencing. These statements will be referenced in this section regarding processing the current record as well as the next section dealing with Final totals at LR time.

Staring below, you can see that the SETOFF operation is turning off the L1 and L1 indicators. To repeat, you could have used any indicator number to represent the fact that it was L1 time or L2 time but since special indicators L1 and L2 are not controlled by RPG in this program, you took control of then. At the need of the L1 and L2 routines, the indicators are set off so that they can be tested properly during the next DO loop iteration.

Earlier you looked at the first READ EMPMAST code and you examined in detail the workings of the PROCES subroutine. From this examination, you know that it moves the record just read into the current record slot (HLDMST) and it calculates gross pay and it prints the detail line. The major DOUEQ loop for RUNREG finds its matching ENDDO statement. As long as indicator 91, which indicates the end of file in the EMPMAST, is not on, the loop continues. But when 91 is on the Do loop ends and control is transferred to the first statement following the ENDDO as you can see below.

Figure 9-18 Record Process, Level Subroutine Calls.

```
C...      SETOFF...                L1L2
C...      EXSR   PROCES
C...      ENDDO
C...      EXSR   LEVEL1
C...      EXSR   LEVEL2
C...      EXCEPTLROUT
C...      ENDSR
```

Final Total Processing

Just as a state change would force a city change (a Level 2 change would force a Level 1 change), so also does a last record change force a next highest level change (L2 in the cycle programs). So, when the RUNREG DO loop is completed at statement 107, the program is all over but the totals.

Since there is no record at this point that was just read, it would not help at all to compare the current record in HLDMST with the record just read. If you were clearing this record out each time prior to reading it in, then that type of code could work. However, it is unnecessary. For when the program is just about done and it has had or it is about to have LR turned on, the record being processed is clearly the last and whether it is a single record or a group of records from the same city, when the next record is no record, there is a level change. In fact, all of the level fields have changed. The contents logically no longer represent the last EMPMAST read because no EMPMAST was read. Logically all of the new fields are zero or blank. So if you were to compare the EMPSTA with the HLDSTA you would get a logical not. HLDSTA would contain the state from the last record actually read and EMPSTA would contain a logical blank.

When LR occurs, there is no need to test the other levels. LR forces all other control breaks. So the record in HLDMST, though it has been fully processed, has not had its City and State totals for this last group written until this point in the program gets the last City total out and another gets the last state total out and prints the final totals and then it runs into the ENDSR for RUNREG. As we have noted several times in discussing the logic of this program, this forces the program back to the last detail calculation, which turns on LR and then drifts quietly in to post detail calc oblivion as the program ends.

Don't forget to do the internal and external versions of this program.

Use the detailed instructions in other labs as well as your own knowledge of the development environment to edit, compile and test these two programs.

If you choose to use Method 1, the above specifications are adequate. You may gain by reading the specifications for method 2, but do not follow them specifically. The specifications for LAB 09 Exercise 1 for Method 2 are discussed before the figures and are not explained in the level of detail of earlier labs. To repeat, use the methods shown in those labs to help you make the changes necessary in the modules to make both the internal and external versions of Lab 09 work to produce the output shown in Figure 9-5.

The Two Big RPG Programs for Lab 09

The two programs, LAB09P4Y and LAB09E4Y get their work done via a series of subroutines that make reading the code more logical. Six character names were used to conform with the RPG/400 language but 10 character names could have been used since this code is all RPGIV. The subroutines are as follows:

- RUNREG
- CHKMST
- CLR
- Level1
- Level2
- PROCES
- MOVMS1
- PAYCLC
- PRNTLN
- NOMAST

Let's take a look at each of these routines and then read the shell code provided here so you can see how this logic is implemented. Following the explanation of the routines, the code that you are to change for LAB09 is included.

RUNREG

RUNREG is the main subroutine for both the internal and external versions of LAB09. It is implemented as a top down module in that all of the major logic of the program is driven from this subroutine. The first action it takes is to call the CHKMST subroutine which analyzes all the data in both the TIMCRD file and the EMPMAST file and it identifies each time card that does not have a master. The CHKMST subroutine calls the NOMAST subroutine for each time card that has no master and it writes a message to the ERROR print file report signifying which employee had the missing master.

Before beginning the loop that reads in all of the EMPMAST records, RUNREG also writes the first page headings of the report. It then calls the PROCES routine which basically processes the first record. It calls three subroutines MOVMS1, which saves the current record in a hold area so it can be compared for a control break later on. It also calls the PAYCLC program which reads in the time card record and calculates the pay for the first employee or it prints the time card missing message. PAYCLC also determines whether the employee is salary or hourly and calculates the pay.

PROCES then calls the PRNTLN program to print the detail line with the gross pay on the main report. RUNREG has the program controlling do loop in it that keeps the program running until there are no more EMPMAST records left to read. After the first record in which it uses PROCES to cal MOVMS1 to store the 1st record in a Hold Structure, it mimics the RPG cycle and keeps looping, reading the Employee Master File, and calling the PROCES subroutine each time. From the second time on, RUNREG executes the LEVEL2 and the LEVEL 1 tests to test for control breaks and direct the proper actions.   The MOVMS1 routine, the PAYCLC, and the PRNTLN routines are called in this Do loop to process records, bring in the time cards (matching) and printing the detail lines on the report.

The CHAIN to the TIMCRD file is actually done in the PAYCLC subroutine which is called each time a Master record is read. PAYCLC chains to the TIMCRD file and if it gets no hit, it does not wait til the PRNTLN routine, it sends out the error message itself to the printer (QPRINT).

CHKMST

Checks for missing EMPMAST payroll master record. At the beginning of the program, RUNREG calls this routine. It reads every time card record, checking for a missing master. When this occurs, it uses the ERROR print file to send out a printed message to the second report file in the program.

CLR

The CHKMST program leaves some entrails when it runs. The CLR routine gets the program reestablished without having clutter in any of the fields that are necessary to check for level breaks etc.

It clears fields from the CHKMST run to begin new register run In essence it clears the fields that were used in the missing master test

Level1

The Level1 routine is called by the RUNREG routine when there is a control break on the city or state. The L1 test is done by RUNREG. It collects the state total and prints the city total when a CITY or state or LR break occurs.

Level 2

The Level2 routine is called by the RUNREG routine when there is a control break on the state. The L2 test is done by RUNREG. It collects the LR total and prints the state total when a state pr LR break occurs.

PROCES

PROCES is a consolidating subroutine. It calls MOVMS1 to save record data, PAYCLC to calculate the gross pay, and PRNTLN to print detail lines and headings if overflow occurs.

PAYCLC

The PAYCLC routine calculates Gross PAY from HRS or Salary. Calculates pay for HELD record. if salaried, it does not need the RATE multiplier

PRNTLN

The PRNTLN routine prints Header and Detail Lines as need be.

NOMAST

The NOMAST Subroutine prints out the error message for a time card without an employee master. It writes the error message for no master to the separate external print file

Figure 9-19 LAB09P4 Full Program -- Internal

```
 1      H* RPG HEADER (CONTROL) SPECIFICATION FORMS
 2      H
 3      F*
 4      F* RPG FILE DESCRIPTION SPECIFICATION FORMS
 5      F*
 6      FEMPMAST    IF   F    70        XXXDISK      KEYLOC(1)
 7      FTIMCRD     IF   F     7        XXXDISK      KEYLOC(1)
 8      FSALFILE    IF   F     9        XXXDISK      KEYLOC(1)
 9      FQPRINT     O    F    77            PRINTER OFLIND(*INOF)
10      FERROR      O    E                  PRINTER
11      D*
12      D*
13      D* This is the DS to hold the prior record read
14      D HLDMST            XX
15      D  HLDNO                     1    3 0
16      D  HREC                      1   XX
17      D  HLDNAM                    4   33
18      D  HLDNM                     4   23
19      D  HLDRAT                   34   38 2
20      D  HLDCTY                   39   58
21      D  HLDSTA                   59   60
22      D  HLDZIP                   61   65 0
23      D  HLDSCD                   66   66
24      D  HLDDPT                   XX   XX
25      I*
26      I* RPG INPUT SPECIFICATION FORMS
27      I*
28      I*
29      I*   EMPMAST is the employee master file
30      I*   One record for each employee - contains payrate and department
31      I*   For salaried employees, Salary is in the SALFILE file
32      I*
33      IEMPMAST    AA  01
34      I                              1   70  EREC
35      I                              1    3 0EMPNO
36      I                              4   23  EMPNM
37      I                              4   33  EMPNAM
38      I                             34   38 2EMPRAT
39      I                             39   58  EMPCTY
40      I                             59   60  EMPSTA
41      I                             61   65 0EMPZIP
42      I                             66   66  EMPSCD               SALCOD
43      I                             67   70  EMPDPT               DPTCOD
44      I*
45      I*   TIMCRD is updated in an independent process.
46      I*   This file provides current time records for the PAYROLL proce
47      I*   For salaried employees, no hours are provided but the TIME re
48      I*   If No TIMCD on Chain - salried person does not get paid
49      I*
50      ITIMCRD     AB  02
51      I                              1    3 0EMPNO
52      I                              4    7 2EMPHRS
53      I*
54      I*   SALCRD is updated in an independent process.
55      I*   This file mimics an extension to the PAYMAST file that was ac
56      I*   For salaried employees, the salary is stored in this file LIN
57      I*
58      ISALFILE    AC  03
59      I                              1    3 0SALENO
60      I                             XX   XXXXSALYR
61      I*
62      C*
63      C* RPG CALCULATION SPECIFICATION FORMS
64      C*
65      C*  Run default register with no prompt input
66      C                  EXSR      XXXXXX
```

```
 67   C                         SETON                                            XX
 68   C*
 69   C*  Body of Code that Controls the running of the Payroll Register
 70   C       RUNREG          BEGSR
 71   C*  Check to see if there is a missing master
 72   C                         EXSR      CHKXXX
 73   C*  Clear fields from CHKMST run to begin fresh register
 74   C                         EXSR      CLRXXX
 75   C                         CLOSE     EMPMAST
 76   C                         OPEN      EMPMAST
 77   C*  First read -- nead a read ahead to be able to check for Levels
 78   C                         READ      EMPMAST                          91
 79   C                         EXCEPT    HEADER
 80   C                         EXSR      PROCESXXX
 81   C*  Run register until end of file is hit... NU1 end program
 82   C       *IN91           DOUEQ     *ON
 83   C*  SECOND READ -- UNTIL EOF NEED FOR LEVEL CHECK
 84   C                         READ      EMPFILEX                         91
 85   C   91                  LEAVE
 86   C*  Replaces L1 coding as in PAREG
 87   C*  LEVEL 1 TEST -- See if current city is different
 88   C       EMPCTY          IFNE      XXXCTY
 89   C       EMPSTA          ORNE      XXXSTA
 90   C                         SETON                                   L1
 91   C                         EXSR      LEVELX
 92   C                         ENDIF
 93   C*  Level 2 test -- See if current state is different
 94   C       EMPSTA          IFNE      HLDSTA
 95   C                         SETON                                   L2
 96   C                         EXSR      LEVELX
 97   C                         ENDIF
 98   C                         SETOFF                                  L1L2
 99   C                         EXSR      PROCEXXXX                              Process HLD
100   C                         ENDDO
101   C                         EXSR      LEVEX1                                 Level 1
102   C                         EXSR      LEVEL2                                 Level 2
103   C                         EXCEPT    LROUT                                  LR - All
104   C                         ENDSR
105   C*
106   C*  Level 1 Subroutine - Control break on City
107   C*
108   C       LEVEL1          BEGSR
109   C       CTYPAY          ADD       STAPAY       STAXXX        9 2
110   C* Send out exception output to the L1OUT excpetion name
111   C                         EXCEPT    L1XXX
112   C                         ENDSR
113   C*
114   C*  Level 2 Subroutine - Control break on State
115   C*
116   C       LEVEL2          BEGSR
117   C       STAPAY          ADD       TOTPAY       TOTXXX        9 2
118   C                         EXCEPT    L2XXX
119   C                         ENDSR
120   C*
121   C*  PAYCLC  Calculates Gross PAY from HRS or Salary
122   C*  Also calculates "net pay" and updates YTD files.
123   C*  Calculate pay for HELD record
124   C*  If Salaried, do not use RATE multiplier
125   C*
126   C       PAYCLC          BEGSR
127   C                         SETOFF                                  9298
128   C                         Z-ADD     0            HLDXXX        6 0
129   C* REPLACES MR CYCLE WORK
130   C       HLDNO           CHAIN     TIMCRD                           92   No TC 92
131   * If no hit on time card read send out Except name NOTIME on report
132   * else multiply hrs by rate using the negative of the NF indicator     Write ERROR
133   C  N92HLDRAT          MULT      EMPHRS       HLDXXX        7 2        EMPHRS-TCD
134   C  N92                Z-ADD     EMPHRS       HLDXXX        9 2
135   C  N92HLDPAY          ADD       CTYPAY       CTYXXX        9 2        Detail City
136   C* Get the salary information from the SALFILE
137   C  N92HLDNO           CHAIN     SXXXILE                          98   Get Sal Rec
```

```
138  C  N98
139  CANN92                 Z-ADD     SALYR          XXXSAL         6 0
140  C* Divide the salary by 52 for weekly salary
141  C  N98
142  CANN92SALYR            DIV       52             XXXPAY                    Calcweek
143  C  N98
144  CANN92HLDPAY           ADD       CTYPAY         XXXPAY         9 2        Detail Sal
145  C  N98
146  CANN92                 Z-ADD     0              HLDHRS                    No HRS for
147  C                      ENDSR
148  C*
149  C* Write error msg for no master to separate External print file
150  C*
151  C     NOMAST           BEGSR
152  C* Write Print Fie Header Record
153  C                      WRITE     HDXXX
154  C* Write the detail record
155  C                      WRITE     DTXXX
156  C                      ENDSR
157  C*
158  C*  Process line item
159  C*
160  C     PROCES           BEGSR
161  C                      EXSR      MOVXXX
162  C                      EXSR      PAYXXX
163  C                      EXSR      PRNXXX
164  C                      ENDSR
165  C*
166  C* Print Detail Line on Register
167  C*
168  C     PRNTLN           BEGSR
169  C  OF                  EXCEPT    HEADRX
170  C  OF                  SETOFF                                            OF
171  C                      EXCEPT    PRTLXX
172  C                      ENDSR
173  C*
174  C* Move Fields to Hold Area for Level Information / Comparison
175  C*
176  C     MOVMS1           BEGSR
177  C                      Z-ADD     EMPNO          HLDNO
178  C                      MOVEL     EMPNAM         HLDNAM
179  C                      Z-ADD     EMPRAT         HLDRAT
180  C                      MOVEL     EMPCTY         XXXCTY
181  C                      MOVEL     EMPSTA         HLDSTA
182  C                      Z-ADD     EMPZIP         HLDZIP
183  C                      MOVEL     EMPSCD         HLDXXX
184  C                      MOVEL     EMPDPT         HLDDPT
185  C                      ENDSR
186  C*
187  C* CLR Clear fields that were used in the missing master test
188  C*
189  C     CLR              BEGSR
190  C                      Z-ADD     0              EMPNO
191  C                      MOVE      *BLANKS        EMPXXX
192  C                      Z-ADD     0              EMPRAT
193  C                      MOVE      *BLANKS        EMPCTY
194  C                      MOVE      *BLANKS        EMPSTA
195  C                      Z-ADD     0              EMPZIP
196  C                      MOVE      *BLANKS        EMPSCD
197  C                      MOVE      *BLANKS        EMPDPT
198  C                      Z-ADD     0              EMPXXX
199  C                      ENDSR
200  C*
201  C*  CHKMST Read time cards looking for missing masters & report
202  C*
203  C     CHKMST           BEGSR
204  C     *IN93            DOUEQ     *ON
205  C                      READ      TIMXXX                                 93
206  C     EMPNO            CHAIN     EMPMXXX                                94
```

```
207    C    94                  EXSR      NOMXXX
208    C                        ENDDO
209    C                        ENDSR
210    C*
211    C*
212    C*
213    C*
214    C*
215    O*
216    O* RPG OUTPUT SPECIFICATION FORMS
217    O*
218    OQPRINT       E           HXXXER          2 06
219    O                                             32 'THE DOWALLOBY COMPANY'
220    O                                             55 'GROSS PAY REGISTER BY '
221    O                                             60 'STATE'
222    O                         UDATE           Y   77
223    O             E           HXXXER          3
224    O                                              4 'ST'
225    O                                             13 'CITY'
226    O                                             27 'EMP#'
227    O                                             45 'EMPLOYEE NAME'
228    O                                             57 'RATE'
229    O                                             67 'HOURS'
230    O                                             77 'CHECK'
231    O             E           NOTIME          1 1
232    O                         HLDSTA               4
233    O                         HLDCTY              29
234    O                         HLDNO               27
235    O                                             53 'No Time Card this pay'
236    O                                             71 ' period for below:'
237    O             E           PRTLN1          0 1
238    O                         HLDSTA               4
239    O                         HLDCTY              29
240    O                         HLDNO               27
241    O                         HLDNM               52
242    O                  NXX    HLDPAY          1B  77
243    O                  NXX    HLDHRS          1B  67
244    O                         HLDRAT          1   57
245    O               XXX                           XX '** No Time Card **'
246    O             E           L1OUT           2 2
247    O                                             51 'TOTAL CITY  PAY FOR'
248    O                         HLDCTY              72
249    O                         CTYPAY          1B  77
250    O             E           L2OUT           0 2
251    O                                             51 'TOTAL STATE PAY FOR'
252    O                         HLDSTA              54
253    O                         STAPAY          1B  77
254    O             E           LROUT           2
255    O                         TOTPAY          1   77
256    O                                             50 'FINAL TOTAL PAY'
```

Figure 9-20 LAB09E4 Shell Full Program -- RPGIV External

```
 1     H* RPG HEADER (CONTROL) SPECIFICATION FORMS
 2     H
 3     F*
 4     F* RPG FILE DESCRIPTION SPECIFICATION FORMS
 5     F*
 6     FEMPMAST  IXX  F      XXX DISK
 7     FTIMCRD   IF  XX      XXXDISK
 8     FSALFILE  IF  XX      XXXX DISK
 9     FQPRINT   O   F   77      PRINTER OFLIND(*INOF)
10     FERROR    O   E          PRINTER
11     D HLDMST      X DS         70   EXTNAME(HLDMAST)
12     D*                          1   30HLDNO
13     D  HREC            1    70
14     D*                          4   33 HLDNAM
15     D  HLDNM           4    23
16     I*                         34  382HLDRAT
17     I*                         39   58 HLDCTY
18     I*                         59   60 HLDSTA
```

```
19   I*                                        61    650HLDZIP
20   I*                                        66    66 HLDSCD
21   I*                                        67    70 HLDDPT
22   C*
23   C* RPG CALCULATION SPECIFICATION FORMS
24   C*
25   C*  Run default register with no prompt input
26   C                    EXSR      RUNREG
27   C                    SETON                              LR
28   C*
29   C*  Body of Code that Controls the running of the Payroll Register
30   C    XXXXXX          BEGSR
31   C* Check to see if there is a missing master
32   C                    EXSR      CHKMST
33   C* Clear fields from CHKMST run to begin fresh register
34   C                    EXSR      CLR
35   C                    CLOSE     EMPMAST
36   C                    OPEN      EMPMAST
37   C* First read -- nead a read ahead to be able to check for Levels
38   C                    READ      EMPR                     91
39   C                    EXCEPT    HEADER
40   C                    EXSR      PROCES
41   C* Run register until end of file is hit... NU1 end program
42   C    *IN91           DOUEQ     XXX
43   C* SECOND READ -- UNTIL EOF NEED FOR LEVEL CHECK
44   C                    READ      XXXXXXX                  91
45   C   91               LEAVE
46   C* Replaces L1 coding as in PAREG
47   C* LEVEL 1 TEST -- See if current city is different
48   C    EMPCTY          IFNE      HLDCTY
49   C    EMPSTA          XXXX      HLDSTA
50   C                    SETON                              L1
51   C                    EXSR      LEVEL1
52   C                    ENDIF
53   C* Level 2 test -- See if current state is different
54   C    EMPSTA          IFNE      HLDSTA
55   C                    SETON                              L2
56   C                    EXSR      LEVEL2
57   C                    ENDIF
58   C                    SETOFF                             L1L2
59   C                    EXSR      PROCES                         Process HLD rec
60   C                    ENDDO
61   C                    EXSR      LEVEL1                         Level 1 Break
62   C                    EXSR      LEVEL2                         Level 2 Break
63   C                    EXCEPT    LROUT                          LR - All breaks
64   C                    ENDSR
65   C*
66   C*  Level 1 Subroutine - Control break on City
67   C*
68   C    XXXXXX          BEGSR
69   C    CTYPAY          ADD       STAPAY      STAPAY       9 2
70   C                    EXCEPT    L1OUT
71   C                    ENDSR
72   C*
73   C*  Level 2 Subroutine - Control break on State
74   C*
75   C    XXXXXX          BEGSR
76   C    STAPAY          ADD       TOTPAY      TOTPAY       9 2
77   C                    EXCEPT    L2OUT
78   C                    ENDSR
79   C*
80   C*  PAYCLC  Calculates Gross PAY from HRS or Salary
81   C*  Also calculates "net pay" and updates YTD files.
82   C*  Calculate pay for HELD record
83   C*  If Salaried, do not use RATE multiplier
84   C*
85   C    PAYCLC          BEGSR
86   C                    SETOFF                             9298
87   C                    Z-ADD     0           HLDSAL       6 0
88   C* REPLACES MR CYCLE WORK
89   C    HLDNO           CHAIN     TIMCRD                   92    No Time Card 92
90   C   92               EXCEPT    NOTIME                         Write ERROR
91   C  N92HLDRAT         MULT      EMPHRS      HLDPAY       7 2   EMPHRS-->TIMECD
92   C  N92               Z-ADD     EMPHRS      HLDHRS       9 2
93   C  XXXHLDPAY         ADD       CTYPAY      CTYPAY       9 2   Detail City
94   C  XXXHLDNO          CHAIN     SALFILE                  98    Get Sal Record
95   C  XXX
```

```
96   CXXXXX              Z-ADD    SALYR         HLDSAL          6 0
97   C N98
98   CANN92SALYR          DIV      52            HLDPAY                       Calc weekly Sal
99   C N98
100  CANN92HLDPAY         ADD      CTYPAY        CTYPAY          9 2          Detail Sal City
101  C N98
102  CANN92              Z-ADD    0             HLDHRS                       No HRS for SAL
103  C                   ENDSR
104  C*
105  C* Write error msg for no master to separate External print file
106  C*
107  C    XXXXXX         BEGSR
108  C                   WRITE    HDR
109  C                   WRITE    DTL
110  C                   ENDSR
111  C*
112  C*  Process line item
113  C*
114  C    XXXXXX         BEGSR
115  C                   EXSR     MOVMS1
116  C                   EXSR     PAYCLC
117  C                   EXSR     PRNTLN
118  C                   ENDSR
119  C*
120  C* Print Detail Line on Register
121  C*
122  C    PRNTLN         BEGSR
123  C  OF               EXCEPT   HEADER
124  C  OF               SETOFF                                  OF
125  C                   EXCEPT   PRTLN1
126  C                   ENDSR
127  C*
128  C* Move Fields to Hold Area for Level Information / Comparison
129  C*
130  C    MOVMS1         BEGSR
131  C                   Z-ADD    EMPNO         HLDNO
132  C                   MOVEL    EMPNAM        HLDNAM
133  C                   Z-ADD    EMPRAT        HLDRAT
134  C                   MOVEL    EMPCTY        HLDCTY
135  C                   MOVEL    EMPSTA        HLDSTA
136  C                   Z-ADD    EMPZIP        HLDZIP
137  C                   MOVEL    EMPSCD        HLDSCD
138  C                   MOVEL    EMPDPT        HLDDPT
139  C                   ENDSR
140  C*
141  C* CLR Clear fields that were used in the missing master test
142  C*
143  C    XXXXXX         BEGSR
144  C                   Z-ADD    0             EMPNO
145  C                   MOVE     *BLANKS       EMPNAM
146  C                   Z-ADD    0             EMPRAT
147  C                   MOVE     *BLANKS       EMPCTY
148  C                   MOVE     *BLANKS       EMPSTA
149  C                   Z-ADD    0             EMPZIP
150  C                   MOVE     *BLANKS       EMPSCD
151  C                   MOVE     *BLANKS       EMPDPT
152  C                   Z-ADD    0             EMPHRS
153  C                   ENDSR
154  C*
155  C*  CHKMST Read time cards looking for missing masters & report
156  C*
157  C    CHKMST         BEGSR
158  C    *IN93          DOUEQ    *ON
159  C                   READ     TIMCRD                                 93
160  C    XXXXXX         CHAIN    EMPMAST                           94
161  C  94               EXSR     NOMAST
162  C                   ENDDO
163  C                   ENDSR
164  C*
165  C*
166  C*
167  C*
168  C*
169  O*
170  O* RPG OUTPUT SPECIFICATION FORMS
171  O*
172  OQPRINT    E         HEADER        2 06
173  O                                        32 'THE DOWALLOBY COMPANY'
174  O                                        55 'GROSS PAY REGISTER BY '
175  O                                        60 'STATE'
```

```
176   O                             UDATE          X    77
177   O              E              HEADER         3
178   O                                                4 'ST'
179   O                                               13 'CITY'
180   O                                               27 'EMP#'
181   O                                               45 'EMPLOYEE NAME'
182   O                                               57 'RATE'
183   O                                               67 'HOURS'
184   O                                               77 'CHECK'
185   O              E              NOTIME         1  1
186   O                             HLDSTA              4
187   O                             HLDCTY             29
188   O                             HLDNO              27
189   O                                               53 'No Time Card this pay'
190   O                                               71 ' period for below:'
191   O              E              PRTLN1         0  1
192   O                             HLDSTA              4
193   O                             HLDCTY             29
194   O                             HLDNO              27
195   O                             HLDNM              52
196   O                      N92    HLDPAY        1B   77
197   O                      N92    HLDHRS        1B   67
198   O                             HLDRAT        1     57
199   O                       92                      76 '** No Time Card **'
200   O              E              L1OUT          2  2
201   O                                               51 'TOTAL CITY   PAY FOR'
202   O                             HLDCTY             72
203   O                             CTYPAY        1B   77
204   O              E              L2OUT          0  2
205   O                                               51 'TOTAL STATE PAY FOR'
206   O                             HLDSTA             54
207   O                             STAPAY        1B   77
208   O              E              LROUT          2
209   O                             TOTPAY        1     77
210   O                                               50 'FINAL TOTAL PAY'
```

*** End of Lab 9 ***

Lecture F: RPG Is Not Just the Cycle

It is CYCLE Plus!

RPG and RPGIV provide a plethora of other ways to achieve the same thing that can be achieved by the cycle. Lab 9 is the embodiment of this notion. It happens that RPG / RPGIV can do report writing just the way every programmer using any computer science programming language such as C or Pascal can achieve. The cycle however permits the job to be done with the least amount of coding. So, in this book of tutorials, we began with the parts you have just read and we have some labs that show you how to deal with the cycle. Then we move from the cycle and your labs show you how to achieve the same thing without the cycle.

We cover four forms of RPG in this tutorial / lab set. RPG/400 as it is called is shown in its internal form (programmer specifies fields for input and output) and its external form (system's integrated database provides the field definitions for input and output). This code is then converted to RPGIV in your labs and you get to create the internal and external form of several programs in RPGIV.

To keep your learning crisp, the RPGIV program definition (the specs) is the same as the RPG/400 definition so when you finish these labs, you will know how the same program looks in all of the four variations of RPG and RPGIV -- internal and external. Since many IBM i RPG shops have all forms of RPG in play as well as some older RPG code, this introduction to the many forms of RPG will be most helpful to you in practice in your RPG shops.

The basic truth is that RPG in any form -- cycle or no cycle, RPG or RPGIV, internal or external, permits programmers to write business code in significantly less statements than in any computer science language. Quite simply, RPG is a business language that was developed for business people who may or may not understand computer science but do understand how to make businesses more productive. RPG programmers haunt IBM to this day with the notion that programming constructs need not be difficult to understand and they hold IBM's feet to the fire so they can accomplish their daily programming tasks without having to know too much about the computer itself. and without being involved in how the computer does its work internally.

Lab 10 Introduction to Interactive RPG Programming

Lab 10 Objectives:

Students learn how to use the Screen Design Aid program (a component of the System i Native Program Development Tools) to produce a simple display panel that will be used to provide input to an Accounts Payable Master File inquiry program written in RPG/400. In Exercise 1, you bring up a pre-written SDA panel to see what it looks like. In Exercise 2, you create that same panel from scratch.

In Exercise 3, you built the first of two RPG programs to run with the screen panel and you exercise the program after you create it. In Exercise 4, you extend your SDA design to display all of the fields in the VENDORP file. In exercise 5, you build the second of two programs that interact with the Vendor Master file VENDORP.

Labs 10 and 11 are based on the VENDORP file. It's DDS description follows in Figure 10-A. This is followed by a look at the data in Figure 10-B

Figure 10-A VENDORP File Description DDS from Field Reference File

```
  Columns . . . :    1  71              Browse                RPGOBJ/SOURCE
   SEU==>                                                            VPREF
   FMT PF .....A..........T.Name+++++RLen++TDpB......Functions++++++++++++++++++++
          ************** Beginning of data ********************************
  0001.00     A           R VNDMSTR                   TEXT('VENDORP  DB FORMAT')
  0002.00     A             VNDNBR      5S 0          COLHDG('VENDOR' 'NUMBER')
  0003.00     A                                       ALIAS(VENDOR_NUMBER)
  0004.00     A             NAME        25            COLHDG('NAME')
  0005.00     A             ADDR1       25            COLHDG('ADDRESS LINE 1')
  0006.00     A                                       ALIAS(ADDRESS_LINE_1)
  0007.00     A             CITY        15            COLHDG('CITY')
  0008.00     A             STATE        2            COLHDG('STATE')
  0009.00     A             ZIPCD       5S 0          COLHDG('ZIP''CODE')
  0010.00     A                                       ALIAS(ZIP_CODE)
  0011.00     A             VNDCLS      2S 0          COLHDG('VENDOR' 'CLASS')
  0012.00     A                                       ALIAS(VENDOR_CLASS)
  0013.00     A             VNDSTS       1            COLHDG('ACTIVE' 'CODE')
  0014.00     A                                       ALIAS(ACTIVE_CODE)
  0015.00     A                                       TEXT('A=ACTIVE, D=DELETE, +
  0016.00     A                                       S=SUSPEND')
  0017.00     A             BALOWE      9S 2          COLHDG('BALANCE' 'OWED')
  0018.00     A                                       ALIAS(BALANCE_OWED)
  0019.00     A             SRVRTG       1            COLHDG('SERVICE' 'RATING')
  0020.00     A                                       ALIAS(SERVICE_RATING)
  0021.00     A                                       TEXT('G=GOOD, A=AVERAGE, +
  0022.00     A                                       B=BAD, P=PREFERRED')
  0023.00     A*          K VNDNBR
          ***************** End of data ********************************
```

Figure 10-B Cropped Query Report of Vendor Master (VENDORP)

```
                               Display Report
                                   Report width  . . . . . :        76
Position to line  . . . . .          Shift to column  . . . . . .
Line      ....+....1....+....2....+....3....+....4....+....5....+....6....+....7..
          VENDR NAME            ADDRESS LINE 1 CITY       ST  ZIP   VND  ACT  BALANCE
          NUMBR                                               CODE  CLS  COD  OWED
000001 00038 John B. Stetz 3817 N. PULAS  SCRANTON   PA 18503  10   A    100.00
000002 00040 Scranton Fabr 2147 S MAIN S  OLD FORGE  PA 18762  20   A    250.00
000003 00042 Pass Pax Inc  1539 OAK HILL  OLD FORGE  PA 19722  10   A    300.00
000004 00044 Cliffy Equipm 2232 FOUEST    SCRANTON   PA 18503  20   A     50.00
000005 00046 Butts & Walla 2150 TOUGHY    SCRANTON   PA 18503  30   A    500.00
000006 00048 Denton and Ba 7934 S SCRANT  SCRANTON   PA 18504  20   A   3500.00
000007 00049 John Studios  2040 N BELTWA  SCRANTON   PA 18505  10   A    325.00
000008 00025 Macone Corp O 1345 Prill Av  Chicago    IL 45903  10   A   7500.00
000009 00026 Lockhart Mach 45 Ginzo Lane  Wokegon    OK 23657  20   A   1495.55
000010 00028 Charley Engra Pedulllion Av  Greghert   IL 45963  20   A    100.00
000011 00030 Detweiller Co 45 Fognetta P  Kernstin   IL 45793  20   A    900.25
000012 00032 Irfing Power  56 Fineel La   Swingder   PA 18503  20   A    250.00
000013 00034 Blind Robin C 11 Robin Lane  Robin      PA 18702  20   A    153.00
000014 00036 Facile Steel  78 Engraved R  Mattusic   PA 18598  30   A    290.00
000015 07000 Microsoft Cor One Microsoft  Redmond    WA 98052  10   A      9.54
000016 07010 Oracle Corpor 1234 Relation  Redwood Sh CA 92626  10   A     95.00
000017 07020 Sun MicroSyst 4150 Network   Santa Clar CA 95054  10   A   8000.00
000018 07030 ATG Dynamo    25 First Stre  Cambridge  MA 02141  20   A    352.56
000019 07040 Education Dir 925 Oak Stree  Scranton   PA 18515  20   A     14.50
000020 07050 Merant Glass  125 Micro Foc  Phoenix    AZ 19954  30   A     56.00
000021 07060 WRQ Reflectio 1556 Emulatio  Tampa Bay  FL 12374  20   A      4.99
000022 07070 Red Hat Club  985 Linus Str  Albany     NY 85743  10   A     78.50
000023 07080 Thompson Corp 5664 Publishe  Austin     TX 98735  20   A      9.65
000024 07090 Fat Brain     65 Books Onli  Clevland   OH 47895  10   A    256.00
000025 07100 Office Max    584 Office Su  Detroit    MI 85742  10   A     19.00
000026 07110 Home Depot    5697 Fix It S  Jackson    MS 65412  30   S     66.54
000027 07120 American Vend 5687 Eating D  Portland   OR 65478  20   D     29.83
000028 07130 McFadyen Cons 521 Wedoitall  Indianapol IN 98523  10   A    250.00
000029 07140 Kensington Mi 78 Clean Stre  Lancaster  PA 65471  20   A     25.25
000030 07150 Texas Instrum 45 Jones Rd.   San Antoni TX 87459  10   A     15.30
000031 77777 Left Outer Jo 1234 Address   Scranton   PA 18515  10   A    500.00
000032 08020 Phillies Phin 391 Carey Ave  Wilkes-Bar PA 18702  20   A  35700.00
000033 08030 Bings Music   91 Peeliere A  Oanoke     VA 58702  20   A  79700.00
```

Nobody expects students in this RPG class to understand the notion of a logical file. However, these programs use logical files. The one you should use instead of VENDORP is VENDMST. However, VENDMAST does exactly the same thing as you can see in the extra source program solutions in your source file called LAB10_2ES2. While you are struggling to get a clean compile, remember that VENDORP itself has no index and thus cannot be processed by key.

Enter the logical file named VENDMST. So, in the XX version of the solution, VENDORP must be replaced in file descriptions with VENDMST. You see VENDMST is a logical file built against VENDORP and all it does is provide an index. In other words, all the good data in VENDORP is visible through VENDMST. Additionally, by using VENDMST, and VENDMAST for that matter, you get all of the data in VENDORP plus an index built on

VNDNBR. So, even though it wil take you a while to appreciate the full power of logical files on IBM i and RPG, you will be using it.

Lab 10 – Exercise 1 Introduction to SDA

Use your screen design aid knowledge obtained from Chapter 20 of the RPG Pocket Guide text or Google screen design aid as400 for IBM's free technical description to design a display panel that can be used in an accounts payable master inquiry program. Use the same one panel design for both input and output.

These examples both work with RPG/400 programs. If you choose to convert the RPG/400 programs to RPGIV using CVTRPGSRC, use the pattern we developed in the earlier labs to accomplish this. Change the names of the programs so that the converted version does not have the same name as the RPGIV version in the SOURCE file.

Those who have chosen to use this Lab / Tutorial as their sole learning vehicle for SDA/Display File DDS, should consider using the IBM manuals in the Infocenter as a reference for anything shown in this tutorial that is not obvious. As noted several times in this tutorial / lab, the best way to use the IBM material is to use the Google search engine. If for example, you want to study about SDA in general, you would type IBM i and SDA on a Google search line and hit the enter key.

A wealth of information is available from IBM as well as sources such as IT Jungle and MC Press.

To be better prepared to write the program and prepare the display file some general DDS and SDA guidance is given before the detailed tutorial Lab Exercises.

Data Description Language

With the delivery of the System/38, IBM also introduced a new data language named after its specification form. It is called Data Description Specifications or quite simply, DDS and it is still used with System i. DDS can be used for externally defined communication files, database files, printer files, and workstation display files. It is the native all-purpose data language for the System i. In this Lab, it shall be used for building a workstation

DDS is far too large a topic for this Lab book. In fact, to help student's gain a command of the DDS language for display files and native database files, I have written three books. All are advertised on the last page of this book. Their names are The IBM i Pocket Developer's Guide; The IBM i Pocket Database Guide; and Getting Started With WebSphere Development Studio Client. So, if DDS is too large a topic for this book and it is needed to create display files, and display files are needed for interactive programming, how can a neophyte RPG programmer create a display file without knowing DDS?

There are two answers to this question. On the still bleeding edge but clotting fast is the very powerful WebSphere Development Studio Client (WDSC) package and its internal screen creation facility know simply as the Designer. The second uses the integrated (with the application development toolset) Program Development Manager (PDM) that we have been using all along in the Labs / tutorials. PDM has been and is the launching pad for its Screen Design Aid facility. All of these products as well as the RPG and COBOL, C, and C++ compilers are shipped by IBM in its latest programmer kit, product number 5722-WDS. For V6R1, IBM has made the buying/using a bit more complicated for the novice to understand. Start by looking up 5761-**WDS** and the rest should flow from there.

WebSphere Development Studio Client (WDSC)

The Eclipse-based WDSC is a Windows oriented intelligent development environment that IBM has earmarked as its replacement for the green screen interactive PDM. The part of WDSC and several earlier incarnations that are germane to display file creation have been around since the mid 990s under the moniker of CODE/400, which stands for the Cooperative Development Environment. The CODE Designer or in WDSC, the Designer is the specific piece of the puzzle that creates display files. In fact, the designer does not really create display files; it creates DDS which then is used to create the display file. Likewise, the IBM Screen Design Aid also creates DDS which is then used to create display files.

In the latest WDSC, the CODE product set has been integrated into the package. A facility called Remote Systems Explorer now provides a navigation tool to your IBM i box, from which you can locate libraries, objects and members and instantly call them up with a fully functional editor that is tuned into the object type. If you have purchased the text book in addition to this lab book / tutorial, you can see an example of this in Figure 10-1 as the TEST3 RPG program is being selected for editing. Figure 10-2 then shows the WDSC source editor with the program in its grasp.

Less than 20% of the IBM i shops of which I am aware use WDSC for RPG and display file development. I would expect that in the next ten years, as WDSC and now the Rational Family of IBM Tools become more and more stable and as intuitive as the green screen tools, these percentages will change in the other direction. Because PDM is still the predominant methodology for AD on IBM i and because SDA is the method most used for designing screen panels, this is the method that we have chosen to use in this Lab book / tutorial. It works!

Introduction to Lab Exercise 10 -1

In the coming hands-on semi-trivial / lab exercise on SDA and Interactive programming, we examine the creation of a display panel using SDA in a brief tutorial fashion. You will be able to use the results of your efforts in this Lab to move on to bigger and more sophisticated programming examples, using subfiles and other different advanced interactive techniques including "green screen" windows.

They key device in RPG which makes workstation files and interactive programming possible is WORKSTN. It is through this mechanism that RPG gets to talk and literally interact with both real and emulated workstation display devices. This device was introduced with the System/34 in 1977, and perfected with the display file as introduced in 1978 with the System/38. AS/400 and System i use the same device facility.

The WORKSTN file gets created using the Data Description language for its externally defined workstation files. DDL is also used in System i for communication files, database files and printer files. It is the native all-purpose data language for the System i.

As noted previously, the Eclipse-based WDSC has a facility called the CODE Designer that in the same spirit of SDA can creates the DDS that creates the display files. SDA is a green screen tool, originally introduced with the System/34 that permits a programmer or analyst to interactively design, create, and maintain display screen panels and menus for applications.

The display panel is the operative part of a WORKSTN file built by DDS. It has a natural affinity for inclusion in RPG, COBOL, and other high level language programs on IBM i. It would be great on other IBM machines such as the Unix (AIX) boxes and the Mainframes, but IBM chooses to keep it IBM i-only. The strong point of SDA as well as the WDSC designer is that you do not need extensive knowledge of DDS coding, its forms, keywords or syntax to use either of these tools.

Though programmers do not have to understand DDS per se to work with SDA or the Designer, it is better if they do. The DDS structure for this Lab enables WORKSTN keywords to be applied to files, fields and formats. When applied to files, the function key for example is applicable to all panels in the display file. When applied at the format level, it has meaning at the screen panel level. And when a keyword is applied at the field level, it has governance only for that particular field.

One of the main productivity features of SDA and the IBM/Rational GUI Designer is that they both provide for database definition inclusion during the design phase. This assures the proper database definitions being used for workstation fields.

In addition to being able to design new panels, the tools also provide a means of adding panels or adding or changing fields or field attributes one existing panels. To use the display file in the RPG program, code the name of the display file in File descriptions. Make it combined and fully procedural and place the WORKSTN device in the device column. Then, in calculations use the appropriate interactive operation, EXFMT, WRITE, or READ to send and receive the specific panels that you request.

What is IBM i SDA?

In much the same fashion as the WDSC Designer, without the use of a mouse, SDA allows a programmer or analyst to interactively design, create, and maintain display screen panels and menus for applications.

When designing screen panels for programs, SDA allows the user to:

1.   Define fields and constants for the screen
2.   Select a data base file and fields from that file
3.   Change attributes (blinking, highlighted, colors, etc.) for fields and
        constants
4.   Move, copy, or remove a field from the screen
5.   Display or change the conditions that control when a field will be
        displayed
6.   Define cursor-sensitive help areas for the screen.

In addition to providing a tool to build workstation display file panels, highlighting the inherent separation of the user interface from the business logic, SDA also provides a facility to test the panels prior to even writing the RPG program to help assure that the panels look and behave properly prior to deployment in an RPG or COBOL program.

Menus

Besides image design and testing, a third capability provided on the SDA main menu is the ability to create and maintain menus with little programming skill required. Menus are a tremendous aid in building applications. This powerful SDA menu build capability takes all of the heavy work from this important task. Your RPG menu for this course was built using SDA.

IBM i menus are very similar to a menu in a restaurant. They tell you what you can have. In essence, they present a list of options. The workstation operator can then make a selection from the available options, and the system does the work of getting that application alive and ready for the user. Online help information can also be built for menus, making it even that much easier to navigate through the options. Online RPG programs are most often launched from menus rather than by name. Since this LAB Exercise deals only with RPG programming factors, the creation of SDA menus is not on its topic list.

Display Panels

Display panels (a.k.a. screens or panels) define the screens a user works with when using interactive application programs. The display files which are produced by SDA have a natural affinity for inclusion in RPG, COBOL, and other high level language programs. Moreover, with the introduction of the WebSphere Development Studio Client, the DDS source produced by SDA for display files can be readily WebFaced into java server pages. This provides the same function for the Web as the display file does for interactive green screen applications. Just as with SDA menus, you can also build online help information for your SDA-created displays.

SDA Features

In a nutshell, SDA provides tremendous facility for programmers. Some of its major features are as follows:

1. Generate data description specifications (DDS)
2. Create menus with message files
3. Present displays in functional groups at file, record and field level
4. Test displays with data and status of condition indicators
5. See the display being designed and changes as work is being done.

*** End of DDS Language Overview ***

Getting Started

You begin using SDA by invoking the STRSDA command from an AS/400 or System i command line. If you press F4 with the command, you will be presented with a fill-in screen. The last option is your first major decision. Do you want to create your display panels or menus in AS/400 mode (*STD), System/38 mode (*S38), or System/36 mode (*S36)? For different reasons, you may choose any of these options. As you would probably expect, AS/400 mode is the default, and there is no IBM i mode. For IBM i, you can use any of the provided options...   but there is no specific IBM i choice because IBM's SDA code existed a long time before IBM i and IBM has chosen not to spend its development dollars to improve it. Regardless of IBM's role in SDA, it is still a fine tool. .

For our labs, use AS/400 mode. Let us begin Lab 10 Exercise 1 at this point to continue this discussion in a tutorial fashion Make sure you have the Labs loaded on your system and you are signed on to your Lab menu, working in your Lab library.

1. Use PDM to copy the source of the DSPF type (not RPG) member named <u>LAB10D1</u> in your source file and create a new member called LAB10D1Y -- of the same DSPF type.

2. Type STRSDA and the first SDA panel you see is shown in Figure 10-1.

Figure 10-1 SDA Prompt Panel

```
                    Start SDA (STRSDA)

Type choices, press Enter.

SDA option . . . . . .    *SELECT         *SELECT, 1, 2, 3
Source file  . . . . .    *PRV            Name, *PRV
  Library  . . . . . .      *PRV          Name, *PRV, *LIBL,
Source member  . . . .    *PRV            Name, *PRV, *SELECT
Object library . . . .    *PRV            Name, *PRV, *CURLIB
Job description  . . .    *PRV            Name, *PRV, *USRPRF
  Library  . . . . . .      *PRV          Name, *PRV, *LIBL,
Test file  . . . . . .    *PRV            Name, *PRV
  Library  . . . . . .      *PRV          Name, *PRV, *LIBL,
Mode . . . . . . . . .    *STD            *STD, *S38, *S36

                                                  Bottom

F3=Exit    F4=Prompt    F5=Refresh    F12=Cancel
F13=How to use this display  F24=More keys
```

If you make no choices on this panel, it will be as if you just typed in STRSDA and did not hit the F4 prompter. You can see in Figure 10-1 that almost all of the options are defaulted to *PRV. This specifies that SDA is to use the name of the source file and library used in your last SDA session for the AS/400 system. There is actually a little item on the AS/400 which the system keeps for each user.

It is called your interactive profile, and the system uses it to remember what parameters you may have used the last time you were in an interactive session with a product. This comes in very handy. For our purposes at this time, let's assume you changed no option on the display panel selected.

Hit Enter and you will see a panel similar to Figure 10-2.

Screen Design Aid Menu Options

When you hit ENTER on this panel or after typing STRSDA, you will see the main SDA Menu. When you examine Figure 10-2, you will notice that it looks a lot like the standard PDM panel but, it is much different.

Figure 10-2 Main Screen Design Panel

```
                    AS/400 Screen Design Aid (SDA)

Select one of the following:

     1. Design screens
     2. Design menus
     3. Test display files

Selection or command
===>1


F1=Help    F3=Exit    F4=Prompt    F9=Retrieve
F12=Cancel    ©) COPYRIGHT IBM CORP. 1981, 2000.
```

Creating a Display File

In Figure 10-2, you are presented with the main SDA Menu. It is good to remember when using SDA that just as many other of the WebSphere Development Studio utilities, SDA comes with significant help facilities. In fact, cursor-sensitive help is always available. This means that whatever field or option you have the cursor on, when you press the help key, detail help text will be displayed. To proceed with creating your first or next SDA menu, such as your RPG Programming Menu, you would pick the option (2) of creating a menu. To proceed with testing an already created display file, you would take option 3. For this coming exercise, do not take either of those options as we are about to create / use / delete a display file.

 I would recommend at this point that you press the help key just to see the definitions of all the function keys. This will help you immensely as you begin designing screen panels.

3. After getting a look at the HELP text, select option 1 from the panel in Figure 10-2 and press ENTER. You will be taken to a panel similar to that in Figure 10-3

Figure 10-3 Design Screens Initial Panel

```
                    Design Screens
   Type choices, press Enter.

       Source file . . . . . . . .  SOURCE ___    Name, F4 for list
          Library . . . . . . . . . YOURLIB___    Name, *LIBL, *CURLIB
       Member  . . . . . . . . . .  LAB10D1Y__  Name, F4 for list



    F3=Exit     F4=Prompt    F12 = Cancel
```

Screen Panel Exercise Objectives

4. In Figure 10-3, specify the new member name, source file, and library where the generated DDS resides (or will reside when generated). Then press ENTER

As you attempt to create the member named LAB10D1Y (Lab 10 display file #1 and the Y means it's yours) in the SOURCE file in your current library by using SDA to build the DDS, let's suppose it is already there. You just put it there in step 1 of this lab via PDM copy.

Just for this exercise, let's just suppose that somebody before you or you as is the case, has created this display file source (DSPF member type). Let's also say that later you learn that it is an unnecessary, bogus object and later, not now, you are authorized to delete it. You will not need it after this next exercise.

Then, after working through this part of the exercise first, you will be able to create your own version of *LAB10D1Y* from scratch.

That's exactly what this display file exercise is all about. You are about to find (in this exercise) that the source for file *LAB10D1Y does* already exist. It has a few intentional errors marked with X. So, when you bring up the *LAB10D1Y* member and take a look at it with SDA's full screen panel editor, you have a chance to see the panel in SDA without having to do very much typing. Display file member named LAB10D1S has the full and complete and correct solution.

After this, you will try to delete it (LAB10D1Y) and you will discover that there is no easy way to get all the pieces. Along the way, you will be shown the tools you need to delete all of the entrails of the SDA application, and you will begin again from scratch to build this simple panel -- but you will have already seen it so it should be easier..

Before we get into the thick of the exercise, let's review a few items that will help put display file DDS in perspective. After all, SDA creates DDS on its way to building the display file object from the DDS that it generates. Sometimes DDS operations can be designed to relate to certain portions of a display file. Some operations pertain to all the panels in a the display file; some pertain to one file, while others may pertain to just one field.

The following brief section is designed to put this in perspective as well as present the nature and consistency of a display file object and its relationship to a calling program.. Then we will resume the Lab exercise / tutorial.

Levels: Files, Records, Fields

It is important to understand the relationship between Files, Record Formats, and Fields within DDS. These important relationships have even more bearing in display formats than in database.

Each record in any display file specifies all the characteristics of one display panel. Thus, operations occurring on one panel are known as *Record Level* operations. A display file record is composed of fields, which exist within a panel and are designated as input, output or both (input and output). Operations on individual fields are known as *Field Level* operations.

Operations that occur in all records within a file are referred to as *File Level* operations. The sum total of all of the screens (record formats, panels etc.), with all of the associated fields and attributes, is referred to as the *display file object*.

The name of the file is important. RPG programs reference the display file by its object name. Therefore the link from program to display file is through the display file name as specified in the program. In RPG for example the display file name would appear in the File Description Specifications as a WORKSTN device file. Remember this so that you can specify it in your own programs and you can recognize it in this exercise.

That's it for the diversion. Now, let's get back to the essence of this Lab exercise. When you have your panel from Figure 10-3 completed, as directed above in Step 4, press ENTER to get to the *Work with Display Records* panel as shown in Figure 10-4.

Figure 10-4 Work with Display Records SDA Panel

```
                        Work with Display Records

   File  . . . . . . :   SOURCE              Member  . . . . . . . :  LAB10D1Y
      Library . . . . :     YOURLIB          Source type . . . . :  DSPF

   Type options, press Enter.
     1=Add           2=Edit comments      3=Copy            4=Remove
     7=Rename        8=Select keywords   12=Design image

   Opt   Order    Record        Type     Related Subfile Date      DDS Error

   12     10    VENDFMT      RECORD                       10/04/90




   F3=Exit                    F12=Cancel       F14=File-level keywords
   F15=File-level comments    F17=Subset       F24=More keys
```

Working with an Existing Source Member

The member named "LAB10D1Y" already exists. Therefore, from your panel input on Figure 10-3, SDA knows enough to find the member, go inside the member and pick up the information about the one record format (screen panel) within that DDS that has been previously built. As you can see in Figure 10-4, the record format name is VENDFMT. Of course, your shell does not say exactly that and you would have to modify it in order for it to work with the RPG program... Observe for now. Do not take this action.

Take note that to add a new format (display panel), from this panel, you would specify the option (OPT) to add (1) and specify the name of the record format. If you want to update the existing format, type the appropriate option number (12) next to the record format name.

As you can see by looking at the options, including option 12, you can use this panel to change information about an existing format, add or change comments, select record level keywords (option 8), or file level keywords (F14), etc. You can also change the image itself using option 12. That is exactly what you are going to do now.

Look at an Existing Screen Image

5.   Type 12 next to VENDFMT as shown in Figure 10-4 and press ENTER with option 12 specified and you will see a panel similar to that shown in Figure 10-5.

Figure 10-5 Screen Image Existing Format

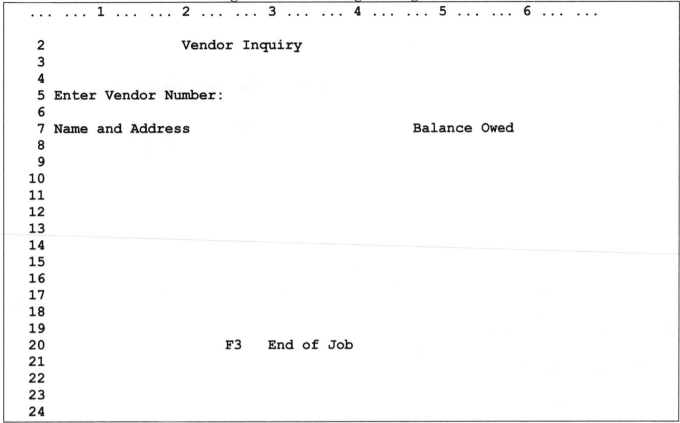

```
 ... ...  1 ... ...  2 ... ...  3 ... ...  4 ... ...  5 ... ...  6 ... ...

    2                     Vendor Inquiry
    3
    4
    5  Enter Vendor Number:
    6
    7  Name and Address                        Balance Owed
    8
    9
   10
   11
   12
   13
   14
   15
   16
   17
   18
   19
   20                      F3    End of Job
   21
   22
   23
   24
```

6. Press F14 now to bring up the "rule."

In order to get your work panel to look like the panel in Figure 10-5, you must press F14. This brings up the "rule." The *ruler* will give you a numeric columnar grid on the left and top so you have an idea on which row and which column you are placing your design.

Your version of LAB10D1Y will be more complete than this sample shown here. It's OK since you are about to delete it anyway. This sample is from the RPG book, not the Lab material in SOURCE. Now that you have reviewed the LAB10D1Y file as it will be built in the next exercise, the first thing that must be done to build a file from scratch is to delete the existing one..

7. Hit F3 to return to a command line to begin the process to delete the LAB10D1Y objects and source..

8. From the command line, type STRPDM and press Enter.

9. Pick Work with Objects, option 2

10. On the Work with objects panel, look for the name "LAB10D1Y" object type *FILE with attributes of display file. If you do not find it, scroll until it appears in the list of objects from your library. You did not compile this but I did so it will be there. This is the display file object that you are deleting, not the source member.

.

11. When you find LAB10D1Y, place a 4 next to it and delete it.

12. Accept the confirmation message to delete the display file object named LAB10D1Y.

13. At this point, the display file is gone. However, the DDS that SDA created is not gone. To find this go out of the Work with Objects panel to get to the PDM Main Menu. (Hint -- hit F3 or F12 twice)

14 Select work with members.

15. Pick the SOURCE source file in your library

16. When you get the Work with members panel look for name LAB10D1Y of type DSPF.

17. If you cannot find it scroll through the list until you locate it.

18. Place a 4 next to it and hit ENTER to delete it.

19. Take the DELETE confirmation message and press ENTER.

The object and the source for LAB10D1Y are both now removed from the system so that LAB10D1Y can now be recreated. That completes Exercise 1 -- Introduction to SDA

Lab 10 Exercise 2:   Building SDA Image from Scratch

In this exercise, you will build, from scratch, the panel similar to what you just saw in Figure 10-5 and which you already deleted.

1. Keep hitting the F3 key until you return to a command line and you have exited SDA.

2. Start your session by typing the start SDA command (STRSDA). Press Enter

The SDA main menu would appear as in Figure 10-2.

3, Type "1" for Design screens.

The Design Screens option panel is presented as shown in Figure 10-6.

4. Fill it in as in Figure 10-6 and press Enter.

Figure 10-6 Design Screens Initial Panel

```
                       Design Screens
   Type choices, press Enter.


      Source file . . . . . . . . SOURCE ___    Name, F4 for list
         Library . . . . . . . . . YOURLIB___    Name, *LIBL, *CURLIB
      Member  . . . . . . . . . . LAB10D1Y___  Name, F4 for list



   F3=Exit     F4=Prompt     F12 = Cancel
```

5. When you complete the panel in 10-6, press ENTER. You will see a panel as in Figure 10-7 below with one big difference. There would be no record format in the file. In fact when you arrive, it says very clearly at the bottom, (*No records in file*) as shown in Figure 10-7.

Figure 10-7 Creating the First Display Panel for the Display File

```
                  Work with Display Records

File . . . . . . :     SOURCE           Member . . . . . . :   LAB10D1Y
  Library . . . . :     YOURLIB            Source type  . . . :   DSPF
Type options, press Enter.
  1=Add              2=Edit comments        3=Copy           4=Delete
  7=Rename           8=Select keywords     12=Design image
Opt  Order  Record      Type   Related Subfile   Date        DDS Error

___  ___  _____
  (No records in file)                                        Bottom


F3=Exit                  F12=Cancel        F14=File-level keywords
F15=File-level comments  F17=Subset        F24=More keys
```

So, your mission is to create one record format for this display file. In the end, the panel you create will look similar to that shown in Figure 10-8

Figure 10-8 Screen Image Existing Format

```
 ... ... 1 ... ... 2 ... ... 3 ... ... 4 ... ... 5 ... ... 6 ... ...

   2                 Vendor Inquiry
   3
   4
   5 Enter Vendor Number:
   6
   7 Name and Address                           Balance Owed
   8
   9
  10
  11
  12
  13
  14
  15
  16
  17
  18
  19
  20              F3    End of Job
  21
  22
  23
  24
```

Figure 10-9 Creating The First Display Panel for the Display File

```
                       Work with Display Records

 File  . . . . . . :      SOURCE            Member . . . . . . :     LAB10D1Y
   Library . . . . :        YOURLIB         Source type  . . . :     DSPF
 Type options, press Enter.
   1=Add                 2=Edit comments        3=Copy          4=Delete
   7=Rename              8=Select keywords     12=Design image
 Opt  Order  Record      Type    Related Subfile   Date         DDS Error
 1    ___    VENDFMT
 ___  (No records in file)                                      Bottom


 F3=Exit                    F12=Cancel        F14=File-level keywords
 F15=File-level comments    F17=Subset        F24=More keys
```

6. To begin this new process with LAB10D1Y, place a "1" in the options column as shown in Figure 10-9, and place the name of the new format (VENDFMT) in the Record column. Press the ENTER key to get the process under way. You will then be asked what *type* of record to add to the display file. This question is shown in Figure 10-10.

Figure 10-10 Add a New Record Selection

```
                          Add New Record

 File  . . . . . . :      SOURCE            Member . . . . . :     LAB10D1Y
   Library . . . . :        YOURLIB         Source type . . :      DSPF

 Type choices, press Enter.

   New record  . . . . . . . . . . . . . . . .    VENDFMT       Name

   Type  . . . . . . . . . . . . . . . . . . .    RECORD        RECORD,  USRDFN
                                                                SFL,     SFLMSG
                                                                WINDOW,  WDWSFL
                                                                PULDWN,  PDNSFL
                                                                MNUBAR



 F3=Exit       F5=Refresh       F12=Cancel
```

Specify Record Format Type

7. Answer the question by filling in the word RECORD for the type.

There are nine choices for the record type, from which you can choose. A normal display file is known as a record. That's what you want to create for this exercise. That's what you pick. When you pick RECORD and hit ENTER, SDA makes that panel image part of the display file SDA source.

SDA is most helpful in being able to build most, if not all of the powerful display facilities supported by DDS. The panel types in Figure 10-10 include record type keywords for subfiles, windows, pull-down menus, and menu bars. As noted, the correct choice for a regular display panel, such as that which we are selecting is *RECORD*.

8. After making this selection, press the ENTER key.

The No-Nonsense Design Image Panel

You will immediately be taken to a completely black design screen. It will look somewhat like Figure 10-8 but there will be nothing filled in. There will be no hints at all as to what you should do next. The closest thing to help you at this point is a little message at the bottom of the black void which says:

```
Work screen for record VENDFMT: Press Help for function
keys.
```

If you follow the message and hit either the Help key or the F1 (Help) key, you will get a ton of help. Do this when you have the opportunity as it is most helpful to learning.

Typing Your Screen Constants

9. When you are finished with the HELP text review, press F14 so that you can see the reference lines on the top and left as shown in Figure 10-11.

Figure 10-11 Screen Image Existing Format

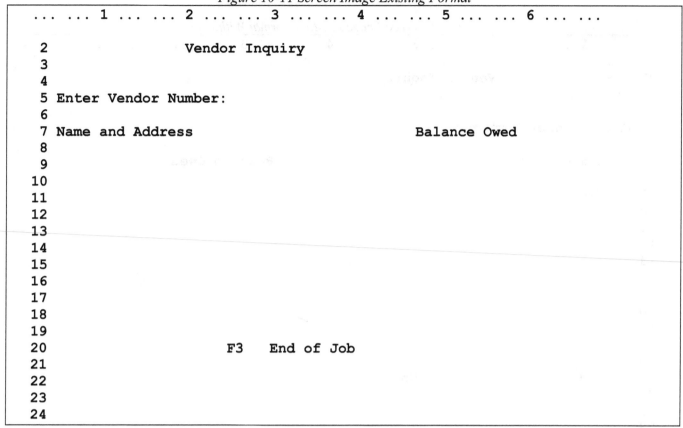

10. After you see the lines, type the constant information as shown in Figure 10-11A.

11. When you have this typing done, you have one more task to do before this phase is completed. On your design panel, after it looks exactly as Figure 10-11A, place a single quote around (*in front of and after*) each set of constant text. Do not place quotes around each individual word. Now, check out Figure 10-11B and make sure that your design panel looks like that.

Figure 10-11B Screen Image Existing Format With Quotes

```
 ... ... 1 ... ... 2 ... ... 3 ... ... 4 ... ... 5 ... ... 6 ... ...

   2                    'Vendor Inquiry'
   3
   4
   5'Enter Vendor Number:'
   6
   7'Name and Address'                       'Balance Owed'
   8
   9
  10
  11
  12
  13
  14
  15
  16
  17
  18
  19
  20                    'F3   End of Job'
  21
  22
  23
  24
```

When you finish, you should have ten single quotes in total, in five pairs, surrounding the five different clumps of text on the panel. When your display looks like the one in Figure 10-11B, press the ENTER key.

12. You will notice that the quotes disappear.

The purpose for the quotes is to define blocks of text to be treated in the same fashion. Without the quotes, SDA builds DDS for each individual "word" or set of continuous letters on the design image. For example, you might be surprised at what happens if the phrase below were typed on the image panel:

F3   End of Job -- Hit the F3 key when you are finished with this panel

Do not do this but know that SDA would build sixteen different lines of DDS code for the sixteen individual blocks of letters above. Each time SDA encounters a blank, it finishes the DDS for the prior "word" and begins to create the DDS line for the next word. Sometimes this is OK and some times it is not.

Suppose you want to highlight the two words, F3 key in the sentence above. Let's say, you want to underline the words or change their color to red. In order to do this, you would want SDA to treat each of the individual pieces of text in the sentence separately so that you could highlight the two words F3 and key individually.

If, on the other hand, you wanted all of the words or phrases in a sentence such as that above to all have the same display attributes, then you would place the quotes around the sentence as follows:

'F3 End of Job -- Hit the F3 key when you are finished with this panel'

Back to our example, if you placed the quotes around the five sets of text as suggested above, and you pressed enter to have the quotes take effect, they disappeared but are in effect. So, if you now want to highlight just the title text, *Vendor Inquiry*, you could do so by placing a highlight (h) code, which is the small letter "h" immediately to the left of the text such as:

```
hVendor Inquiry
```

Remember, because you placed quotes around both words, SDA remembers that this block works as a unit. Press Enter. When you press the ENTER key from the design panel, immediately, you would see this text highlighted, such as the following:

Vendor Inquiry

Notice the h for highlight is no longer visible

Instantaneous Feedback upon ENTER

You may also notice that after you press ENTER, any SDA commands on the design screen, such as the quotes to block text together or the "h" command to highlight a block of text, are all gone. ENTER causes a design panel interaction with SDA. SDA does its work during these interactions. The panel returns to a WYSIWYG form so that you know what the effect of your change has been immediately. For example, your highlighted field will immediately appear highlighted

At this point, the panel is almost complete. You keyed the constants at the desired locations and it is starting to look like a real display. However, the panel is really quite incomplete. It does not yet include any variable fields - either input or output. You are about to add fields from the database to this panel. but first save your work.

Intermediate Exit and Creation

To know which command keys to hit for ending the database design session (F3 or F12) and to know the various attribute commands, such as "h" for highlight, you may have already toured the Help text (by hitting the Help key or F1.) During the tour, the Help text would tell you about using F14 for the ruler and it would tell you that the F10 key is to be used to bring in field descriptions from the data base file – for both prompt and field reference purposes.

As a final review point before moving on, we also demonstrated how to deal with the notion of multi word constants. You enclosed them in quotes on Figure 10-11B. Overall, blocking constant text in this fashion, results in fewer DDS statements, and it makes working with / examining the SDA-created DDS substantially easier.

Before we add input fields to the display file DDS that SDA is about to create, let's exit SDA from the display panel, without adding any variables.

13. Do this by pressing F12 twice.

14. Then hit ENTER after reviewing the "defaults" specified on the SDA exit panel.

When you get to a command line, the file LAB10D1Y has been created, though it is incomplete. SDA has created a set of incomplete DDS specs for you in a source member.

Now, you need to take a look at the DDS in Figure 10-12. SDA just created this for you. This is what it looks like prior to completing the panel with input.

15. To actually see this, you need to STRPDM, press ENTER until you get to Work With members.

16. Scroll to LAB10D1Y and pick option 5 to display the member. Your panel will look similar to that shown in Figure 10-12.

Figure 10-12 **LAB10D1Y** *Source with Only Constant DDS*

```
 Columns . . . :    6  76          Browse              RPGOBJ/SOURCE
 SEU==>                                                LAB10D1S
 FMT A* A*. 1 ...+... 2 ...+... 3 ...+... 4 ...+... 5 ...+... 6 ...+... 7 ...+.
 *************** Beginning of data **************************************
 01.00 A*%%TS  SD  20020513  111307  BKELLY      REL-V5R1M0  5722-WDS
 02.00 A*%%EC
 03.00 A                              DSPSIZ(24 80 *DS3)
 04.00 A                              CF03(03 'end-of-job')
 05.00 A           R VENDFMT
 06.00 A*%%TS  SD  20020513  105803  BKELLY      REL-V5R1M0  5722-WDS
 07.00 A                            2 24'Vendor Inquiry'
 08.00 A                            5  9'Enter Vendor Number:'
 09.00 A                            7  9'Name and Address'
 10.00 A                            7 51'Balance Owed'
 11.00 A                           20 29'F3   End of Job'

 F3=Exit    F5=Refresh    F9=Retrieve   F10=Cursor   F11=Toggle   F12=Cancel
 F16=Repeat find          F24=More keys
```

17. Note that there are no input fields, exit SEU and exit PDM and come back to the command line.

Sidebar: A Quick way of checking Intermediate DDS with SEU is described below:

The quick way to check your DDS is as follows:

Use PDM to *Work with members*; select SOURCE in your library. Press ENTER to get the list of SDA members. Display member LAB10D1Y (PDM option 5), which is the newly created DDS from SDA. The source should look similar to that in Figure 10-12. Notice the big chunks of text. If you had not used the quotes around the constant text blocks as suggested, there would be many more, but smaller DDS statements. SDA would make each word a statement by default.

Looking at the DDS in Figure 10-12, you can see a number of lines of DDS. You can also see that of these lines, there is one line for each quoted block of constant text and there is a record format ("R" in column 17) statement line in which the screen panel is named (VENDFMT). The file level keyword DSPSIZ is created and there are no other keywords. Moreover, as predicted, there are no variable fields defined in DDS.

The numbers you see prior to the text represent the screen panel location information for the row and column starting positions. This is where you placed the text on the screen. These positions are determined based on where you keyed the text on the design panel.

This is one of the major timesaving benefits of SDA. Can you imagine manually coding these DDS statements in such detail, as well as having to specify the exact "from" and "to" positions?

Adding Variable Fields from the Database

So we have exited SEU and PDM.

18. Bring back your SDA design panel as it was when you added the quotes in Figure 10-11B. Get there by the following:

- F3 from PDM
- STRSDA
- Design Screens - option 1
- Specify SOURCE in YOURLIB, member LAB10D1Y
- Place a 12 next to VENDFMT in the record list and hit Enter.

You will be looking at the SDA Design Panel as in Figure 10-11B.

19. Begin by adding input and output information to this panel. First press F10 to get at the database.

20. Pick the VENDORP database file that exists in the your library. You will see a panel similar to that in Figure 10-13.

Figure 10-13 Select Database Files For Screen Reference

```
                      Select Database Files

 Type options and names, press Enter.
   1=Display database field list
   2=Select all fields for input (I)
   3=Select all fields for output (O)
   4=Select all fields for both (B) input and output


 Option     Database File    Library       Record
   1_          VENDORP         YOURLIB       VNDMSTR




 F3=Exit    F4=Prompt    F12=Cancel
```

21. To get a look at all of the fields in the VENDORP file, which you might choose to use as input or output references, select option 1, and specify the location for the VENDORP database file as shown in Figure 10-13. In this panel, select the data base file, library and the specific record format, to serve as a reference for the fields being defined on the screen image panel. Of course, this all depends on the VENDORP database file already having been created. When finished press ENTER to continue and you will see a panel such as that shown in Figure 10-14.

Figure 10-14 Select Database Fields for use on Design Display

```
                     Select Data Base Fields

  Record . . . :   VNDMSTR
 Type information, press Enter.
  Number of fields to roll  . . . . . . . . . . . . . . . .    _8
   Name of field to search for . . . . . . . . . . . .  _____


 Type options, press Enter.
  1=Display extended field description
  2=Select for input (I),3=Select for output(O),4=Select/both(B)


  Option    Field         Length    Type     Column Heading
    4       VNDNBR         5,0       P        VENDOR NUMBER
    3       NAME            25       A        NAME
    3       ADDR1           25       A        ADDRESS LINE 1
    3       CITY            15       A        CITY
    3       STATE            2       A        STATE
    3       ZIPCD          5,0       P        ZIP CODE
    _       VNDCLS         2,0       P        VENDOR CLASS
    _       VNDSTS           1       A        ACTIVE CODE
                                                      More...
  ...
    3       BALOWE         9,2       P        BALANCE OWED

 F3=Exit    F12=Cancel
```

Selecting Database Fields for Use

After picking F10 from the image panel and option 1 on VENDORP, it is time to pick the fields that should appear in the particular image panel that you are building with SDA. As you pick the fields as listed in Figure 10-14, you also must tell SDA to select the field for the use you intend -- input, output or for both purposes. Both is short for both output and input. Both means that the field, when it appears on the screen as output, will have any changes received back into the file on the input cycle (Enter key etc.). For each database field that you want to be used in the panel, Enter a "2" to select it for input, a "3" for output, and a "4" for both (output and input).

22. Working with a panel as in Figure 10-14, select the VNDNBR field as both (option 4), and selected the six other fields as output only (3).

23. To get to see field six, BALOWE on this panel, hit Page Down or Roll Down.

24. Then, select the BALOWE field as an output field (3). In Figure 10-14, field BALOWE is superimposed at the bottom of the panel, so you could see it in better context.

The idea with this application as you may have already surmised is that just this one panel is to be used to enter a vendor number and it also displays the results -- nothing fancy -- no tricks. A few tricks get added in the next set of exercises after you create the RPG program for this panel. The program looks up the vendor information, and redisplays the vendor number as a both field. After looking up the vendor information, the program writes the data to the same display panel with the same "write/read" operation (EXFMT in RPG). Because the vendor information is sent to the screen as both, it can be read back in. It can also be changed. In other words, the next vendor # may be entered while the prior vendor information is on the screen. Then, when you press Enter, the new vendor information appears.

25. When you are done with this panel hit F3 or ENTER to return to the design panel.

26. When you get back to the design panel, you should be pleased to see that the selected fields are displayed on the bottom row of the work screen where you design your display. Press page down (Roll on some terminals) to display more data base fields if all of them are not visible. They should all be visible as in Figure 10-15

Exiting the Data Base Option

27. Press ENTER on the display shown in Figure 10-14 to return to the *Select data base files* display if you want to reference another file for input, or if you are on your way to exiting.

28. In this example, press F3 or ENTER again from the database files display, to return to the design panel. You will see a screen similar to that shown in Figure 10-15.

Figure 10-15 Vendor Inquiry Panel With Fields in On-Deck Circle

```
 ... ...  1 ... ...  2 ... ...  3 ... ...  4 ... ...  5 ... ...  6 ...
  2                     Vendor Inquiry
  3
  4
  5   Enter Vendor Number:
  6
  7   Name and Address                        Balance Owed
  8
  9
 10
 11
 12
 13
 14
 15
 16
 17
 18
 19
 20                      F3    End of Job
 21
 22
 23
  1:VNDNBR 2:NAME 3:ADDR1 4:CITY 5:STATE 6:ZIPCD 7:BALOWE
```

29. Look at the bottom of Figure 10-15 for the selected fields.

When you are looking for a field and it is not in the list, remember that the bottom line of the screen can hold only so many fields. The fields are inserted and appear in a multiple-field mode at the bottom of the work screen as shown in Figure 10-15. This is what we referred to as the "On-Deck Circle." A "+" at the end of the field name horizontal list indicates there are more field names. Just position the cursor in that area of the screen and press page down to display more field names.

SDA Image Commands

Notice in Figure 10-15 that the text fields are in tact, and the design panel is in somewhat of a wait state. It is waiting for you to do something with these fields. They don't just pop up into the screen panel. You have to place them. To do this, SDA has given you some handy commands. The first command is the " &." With this command, you tell SDA to "place a database field right here!" Following the "&" command, you then tell SDA which database field to place by specifying its number.

30. Type the SDA database commands "&" along with the field numbers exactly as shown in the panel in Figure 10-16. These reference, by number, the on-deck fields that SDA lists at the bottom of the panel after you select them in the panel shown in Figure 10-14.

In real life, you would not split your design by (1) implementing the constant fields, (2) saving the panel, (3) creating the file, and (4) coming back in update mode to add the variables with database fields, as we did for this training example. You would to the constants and the variables at the same time in the same SDA work session.

Figure 10-16 shows how the panel should look when you build it with all the necessary information specified at once. In other words, the quote commands surround the text as they should have at the time we built the constants-only panel.

Figure 10-16 Database Fields Selected for Action

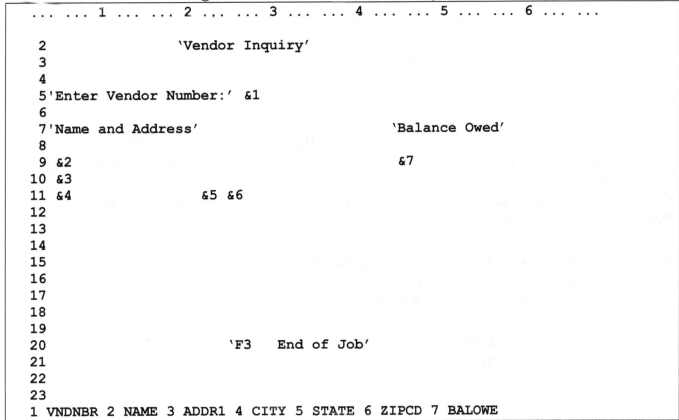

```
... ... 1 ... ... 2 ... ... 3 ... ... 4 ... ... 5 ... ... 6 ... ...

   2                    'Vendor Inquiry'
   3
   4
   5 'Enter Vendor Number:' &1
   6
   7 'Name and Address'                        'Balance Owed'
   8
   9 &2                                        &7
  10 &3
  11 &4                    &5 &6
  12
  13
  14
  15
  16
  17
  18
  19
  20                    'F3    End of Job'
  21
  22
  23
   1 VNDNBR 2 NAME 3 ADDR1 4 CITY 5 STATE 6 ZIPCD 7 BALOWE
```

Column Headings from the Database

As you can see in Figure 10-16, in addition to the blocked text shown with quotes, we have placed the "&" command plus the field number at the location desired for each field. If you want to be more productive than this, or perhaps you are feeling a little lazy during your design trip, SDA gives you a few more tools to eliminate even more keying and more guesswork.

You can ask SDA to get you the column headings from the database and you can then use them as your prompts. If you have good column headings, the idea is that there should be lots less keying and lots less opportunity for misinterpretation of field meanings. Moreover, you can tell SDA to place the prompt text to the left or to the right of the inserted database input or output field, so you have initial design flexibility. Additionally, you can tell SDA to place the column heading right on top of the field being defined.

You add the column heading and provide its placement with one-letter commands. You place the letter "L" for left, or the letter "R" for right or the letter "C" for center, along with the "&" command and the field number. This is how you tell SDA to grab the column heading, along with the field definition, and place them on your design panel – based on the specific command you used.

For example to include the prompt for vendor number to the left of the variable as it is inserted on a design image panel, you would type the following:

@1l (At sign , a one, followed by an L for left)

To put the title on top of name, you would type the following:

@2C

In this panel, we chose to use our own prompts so these two examples above are not used. For your own practice, however, before you close our this panel, try putting the headings from the database in different places, -- left, right, and center. After you have learned how this works, exit SDA without saving it and come back in at Figure 10-13. You will benefit from doing it a second time.

When you press ENTER on the display, you see how nice or how ugly the text prompts appear in the work display. If they are not so nice, without re-keying or excess typing, you can simply change them and move them accordingly.

31. Hit ENTER with the display filled as in Figure 10-16. Your display panel should look similar to that in Figure 10-17.

Figure 10-17 The Resulting Display Panel

```
...  ... 1 ...  ... 2 ...  ... 3 ...  ... 4 ...  ... 5 ...  ... 6 ...  ...
   2                     Vendor Inquiry
   3
   4
   5  Enter Vendor Number:*99999-
   6
   7  Name and Address                        Balance Owed
   8
   9  OOOOOOOOOOOOOOOOOOOOOOOOO               *666666666
  10  OOOOOOOOOOOOOOOOOOOOOOOOO
  11  OOOOOOOOOOOOOOO   OO*66666
  12
  13
  14
  15
  16
  17
  18
  19
  20                     F3    End of Job
  21
  22
  23
  24
```

The field *Vendor Number*, which is represented by all 99999s, is an output/input (both) field, and it is defined as numeric. The fields defined at lines 9 to 11 are a combination of alphabetic output (O) and numeric output (6). If you were not using SDA database referencing to supply the field attributes and lengths, you would have had to count field spaces and assure that your coding lined up properly. This would be another thing you would have to do that would not be much fun! SDA helps keep it light-hearted. The database referencing ability is just another way that SDA saves this type of drudgery, and in so doing, it saves time. Who wants to be counting O's as you are hitting the O key, hoping not to have one too many or one too few?

Adding Fields & Changing Field Attributes

Oh! It's not that you can't make a mistake with SDA. You can make as many as you please, and you can fix them just as fast – long before you'd know you'd made them if you were dealing just with DDS. You can add fields and/or change the attributes of fields after they are on your work display — years after you've first created your display file. As you can see in Figure 10-17, we are doing exactly that for the vendor number field and the balance owed field

32. Place an asterisk next to fields to be edited for highlighting or perhaps to display their attributes as shown in Figure 10-17.

The "*" is just another tool that enables you to open the fields up for many different combinations of changes, without once having to refer to your DDS manual.

33. Press Enter to see your options and then move to the second field. Press F12 to return to the design panel. See Figure 10-18 and 10-19. Perform the instructions noted for those two panels and then reverse them. We will continue with the * command in a few pages but first let's talk about using some direct and immediate SDA field manipulation commands.

Field Manipulation Commands

There are also one-character commands which immediately highlight a field. You have already seen the highlight command which is simply a small "h." A few more examples include the "r" for reverse image, and the "u" for an underline.

Delete Field Command

Some one-character commands do more than just highlight. They are much more powerful. The "d" command, for example, is for *dangerous*. OK, it is not. But it is dangerous! You can place a "d" next to any field you want to delete from the panel. It's that easy. Press ENTER and it's gone. It stands for delete.

Two Forms of Move Commands

Two other powerhouse commands are the two forms of "move." To move fields you have two choices. And, they are both good! To move them a little, use the symbols " >>>>" and "<<<<." There is a one-to-one relationship between symbols used and characters moved. These field move commands move fields, and blocks of fields, to the left (<) or to the right (>) as many positions as symbols you type. If you type four ">>>>" signs, for example, and you place them next to the rightmost character of text to be moved, when you press ENTER, the text will be four positions over to the right. Likewise if you wanted to move to the left, you would type the "<" symbols to the left of the text to be moved.

33. Remember where the text is originally aligned and try these >>> and << <<<< commands so that you can see their effects on the design image. Then, get even more SDA experience by moving them back. Even the WDSC GUI Designers use facilities such as this so learning how to use SDA will also give benefits in the future.

Another tremendous tool is the "block move" operation. To move fields a lot, use this command. This move command is a simple dash "-" preceding the field or text block to be moved. Just like SEU, it needs a corresponding to-position indicator to get its job done. SDA has chosen the equal sign "=" for this. An example of the way this works is as follows: If you place a dash on text at, say line 23, and you put an equal sign in some column on say, line 5, after you hit the ENTER key, the block of text from line 23 is now on line 5, starting at your designated column position. It is no longer on line 23. The move operations make it so easy to redesign the work panel on the fly that it actually isn't any fun getting it right the first time.

34. Use the block move described above to put the fields back to their original spots.

Adding a New Field to Your Display

There will also be times that you must add a field to the panel which is not in a database. For example, if your program is calculating a result which goes nowhere else but the screen panel, your panel must know about that field somehow. SDA handles it. You can easily add your own fields to the work screen. Just key a "+" to specify a user-defined field. For numeric, "3" is input, "6" is output and "9" is both. For alphabetic, "I" is input, "O" is output, and "B" is both. For example: +6 (8,2) creates a field named FLD001 (default field name) with a length of eight, and with two decimals for output only.

35. Find a clean spot on the panel and type +33333 to indicate a numeric input field of five positions. Hit ENTER.

36. Place a D to the very left of the 33333 input field to delete it. Press ENTER and it is gone. To name or change the attributes of the field, you may type an * as in the above and below examples.

Changing Display Attributes

It's been so long, we would like to remind you that, in our example panel in Figure 10-17, we have placed asterisks "*" next to the vendor number field (VNDNBR), the balance owed field (BALOWE), and the zip code (ZIPCD) field . When you hit ENTER, with these asterisks positioned where they are, you will first see a panel similar to that in Figure 10-18.

Figure 10-18 Select Field Keywords

```
                    Select Field Keywords

   Field . . . . . :  VNDNBR      Usage . . :  B
   Length  . . . . :  5,0         Row . . . :  5      Column . . . :  31


   Type choices, press Enter.
                                        Y=Yes   For Field Type
      Display attributes . . . . . . .    Y     All except Hidden
      Colors . . . . . . . . . . . . .    __    All except Hidden
      Keying options . . . . . . . . .    __    Hidden, Input or Both
      Validity check . . . . . . . . .    __    Input or Both, not float
      Input keywords . . . . . . . . .    __    Input or Both
      General keywords . . . . . . . .    __    All types
      Editing keywords . . . . . . . .    Y     Numeric Output or Both
      Database reference . . . . . . .    __    Hidden, Input, Output, Both
      Error messages . . . . . . . . .    __    Input, Output, Both
      Message ID (MSGID) . . . . . . .    __    Output or Both


      TEXT keyword . . . . . . . . . .    VENDOR NUMBER
   F3=Exit    F4=Display Selected Keywords    F12=Cancel
```

You will see a panel similar to Figure 10-18 once for each of the fields selected with the "*" command.   DDS is used to build your display file and DDS has lots of display file commands. Figure 10-14 organizes these commands into various types.   So reading down the options, you can change the display attributes (highlight, underline, reverse image etc.), the colors of the field. the keying options for the text etc. Moving further down, you see that in addition to the display attributes, we selected Editing Keywords. Since we placed a "Y" on two of these options, we will receive two option menus in order to specify the (1) display attributes and then (2) the editing attributes.

From this field keywords panel, for VNDNBR, change the *Display attributes* and *Editing keywords* by placing "Y" responses in this panel. For BALOWE and ZIPCD, change just the *Editing keywords* by typing a "Y." To proceed from this panel for the field VNDNBR, type "Y" in the appropriate columns as shown in Figure 10-18. You will first be taken to a panel similar to the *Select Display Attributes* panel as in Figure 10-19.

By placing the "*" next to the vendor number field (VNDNBR), you first get the panel in Figure 10-18. From there, you determine which type of attribute you want to change. By selecting a "Y" for Display Attributes, you get to work with the panel in Figure 10-15. By selecting a "Y" for editing keywords, you get to work with a panel similar to that in Figure 10-16.

Figure 10-19 Select Display Attributes

```
                    Select Display Attributes

   Field . . . . . :    VNDNBR          Usage . . :  B
   Length  . . . . :    5,0             Row . . . :  5      Column . . . : 26

   Type choices, press Enter.
                                        Keyword   Y=Yes    Indicators/+
      Field conditioning . . . . . . . . . .
      Display attributes:                   DSPATR
        High intensity . . . . . . . . . .    HI      _      __ __ __
        Reverse image  . . . . . . . . . .    RI      Y      _44 __ __
        Column separators  . . . . . . . .    CS      _      __ __ __
        Blink  . . . . . . . . . . . . . .    BL      _      __ __ __
        Nondisplay . . . . . . . . . . . .    ND      _      __ __ __
        Underline  . . . . . . . . . . . .    UL      _      __ __ __
        Position cursor  . . . . . . . . .    PC      _      __ __ __
        Set modified data tag  . . . . . .    MDT     _      __ __ __
        Protect field  . . . . . . . . . .    PR      _      __ __ __
        Operator ID magnetic card  . . . .    OID     _      __ __ __
        Select by light pen  . . . . . . .    SP      _      __ __ __
     F3=Exit    F12 = Cancel
```

Making the Attribute Change

Our display objective for the VNDNBR field is to make it a reverse-image, if a certain condition occurs in the program. To display the field in reverse-image (like a negative) under certain conditions, specify the attributes as shown in the panel in Figure 10-19. When you come back to the design work panel, the field VNDNBR will show in reverse-image.

Conditional Attributes Using Indicators

However, it will not be shown in reverse-image when put out by the program unless indicator 44 is on in the controlling program at the time of the output operation. You set the condition (indicator 44 in this case) for the field to be shown in reverse-image within the high-level language program. If the indicator is on, the VNDNBR field will be lit up in reverse-image when the program sends out this screen panel. Field conditioning and un-conditioning can be achieved by entering a "Y" by the desired display attribute (DSPATR) when you select an indicator to condition the attribute.

For the first RPG program, do not set on 44 but do set it on in the second program. The instructions for the second program are in exercise 5.

Adding Editing Keywords

37. When you have changed the attributes in Figure 10-19 to your satisfaction, press the ENTER key until the display changes to *Select Editing Keywords* for VNDNBR. This panel is shown in Figure 10-20. Type the "3" edit-code for the field since, for this field type so that for a zero value, the vendor numbers (even if zero) will show, and there will be no commas, and no decimals in the vendor number field. Keep pressing enter until the field name changes to BALOWE.   If you care to edit BALOWE, continue, otherwise, hit F12 til you get to the design panel

Figure 10-20 Selecting Editing Keywords or Codes.

```
                     Select Editing Keywords
   Field . . . . . :   VNDNBR  Usage . . :  B
   Length  . . . . :   5,0     Row . . . :  5  Column . . . :  31


   Type choices, press Enter.
                                             Keyword              More
     Edit code  . . . . . . . . . . . . . . . EDTCDE    3 A-D,J-Q,W etc.
        Replace leading zeros with . . . .                  *, $

     Edit word  . . . . . . . . . . . . . . . EDTWRD

     Edit mask  . . . . . . . . . . . . . . . EDTMSK

   F3=Exit    F12=Cancel
```

After you finish with the VNDNBR field for both attributes and editing, keep pressing the ENTER key until the field name changes to BALOWE. It should be right away. By having placed the "*" next to the balance owed field, you also get a panel similar to that in Figure 10-18. However, the field name is primed with BALOWE instead of VNDNBR, since that is the field you now want to adjust. Since it is a nice big numeric field, it would be nice for it to show up edited on the final display.

You do not need a Y for *Display Attributes*, as in VNDNBR, since the attributes are fine. However, to make the field look right, you need to do some editing of the output. If you look down, near the bottom of the panel in Figure 10-18, you will notice Editing Keywords. Place your "Y" in this field. Make sure there is not a "Y" in any of the other attributes, and press ENTER. You will see a panel similar to that in Figure 10-20. Instead of *VNDNBR*, however, the field name will be *BALOWE*.

If you hit Help on the Edit-codes field, it will tell you which code produces which level of editing. This is very handy. I like to show dollar fields with commas and have zero balances appear on the report rather than be hidden. Also, I like to have a minus sign show to the right of the number if the value is negative. If you hit the Help or F1 key now, you will see that the edit-code to do all of that is a "J." To select "J," type it into the edit-code instead of the "3" as in Figure 10-20 and press Enter.

You should see the panel as in Figure 10-18 again, except this time, the field name should be *ZIPCD*. Follow the same process for editing this field as you did for *VNDNBR,* but leave the attributes alone. Change the edit-code to "3". When you have made all of your editing and attribute changes for the asterisked "*" fields, you should return to the SDA work panel. Your display should no longer show the "-" sign to the right of *VNDNBR* and *ZIPCD* and the *BALOWE* field should appear nicely edited. See Figure 10-21 for the final display panel.

Figure 10-21 Final Version of Display Panel

```
 ... ...  1 ...  ...  2 ...  ...  3 ...  ...  4 ...  ...  5 ...  ...  6 ...  ...  7
  2                  Vendor Inquiry
  3
  4
  5  Enter Vendor Number: 99999
  6
  7  Name and Address                        Balance Owed
  8
  9  OOOOOOOOOOOOOOOOOOOOOOOOOOOO            $6,666,666.66-
 10  OOOOOOOOOOOOOOOOOOOOOOOOOO
 11  OOOOOOOOOOOOOOO   OO 66666
 12
 13
 14
 15
 16
 17
 18
 19
 20                 F3    End of Job
 21
 22
 23
 24
```

The example in Figure 10-21 shows the final form of the screen as it was just designed. Remember, as you look at your panel, you can move any of the fields around, delete fields, or add more fields and more constants.

Assigning End-of-Job Indicator

Before you close this out, there is one more job to do. You need to enable a command key (CF03) and assign an indicator (switch) value to the command key so that the program can get a signal from the display panel when the operator decides that it is time to end it. Since there is only one display panel, and since other panels, if added, may very well want to end the program in the same fashion, the recommendation is to add the CF03 function key at the file level so it applies to all display panels (formats).

Repeat of Figure 10-4(10-22) Work with Display Records SDA Panel

```
                        Work with Display Records

   File  . . . . . . :   QDDSSRC          Member  . .  . . :   LAB10D1Y
     Library . . . . :     HELLO          Source type    . . :   DSPF


   Type options, press Enter.
     1=Add            2=Edit comments      3=Copy            4=Remove
     7=Rename         8=Select keywords   12=Design image

   Opt  Order   Record        Type    Related Subfile Date      DDS Error

   __   ____    VENDFMT       RECORD                  10/04/90
    8



   F3=Exit                    F12=Cancel      F14=File-level keywords
   F15=File-level comments    F17=Subset      F24=More keys
```

38. From Figure 10-21, press F24 to return to the *Work with Display Records* panel similar to that in Figure 10-22 (Figure 04) as repeated above.

39. From this screen, to assign the indicator to just this one panel design, type an "8" (select keywords) next to the format name and press ENTER.

40. Select *Indicator keywords* by placing a "Y," next to the prompt. Hit Enter again. You would then see a panel similar to Figure 10-23.

Figure 10-23 Defining Command Keys and Indicators

```
                       Define Indicator Keywords

 Member . . . :    LAB10D1Y


 Type keywords and parameters, press Enter.
    Conditioned keywords:     CFnn CAnn CLEAR PAGEDOWN/ROLLUP
                              PAGEUP/ROLLDOWN
                              HOME HELP HLPRTN
    Unconditioned keywords:  INDTXT VLDCMDKEY


 Keyword    Indicators/+ Resp Text
 CF03       __  __  __    03   end-of-job



    . . .
                                               Bottom
 F3=Exit    F12=Cancel
```

41. On the panel in Figure 10-23, type *CF03* for the keyword. Type the response indicator as 03. This means that command key 03 will turn on indicator 03 in the RPG program. Type *"end-of-job"* for text for documentation and to help in Web conversions.

This creates the indicator reference at the record format (display panel) level. Since we have just one panel in this version of the display file, this is fine and this is all we need at this time..

Indicator at File Level

However, if we have more than one display panel in our file but we just have not yet built them, we would press F14 for "File-level keywords." From there, select "Indicator keywords" as above for the record level. After all that, you would get a panel, which looks the same as the panel used for record function keys, as shown in Figure 10-23. Then, press ENTER to return to the Work with Display Records panel.

After defining the command keys, there is no more design work to do for this simple project. From here then, it is time to compile and test your display file.

42. Press F3 to exit. You will get the SDA exit panel.

43. Take the options to exit and create the objects. The source will be saved and your updated file will be created. At this point of success, you now have created the display file object and you can test it.

44. From the Main SDA Menu, STRSDA, take the option (3) to test your display file objects. You will get a panel like Figure 10-24

Figure 10-24 Test Display File

```
                        Test Display File

Type choices, press Enter.

  Display file . . . . . . . . . . . . .   LAB10D1Y     Name, F4 for list
    Library  . . . . . . . . . . . . . .     YOURLIB    Name, *LIBL ...

  Record to be tested  . . . . . . . . .   VENDFMT      Name, F4 for list

  Additional records to display  . . . .                Name, F4 for list




F3=Exit     F4=Prompt     F12=Cancel
```

45. Fill in the information as above and hit Enter.

Figure 10-25 Fill in Test Data

```
                      Set Test Output Data

  Record . . . :    VENDFMT

  Type indicators and output field values, press Enter.

  Field          Value
  VNDNBR         99999:
  NAME           OOOOOOOOOOOOOOOOOOOOOOOOOOO:
  BALOWE         666666666:
  ADDR1          OOOOOOOOOOOOOOOOOOOOOOOOOOO:
  CITY           OOOOOOOOOOOOOOO:
  STATE          OO:
  ZIPCD          66666:


                                                           Bottom

F3=Exit     F12=Cancel
```

46. Change the data. Type real vendor information and press Enter.

This completes Lab 10 Exercise 2. At this point, your display file is created and tested now you can use it in an RPG program or a program written in RPGIV or COBOL.

The Display file DDS looks like that shown below in Figure 10-26:

Figure 10-26 **LAB10D1Y** *Source with Only Constant DDS*

```
Columns . . . :   6  76              Browse              RPGOBJ/SOURCE
SEU==>                                                   LAB10D1S
FMT A* A*. 1 ...+... 2 ...+... 3 ...+... 4 ...+... 5 ...+... 6 ...+... 7 ...+.
 *************** Beginning of data *********************************
01.00 A*%%TS  SD  20020513  111307  BKELLY     REL-V5R1M0  5722-WDS
02.00 A*%%EC
03.00 A                                DSPSIZ(24 80 *DS3)
04.00 A                                CF03(03 'end-of-job')
05.00 A           R VENDFMT
06.00 A*%%TS  SD  20020513  105803  BKELLY     REL-V5R1M0  5722-WDS
07.00 A                               2 24'Vendor Inquiry'
08.00 A                               5  9'Enter Vendor Number:'
09.00 A                               7  9'Name and Address'
10.00 A                               7 51'Balance Owed'
11.00 A                              20 29'F3    End of Job'
12.00 A           VNDNBR    R      B  5 31REFFLD(VNDMSTR/VNDNBR RPGOBJ/VPR
13.00 A                                EDTCDE(3)
14.00 A           NAME      R      O  9  9REFFLD(VNDMSTR/NAME RPGOBJ/VPREF
15.00 A           BALOWE    R      O  9 51REFFLD(VNDMSTR/BALOWE RPGOBJ/VPR
16.00 A                                EDTCDE(J)

 F3=Exit    F5=Refresh    F9=Retrieve  F10=Cursor   F11=Toggle   F12=Cancel
 F16=Repeat find         F24=More keys
```

Lab 10 Exercise 3 Using Display File in an RPG Program

Objectives:

Students learn how to write an interactive RPG/400 program that inquires into the vendor master file (VENDORP) using a random read operation by key.

Begin this exercise by copying with PDM, the RPGIV member named LAB10_1E to a new member that you should call LAB10_1EY. The Y is for Your Code.

In this exercise, you will modify the RPG/400 program LAB10_1EY that sends out the LAB10D1Y display file format VENDFMT using EXFMT. This is the panel you just created in the prior lab. Modify the program so that it reads in a vendor number, looks up the vendor in the VENDORP file by using a CHAIN operation., and send out the information achieved from the Vendor Lookup (chain to the VENDORP file.) From here the user can type in the next vendor number and press enter to get its information as formatted via the panel as created and shown in Figure 10-17. This process can be repeated until the user hits the end of job command key (F3) which turns on indicator 03. If this happens, you should assure that the program code ends the program.

After testing the SDA panel using the SDA testing facility (option 3 from the SDA Main menu - Figure 10-2), the next step is to merge the file with your RPG program. This is the merging of the user interface with the business logic. Figure 10-19 shows the RPG program named LAB10_1EY. As defined in the specifications, the program is to send out a display of vendor information from the database using this panel we created.

47. From PDM, use SEU to modify this program to have it perform the functions as described -- member is called LAB10_1EY. Remove the XXs from the source member and anything else that would impede a clean compile and a proper execution. Compile it when completed. (option 14 in PDM). The logic of the program is as follows:.

RPG Display File Program Logic

The Display file solution is called LAB10D1S as you may recall from the prior two labs. The LAB10D1Y workstation (WORKSTN) file is to be defined as combined (C) and Fully procedural (F) and it is to be externally described. (E).

This means that the input and output that has been created with SDA does not have to be repeated by the RPG programmer. No input specs are required. RPG will use the internals of the display file and bring in the input and output specs as needed. A "combined file" is used for a device such as a workstation to reflect that the program will be able to send data to the device and receive data from the device. The notion of send and receive to the same device (not a database) is referred to as a combined operation and is coded accordingly in RPG. If it were a database file, the file would be Update. However, Update is an invalid entry for a Workstation file.

The VENDMST database (disk) file is defined as input (I) and Fully procedural (F) and it too is externally described. (E). This means that the data definitions as created with DDS do not have to be repeated in the program. Therefore the programmer does not have to type them into the program as would be the case for internally described data. RPG will use the internals of the database file which include the data definition for input as appropriate. Since this is an input database, there will be no output or update specifications brought in to this program for VENDMST. The compiler produces a listing that includes the input and output -- even though the programmer did not have to type the code for the fields within the program. .

As you scan the program, you will notice that all of the code is not complete. It is your job to think through what should be where the X's are and then to make the changes to get a clean compile. The first set of work is with the file descriptions which need to be completed to include the notions of combined,, input, external definitions and key processing. At statement 6, an input spec (I) is used to define a named constant called ERRMSG. This error message constant is constructed so that if a vendor is not found, it is convenient to send this message to the display panel.

The program logic begins with a Do-While-Equal statement shown as Xs in Figure 10-27. This tells the compiler to keep running the same set of statements, from the DOW statement to the ENDDO until something happens. That "something" occurs if indicator 03 (a switch that gets tested) has turned to the ON state from the OFF state.

Figure 10-27 RPG program (LAB10_1EY) for Display File (LAB10D1S)

```
. . . :      6  76              Browse                    RPGOBJ/SOURCE
                                                          LAB10_1EY
 *. 1 ...+... 2 ...+... 3 ...+... 4 ...+... 5 ...+... 6 ...+... 7 ...+.
F* MAKE NEW FULLY PROCEDURAL EXTERNALLY DEFINED WORKSTN FILE
FLAB10D1YCXX E                      XXXXXXX
F* PHYSICAL FILE VENDORP WITH KEY
F* MAKE VENDORP FULLY PROC EXT DEFINED DISK FILE USED FOR INPUT
FVENDORP XXX E          X          DISK
I                'VENDOR NOT FOUND      'C         XXXXXX
C* WRITE A DO WHILE EQUAL STATEMENT TO RUN TIL IND 03 IS *OFF
C           *IN03     XXXXX OFF                CF03 = 03
C                     EXFMTVENDXXX
C           XXXXXX    CHAINVENDORP           90     90 = NOT FOUND
C           *IN90     IFEQ *ON
C                     MOVELERRMSG     NAME
C                     ENDIF
C                     ENDXXX
C                     MOVE *ON        *INLR
```

You may recall that in our SDA display panel, we assigned Command Key 03 to the indicator 03. Thus, when indicator 03 (*IN03) is turned on by the user of the display file while on a workstation pressing the F3 key, it is a signal to the program that the program user wants to end the program. F3 is changed to indicator 01 by the user interface. The DOW then moves to the statement following the ENDDO and sets on LR (last record), which as we know is how RPG programs end.

Within the repeating Do-Loop, the program sends out the VENDFMT panel from our SDA-built display file. The EXFMT operation in RPG sends this panel and then waits in the program for a user to enter data and hit ENTER. When the user types the vendor number and hits ENTER, the typed information becomes available in the program, inside the field *VNDNBR*.

In the next statement, the program needs to use the VNDNBR data to CHAIN to (access) the vendor file. If the vendor number entered is on file, the database information for that vendor is available to the program immediately after the CHAIN operation. If the record is not found, the operation turns on switch # 90 (indicator 90) to let the program know that a record was not found.

The program tests the status of indicator 90 to see if it is on - meaning that a record was not found. If the record was not found, the program loads an error message into the *Vendor Name* field of the display panel. The ENDIF ends this not-found error routine that began with the IFEQ statement.

Eventually we hit the ENDDO. This works with the DOWXX at the top to define the part of the program which repeats until the user hits Command Key 3. The ENDDO passes control back to the DOWXX and if the user has not hit Command Key 3, control is passed to the statement following the DOWEQ statement .

The second and subsequent times through the DOWEQ loop, the output part of the operation sends out the data from the database, or the error message in NAME, while the input part of the operation brings in the next VENDOR number as well as an indication that the ENTER key or Command key 03 has been pressed. The program continues in the loop until the user takes the appropriate ending action - by pressing Command key 03.

Simple RPG Inquiry with Display File

In this inquiry example, the input is vendor number and the output is name and address information, as defined on the panel, which you built in this Lab. After you have compiled your RPG program, you can call the program (CALL LAB10_1EY), enter a vendor number, and press ENTER. The name, address and balanced-owed information are then displayed. When this happens, your efforts have been successful and this exercise in Lab 10 is completed.

Other Display Operations

The EXFMT (execute format) operation is very powerful and is the most used of the RPG interactive display operations. Without IBM implementing EXFMT, the programmer would be forced to use the WRITE operation followed by the READ operation to perform the same function. When a WRITE followed by a READ occurs to a displays station and the panel contains input fields or command keys, the RPG program halts on the "READ" so that the user can interact with the workstation. When the user hits a command key or other function key or the ENTER key, the READ operation brings in the input or both data from the workstation. If the EXFMT in this Lab were replaced by the WRITE / READ operations, the code would look as follows:

```
C...        WRITE  VENDFMT
C...        READ   VENDFMT
```

A WRITE operation is also used when the programmer wants to output information to a display and accept no input. The READ operation cannot be used without a prior WRITE operation since the WRITE places the format on the workstation that the READ accepts the entered data.. However, there are mechanisms, using facilities referred to on the System i as shared access paths that permit program A to use a WRITE operation to place a panel on the workstation, set on LR and end, and then have program B come alive and READ the panel sent by program A.

This notion is called request under format (sharing formats) and was used frequently when memory was expensive and processor speeds were very limited. While the user was typing in the data on the panel sent by program A, the system would be loading program B, thereby giving the illusion of better performance.

Lab 10 Exercise 4 Adding Fields & Function to existing panel.

In this exercise, you will build, from scratch, the panel shown in Figure 10-28

Figure 10-28 Extended Vendor Inquiry Panel

```
                    Extended Vendor Inquiry


     Enter Vendor Number:   99999


     Name and Address                        Balance Owed


     OOOOOOOOOOOOOOOOOOOOOOOOOOO             6,666,666.66-
     OOOOOOOOOOOOOOOOOOOOOOOOOO
     OOOOOOOOOOOOOOO   OO 66666




     Vendor Class       66
     Vendor Status      O
     Service Rating     O




                    F3     End of Job

 Work screen for record VENDFMT: Press Help for function keys.
```

0. Start the exercise by copying the member LAB10D2 in your source file to LAB10D2Y in your SOURCE file using PDM

1. Use the STRSDA command to start the process and hit the enter key

2, Type "1" for Design screens.

The Design Screens option panel is presented as shown in Figure 10-29

Figure 10-29 Design Screens Initial Panel

```
                    Design Screens
  Type choices, press Enter.

     Source file . . . . . . . . .  SOURCE ___    Name, F4 for list
        Library . . . . . . . . .  YOURLIB___    Name, *LIBL, *CURLIB
     Member  . . . . . . . . . . .  LAB10D2Y   Name, F4 for list



  F3=Exit     F4=Prompt    F12 = Cancel
```

3. Fill it in as in Figure 10-29 using your source file, your library and your member, LAB10D2Y.

4. When you complete the panel in 10-29, press ENTER. You will see a panel as in Figure 10-30 .

Figure 10-30 Creating The Extended Display Panel

```
                      Work with Display Records

  File  . . . . . . :    SOURCE              Member . . . . . . . :    LAB10D2Y
    Library . . . . :      RPGOBJ            Source type  . . . :    DSPF

  Type options, press Enter.
    1=Add               2=Edit comments        3=Copy            4=Delete
    7=Rename            8=Select keywords     12=Design image

  Opt   Order    Record         Type       Related Subfile    Date        DDS Error

   12     10     VENDFMT        RECORD                        07/16/07


                                                                        Bottom
  F3=Exit                   F12=Cancel        F14=File-level keywords
  F15=File-level comments   F17=Subset        F24=More keys
```

5. Place a 12 next to the VENDFMT panel and press enter.

6A. Your mission is to examine this one record format for this LAB10D2Y display file. In the end, the panel you get to look at will look like that shown in Figure 10-28.

6B. Now that you got this far, you should know that there are XXs in the source member that you copied into your source file LAB10D2Y and so, these must be removed for this display to work with your program. They must be replaced with valid and correct code. You can exit SDA and go to SEU to make the changes and then come back here for the rest of the exercise or you can try to wait til the end of this exercise and before you connect to the program in Exercise 5, alter the XXs from the new DDS built in this exercise and see if that works for you. The correct DDS is shown in member LAB10D2Y in your SOURCE file in your library if you need to look at it as a reference. Yes, DDS created by SDA can be modified by SEU.

7. Depending on your choice, at this point you have made it. So, Press Enter and you will see the panel shown in Figure 10-28.

8. When you have observed the panel sufficiently, place an asterisk next to all of the fields as shown in Figure 10-31 below:

Figure 10-31 Checking Out the Attributes -- See the asterisks

```
                        Extended Vendor Inquiry


        Enter Vendor Number:   99999

        *Name and Address                          *Balance Owed

         OOOOOOOOOOOOOOOOOOOOOOOOOOO               *6,666,666.66-
        *OOOOOOOOOOOOOOOOOOOOOOOOOOO
        *OOOOOOOOOOOOOOO    OO 66666




        *Vendor Class      *66
        *Vendor Status     *O
        *Service Rating    *O




                    *F3     End of Job
```

8. Press Enter to select the type of keywords. You will get a panel that looks like the one in Figure 10-32

Figure 10-32 Selecting the Field Keyword Groupings

```
                         Select Field Keywords

Constant  . . .  :     Name and Address
Length  . . . .  :     16                        Row . . . :  7    Column . . . :  9

Type choices, press Enter.
                                      Y=Yes    For Field Type
   Display attributes . . . . . . .    Y       All except Hidden
   Colors . . . . . . . . . . . .             All except Hidden



   General keywords . . . . . . . .            All types

   TEXT keyword . . . . . . . . . .


F3=Exit    F4=Display Selected Keywords    F12=Cancel
```

9. Place a Y in Display Attributes and press ENTER. You will see a panel such as that shown in Figure 10-33.

Figure 10-33 The Name and Address Prompt -- Indicator Settings

```
                        Select Display Attributes
Constant  . . . :  Name and Address
Length  . . . . :  16                  Row . . . :   7    Column . . . :   9
Type choices, press Enter.
                                            Keyword   Y=Yes   Indicators/+
                                                                  20
  Field conditioning . . . . . . . . . . .
  Program-to-system field  . . . . . . . .
  Display attributes:                       DSPATR
    High intensity . . . . . . . . . . . .   HI
    Reverse image  . . . . . . . . . . . .   RI
    Column separators  . . . . . . . . . .   CS
    Blink  . . . . . . . . . . . . . . . .   BL
    Nondisplay . . . . . . . . . . . . . .   ND
    Underline  . . . . . . . . . . . . . .   UL        Y
    Position cursor  . . . . . . . . . . .   PC
F3=Exit    F12=Cancel
```

10. Our objective is to merely observe so take your time. Note that indicator 20 is used to condition this prompt and in fact every other field (variable) or constant that you placed an asterisk against in Figure 10-31. This means that unless Figure 20 is on, this prompt and the other fields and prompts that you will observe will not appear on the panel. Thus, the RPG program must turn on indicator 10 to provide this function.

11. Keep pressing ENTER to go through all of the other variables and constants and note that they are conditioned by indicator 20. For each when the display looks like that in Figure 10-32, take a Y on display attributes so that you can see that indicator 10 is assigned. When you finish this activity, you will be back at the design panel as shown in Figure 10-31.

12. From here, it is time to exit and create the Display file. Press F12 to get back to the records panel as shown in Figure 10-30.

13. press F3 to exit SDA.

14. On the Save DDS - Create Display File panel which appears, take all the defaults to create this display panel.

15. press F3 to exit SDA.

You have completed Lab 10 Exercise 4.

Lab 10 Exercise 5 Extended Vendor Inquiry RPG Program

This new program sends and receives via EXFMT the new display file LAB10D2Y with modified format VENDFMT. The new format contains three additional fields. The format and the VENDORP DB have the same field names so no moves are to be required. To avoid clutter on the screen when there is an error message to be sent, no other data other than the vendor number is to be shown on the screen (indicator 20 off). Additionally, the VNDNBR should be highlighted if an error condition exists. One more thing. Because the named ERROR constant is smaller than the NAME field in which it is displayed, clear the field first for each error condition by moving blanks to the NAME field.

Method 1: Not recommended. More difficult. Copy the LAB10_1EY program into your library as LAB10_2EY . Modify this RPG/400 program. LAB10_2ES is in your SOURCE file as a solution that you may reference From Lab 3 you may recall that this sends out the LAB10D1Y display file format VENDFMT using EXFMT. The new program name is LAB10_2EY. This program needs to interface with display file LAB10D2Y using format VENDFMT with the EXFMT RPG operation. This is the panel you just examined and compiled.

Modify the program so that it sets on indicator 44 when there is an error condition and it sets it off when needed. Also, modify this program so that it turns on indicator 20 to send good data and turn off indicator 20 to send an error message. Because the named ERROR constant is smaller than the NAME field in which it is displayed, clear the field first for each error condition by moving blanks to the NAME field.

Method 2: Recommended approach... Program shell LAB10_2E is already in your library with X's in places where you must modify the code to perform the functions necessary to accommodate the added function. LAB10_2ES is also in your SOURCE file as a solution that you may reference. Begin by copying LAB10_2E to LAB10_2EY using PDM copy. The new program is to interface with display file LAB10D2Y using format VENDFMT with the EXFMT RPG operation. This is the panel that in Exercise 4, you just examined and compiled.

The program needs to set on indicator 44 when there is an error condition and it sets it off when needed. The program is to it turn on indicator 20 to send good data and to turn off indicator 20 to send an error message. Because the named ERROR constant is smaller than the NAME field in which it is displayed, clear the field first for each error condition by moving blanks to the NAME field.

Figure 10-26 RPG program (LAB10_2EY) for Display File (LAB10D2S)

```
*************** Beginning of data ***********************************
F* PROGRAM SENDS OUT MORE FIELDS & HIGHLIGHTS INVALID VENDOR
F* USE 44 TO HIGHLIGHT VNDNBR  USE 20 TO SEND ALL PANEL FIELDS
F* DISPLAY FILE NEW2 -- NEW WITH ALL FIELDS
FLAB10D2SCF  E                 WORKSTN
F* PHYSICAL FILE VENDORP WITH KEY
FVENDORP IF  E           K        DISK
I* NAMED CONSTANT FOR ERROR MESSAGE
I               'VENDOR NOT FOUND      'C          ERRMSG
C*
C           *IN03       DOWEQ*OFF                        CF03 = 03
C                       EXFMTVENDFMT
C                       SETOF                 XX
C                       SETON                 20
C           VNDNBR      CHAINVENDORP          90    90 = NOT FOUND
C           *IN90       IFEQ XON
C                       MOVE XBLANKS     NAME
C                       SETON                 44
C                       SETOF                 XX
C                       MOVELERRMSG      NAME
C                       ENDIF
C                       ENDDO
C                       MOVE *ON         *INLR
***************** End of data *****************************************
```

Instructions for method 2

1. Use PDM / SEU copy to copy the shell to LAB10_2EY program and then take PDM option 2 to edit this RPG source member with SEU.

2. Check out the program logic and compare to the write-up above. Remove all X's from the program and make changes to code at the point of the X as appropriate to support the program logic.

3. Save your work as LAB10_2EY.

4. Compile LAB10_2EY and place the object in your current library.

5. Run the program to see how it behaves. Repeat steps until clean compile and clean execution.

You have completed Lab 10 Exercise 5.

Lab 11 Use Display Files with RPG Programs to Update DB Files

Lab 11 Objectives:

Students learn how to write an interactive RPG/400 program that updates the vendor master file (VENDORP).

Lab 11 Exercise 1 Creating Update Enabling Display Files - Multiple Formats

In this exercise, you will examine two panels in the display file named LAB11D1. Start this exercise by using a PDM copy and create the LAB11D1Y Display file member (DSPF) with the contents.

The two panels are shown in Figures 10-27 and Figure 10-28. The big difference in the display file in this exercise and the ones in Lab 10 is that this display file has two screens (panels - formats) and this display file is built to accept changes to the data that is displayed -- as the vehicle for input to the Vendor Maintenance Program that we discuss in Lab 11 Exercise 3.

These display panels already work in the solution, but since nobody is becoming an expert in DDS for display files by studying this stuff, it won't hurt to get a little more learning in DDS and display files along the way. Since this is not a DDS or SDA self-study, you are not be forced to build the new panel from scratch. The screen panel for this exercise is called LAB11D1Y as you have just created via PDM copy.

It consists of two different formats shown in Figure 11-1 and 11-2 below. Your mission in this Lab exercise is to examine the differences compared to the display files that were used for inquiry (read) only. Additionally, there are a few XXed out areas in the DDS for these. So, use SEU inside of LAB11D1Y and search for the Xs and then correct them. Come back to PDM and place a 14 on the display file to compile it. If for whatever reason, you cannot make it work. Compare it to LAB11D1S line by line as this is the solution.

Figure 11-1 Vendor Maintenance Multi Format Display File - Panel 1

```
                          Vendor Maintenance



         Enter Vendor Number:   99999




         OOOOOOOOOOOOOOOOOOOOOOOOOOOOOO




                          F3    End of Job

Work screen for record FIRST: Press Help for function keys.
```

Figure 11-2 Vendor Maintenance Multi Format Display File - Panel 2

```
                          Vendor Maintenance


         Enter Vendor Number:   66666

         Name and Address                      Balance Owed

         BBBBBBBBBBBBBBBBBBBBBBBBBB            9,999,999.99-
         BBBBBBBBBBBBBBBBBBBBBBBBBB
         BBBBBBBBBBBBBBB   BB 99999-



         Vendor Class     99-
         Vendor Status    B
         Service Rating   B




                          F3    End of Job

Work screen for record VENDFMT: Press Help for function keys.          .
```

In this Lab 11, Exercise 1, your display file must accommodate the reading in of a vendor number and the subsequent display of that vendor's information on the screen.   Additionally, since this file is used as a maintenance enabler, the data that is displayed must also be read back into the program. You may recall that the VNDNBR field in the prior files was "BOTH" input and output capable, the big change that needed to be made to the major information format was to make it capable of passing back changes to the program. In this case, there is a separate panel with VENDNBR

So, in addition to performing the inquiry function, this exercise needs to create a file that permits the user to modify the data on the screen so that the RPG program will update the database accordingly.

Use these steps to get this mission accomplished:

1. Use the STRSDA command to start the process and hit the enter key

2, Type "1" for Design screens.

The Design Screens option panel is presented as shown in Figure 11-3

Figure 11-3 Design Screens Initial Panel

```
                        Design Screens
     Type choices, press Enter.

          Source file . . . . . . . .  SOURCE ___    Name, F4 for list
             Library . . . . . . . . .  YOURLIB___   Name, *LIBL, *CURLIB
          Member  . . . . . . . . . .   LAB11D1Y_    Name, F4 for list



     F3=Exit     F4=Prompt     F12 = Cancel
```

3. Fill it in as in Figure 11-3 and press Enter.

4. When you complete the panel in 11-3, press ENTER. You will see a panel as in Figure 11-4.

Figure 11-4 Creating The First Maintenance Display Panel

```
                    Work with Display Records

   File  . . . . . . . :    SOURCE          Member . . . . . . . :   LAB11D1Y
      Library . . . . :      RPGOBJ          Source type  . . . :    DSPF

   Type options, press Enter.
     1=Add              2=Edit comments      3=Copy         4=Delete
     7=Rename           8=Select keywords    12=Design image

   Opt   Order    Record        Type     Related Subfile   Date         DDS Error
    __     10     FIRST         RECORD                      07/16/07
    __     10     VENDFMT       RECORD                      07/16/07


                                                                  Bottom
   F3=Exit                    F12=Cancel        F14=File-level keywords
   F15=File-level comments    F17=Subset        F24=More keys
```

5. Place a 12 next to the FIRST panel and press enter to get a look at the panel.

6. Your mission is to examine the two record formats for this LAB11D1Y display file. In the end, the first panel you get to look at, will look like that shown in Figure 10-27.

7. Press Enter and you will see the panel shown in Figure 10-27.

8. When you have observed the panel sufficiently, place an asterisk next to any fields that you would like to examine further and look at the SDA attributes that may be associated with the fields and constants. This is not required, however.

9. Place a 12 next to the VENDFMT panel and press enter.

10. Your mission is to examine this second record format for this LAB10D1Y display file. In the end, the panel you get to look at will look like that shown in Figure 10-28.

11. Press Enter and you will see the panel shown in Figure 10-28.

12. When you have observed the panel sufficiently, place an asterisk next to any fields that you would like to examine further and look at the SDA attributes that may be associated with the fields and constants. This is not required, however.

13. Your objective in this exercise is to first observe and then to compile the SDA generated DDS into a display file --- so take your time. Note that the code is "B" for the formerly "O" fields. "O" fields do not return anything to the RPG program. Therefore, "B" for both output and input are used. Take notice to the B fields and take notice that they are all underlined -- the SDA default for fields that are returned back to the program and are available for user input. In our case, the data from VENDORP will populate the fields and then the user can change the data, hit ENTER and the program will receive the changes and update the database accordingly.

14. Now it is time to exit and create the Display file. If you have displayed any attributes for fields, press F12 to get back to the records panel as shown in Figure 10-27 or 10-28.

15. Press F3 to exit SDA.

16. On the Save DDS - Create Display File panel which appears, take all the defaults to create this display panel.

17. Press F3 to exit SDA.

You have completed Lab 11 Exercise 1.

Lab 11 Exercise 2 Extended Vendor Maintenance (UPDATE) RPG Program

Start by performing a PDM copy on the RPG shell for the exercise, LAN11_1E and copy it to LAB11_1EY. Make the LAB11_1EY program sends and receive (using EXFMT) the new display file from Exercise 1, LAB11D1Y. Remember it has two formats, FIRST and VENDFMT. The new DSPF file contains the two screen panels.

After you do the copy, take a look at the code. See if you can decode it and then come back here.

The VENDFMT format and the VENDORP DB have the same field names so just as in Lab 10 Exercise 5, no moves should be required to move data from one file to another.   This code does not contain the references to indicator 20 which were needed in the last program to avoid clutter and residuals when, for example a vendor was not found. Without indicator 20 conditioning, since there was just one format, all fields would display with a vendor not found condition, and thus the good information from the prior record would appear on the Error panel. Indicator 20 conditioning prevented this.

Since there are two panels in this maintenance program (update), the vendor number input panel (FIRST) is small enough to contain just enough room for the vendor number and the error message. No other information is displayed on this "FIRST" panel. Since the vendor input is taken care of in its own panel, there is no need to condition the constants and variables of the modified VENDFMT panel with indicator 20 and thus, it is not needed in this the LAB11_1EY program.

Other than the aforementioned factors, the inquiry logic of the maintenance program is very similar to that of the extended inquiry program in Lab 10 Exercise 5. Since there are two panels, there are two different EXFMT operations in the program. In the beginning of the calculations code, the FIRST panel is put out and the vendor # is read into the program. the VNDNBR field is used to randomly read (CHAIN) to the VENDORP file as before. However, before that the program tests to see if F3 were pressed on the FIRST panel.

If F3 had been pressed, the code should LEAVE the DO loop and go on to end the program by setting on LR in detail calculations. In this case, in which the user has buyers remorse and ends before anything is done, no second panel (VENDFMT) should be presented.

Without this "second" test for F3 being pressed, the DO loop would not be tested until the beginning DOWXX statement. Thus, the second EXFMT would execute and show data from whatever was keyed in the VNDNBR field. This could very well have been the last record's information.

Nobody wants to get a second panel after hitting a key to end a program so the F3 needs to cause the DO loop to be exited with a LEAVE operation. An ITER would appear to do the same thing but it would actually begin the DOW again and fail because *IN03 is on.

If there is a found condition the program should use the ELSE condition (meaning found record) to send out the VENDFMT with the current vendor information. Since the fields are both input and output, the user can then change the data on the display with the keyboard as they see fit, and press ENTER.

The ENTER key should then cause an UPDAT operation to occur against the VNDNBR that is being modified to effect the change. As a point of note, the UPDAT operation in RPG requires the record format name of the VENDORP file rather than the File name.

Two Methods to Do this Lab Exercise

Method 1: Not Recommended. Copy the LAB10_2EY program into your library as LAB11_1EY . Modify this RPG/400 program LAB11_1EY program. From Lab 5 you may recall that this sends out the LAB10D2Y display file format VENDFMT using EXFMT. The new program name as noted is LAB11_1EY. It needs to interface with display file LAB11D1Y using formats FIRST and VENDFMT with two EXFMT RPG operations. This is the panel you just examined and compiled in Lab 11, Exercise 1.

Modify the program so that it no longer sets on indicator 20 and it accommodates the changes outlined above to provide for an update facility using the both type fields in the modified VNDFMT panel.

Method 2: Recommended: Copy member LAB11_1E as RPG program member LAB11_1EY. Then edit LAB11_1EY. It has X's in places where you must modify the code to perform the functions necessary to accommodate the added function. The program interfaces with display file LAB10D1Y display file using formats FIRST and VENDFMT with two EXFMT RPG operations. This is the panel that in Exercise 1, you just examined and compiled / created.

The program still needs to set on indicator 44 when there is an error condition and it must set it off when needed. The program does not need to turn on indicator 20 as described above to send good data and to turn off indicator 20 to send an error message. When the record is found, display the record for change and then update the VENDORP file using the DB record format name.

Detailed Instructions for method 2

1. Use PDM / SEU to edit the LAB11_1EY program after copying in the shell..

2. Remove all X's from the program and make changes to code at the point of the X as appropriate to support the program logic.

3. Save your work as LAB11_1EY.

4. Compile LAB11_1EY and place the object in your current library.

5. Run the program to see how it behaves.

6. Repeat until it works.

You have completed Lab 11 Exercise 2.

Lab 12 Adding Capabilities to the Payroll Program - Creating Menu and Maintenance Functions

Lab 12 Objectives:

Add advanced RPG facilities to the Lab 6 - 9 programs and make the program provide the function of four programs:

We took a two-lab (lab 10 & 11) diversion from the general theme of this lab book to present several programs that helped teach how to use interactive RPG. We're back on track for the last lab. We took the diversion so that you could get some practice with interactive displays before we got to this display file which controls multiple functions and the program that processes it.

This is a much more complex program than Lab 06. Even before you make your changes to get it to work, it is important that you understand its theme and its general principles. The good news about this program and this lab is that it is based on the work that you have already completed. So, all of the difficulty in figuring out how to do matching records without the RPG cycle is behind us and is that is a big part of this program.

In many ways this is not just one program. It is several programs all rolled into one and depending on the options that are taken by the user, this program performs any of several tasks. The main tasks are listed right on the menu panel shown in Figure 12 -1 and they are repeated below for you convenience. As you can see the options are provided as function keys and not as numbers or letters to select on a menu. If this application were ever WebFaced or implemented on the Web in any other way, the function keys would translate easily into buttons or icons and the buttons would be able to be clicked by a mouse to give the client / server and the Web look and feel to the migrated application.

The major program options in Program LAB12E4Y which drives the four panel display file application are as follows:

F10 to Create New Master Payroll Records
F11 to Update Master Payroll Records
F20 to Run the Payroll Register
F21 to Accept this Payroll as Correct and Write History File
F22 to Create Archive History Report for Pay Period 66

In order to implement all of this function, several new files and a data area are introduced with this program so there is a lot of learning ahead. We'll save the file definitions for Exercise 2 as we fully describe the function of program LAB12E4Y. For now, let's take a look at the display panels in display file LAB12D1Y that are necessary to make this all work. In figure 12-1 take a look at the initial panel used in the program:

Figure 12- 1 Payroll Input Menu Display FIle LAB12D1Y Format PROMPT

```
                      The Dowallaby Company
                         Payroll Input
                             66

      Press F10 to Create New Master Payroll Records

      Press F11 to Update Master Payroll Records

      Press F20 to Run the Payroll Register

      Press F21 to Accept this Payroll as Correct and Write History File

      Press F22 to Create Archive History Report for Pay Period  66


      Press F3 to END THE JOB




Work screen for record PROMPT: Press Help for function keys.
```

Figure 12-2 shows the format of the ADD Record panel for the Employee master.

Figure 12-2 Payroll ADD to Master Panel

```
                     The Dowallaby Company
                     Add to Employee Master


            Employee Number      666
            Employee Name        IIIIIIIIIIIIIIIIIIIIIIIIIIIIII
            Employee Pay Rate    33333-
            Employee City        IIIIIIIIIIIIIIIIIII
            Employee State       II
            Employee Zip Code    33333-
            Employee Salaried?   I
            Employee Dept Code   IIII


      Press Enter to continue...    Press F12 to end the ADD
Work screen for record ADD: Press Help for function keys.
```

Figure 12-3 shows the format of the UPDATE Record panel for the Employee master when there is a not found record condition.

Figure 12-3 Payroll Update to Master Panel -- Error Condition Panel

```
                     The Dowallaby Company
                        Payroll Input
                           UPDATE


        Enter the Employee # you wish to UPDATE



           EMP NBR:   333-




           EMPLOYEE # NOT FOUND     666


     Press F12 to End The Update

Work screen for record UPDATE1: Press Help for function keys.
```

Figure 12-4 shows the format of the UPDATE Record panel for the Employee master when the record requested is found.

Figure 12-4 Payroll Update to Master Panel -- Good Record

```
                    The Dowallaby Company
                  Update to Employee Master


              Employee Number      666
              Employee Name        BBBBBBBBBBBBBBBBBBBBBBBBBBBBBB
              Employee Pay Rate    99999-
              Employee City        BBBBBBBBBBBBBBBBBBBBB
              Employee State       BB
              Employee Zip Code    99999-
              Employee Salaried?   B
              Employee Dept Code   BBBB

       Press Enter to continue...    Press F12 to end update
```

Lab 12 Exercise 1 Examine with SDA and Compile Multi-Format Display File

Each of these panels are already completed and are awaiting your review. There is no shell. There are no X's. You need to examine them with SDA first and then and SEU and look at their keywords and indicators before commencing with the Exercise 2 part of this Lab. You need to be familiar with the panels that are used and when to send / receive which panel.   Starting with panel named PROMPT in LAB12D1Y and moving through ADD, UPDATE1, and the UPDATE panel, use SDA to review the panels and the display and indicator keywords that are used in this application. After you use SDA, before you try to make Exercise 2 work, you owe it to yourself to look at the generated DDS for this "monster." The steps for PROMPT are shown below. Repeat these instructions for each of the panels in LAB12D1Y.

1. Use the STRSDA command to start the process and hit the enter key

2, Type "1" for Design screens.

The Design Screens option panel is presented as shown in Figure 12-5.

Figure 12-5 Design Screens Initial Panel

```
                        Design Screens
   Type choices, press Enter.

      Source file . . . . . . . . SOURCE ___    Name, F4 for list
         Library . . . . . . . . YOURLIB___    Name, *LIBL, *CURLIB
      Member  . . . . . . . . . . LAB12D1Y___   Name, F4 for list


   F3=Exit     F4=Prompt     F12 = Cancel
```

3. Fill it in as in Figure 12-5 and press Enter.

4. When you complete the panel in 12-5, press ENTER. You will see a panel as in Figure 12-6.

Figure 12-6 Creating The Extended Display Panel

```
                      Work with Display Records

File  . . . . . . :    SOURCE              Member . . . . . . :    LAB12D1Y
  Library . . . . :    RPGOBJ              Source type  . . . :    DSPF

Type options, press Enter.
  1=Add               2=Edit comments       3=Copy          4=Delete
  7=Rename            8=Select keywords    12=Design image

Opt  Order    Record         Type    Related Subfile   Date      DDS Error

 12    10     PROMPT         RECORD                   06/13/06
 __    20     ADD            RECORD                   06/13/06
 __    30     UPDATE1        RECORD                   06/13/06
 __    40     UPDATE         RECORD                   06/13/06


                                                       Bottom
F3=Exit                   F12=Cancel      F14=File-level keywords
F15=File-level comments   F17=Subset      F24=More keys
```

5. Note the four record formats (display records). Place a 12 next to the PROMPT (first) panel and press Enter.

6. Your mission is to examine this one record format for this LAB12D1Y display file. In the end, the panel you get to look at will look like that shown in Figure 12-1.

7. Press Enter and you will see the panel shown in Figure 12-1 as repeated below for your convenience as Figure 12-7:

Figure 12-7 Payroll Input Menu Display File LAB12D1Y Format PROMPT

```
                    The Dowallaby Company
                       Payroll Input
                            66

    Press F10 to Create New Master Payroll Records

    Press F11 to Update Master Payroll Records

    Press F20 to Run the Payroll Register

    Press F21 to Accept this Payroll as Correct and Write History File

    Press F22 to Create Archive History Report for Pay Period  66


    Press F3 to END THE JOB




Work screen for record PROMPT: Press Help for function keys.
```

8. When you have observed the panel sufficiently, you may choose to place an asterisk next to the fields you want to examine in more detail. From there you would go through the attributes panels as you did in Lab 10.

9. When you are ready, press F12 which will take you back to the Work with Display Records panel 12 as shown in Figure 12-6.

10. Go through all of the other three panels following the instructions for the PROMPT panel, which you just completed.

12. When you have finished, begin the exit process and create the Display file. The specifics to do this follow:

13. Press F12 to get back to the records panel as shown in Figure 12-62.

14. press F3 to exit SDA.

15. On the Save DDS - Create Display File panel which appears, take all the defaults to create this display panel. Yes, I already created it but let the compiler overlay my work.

16. press F3 to exit SDA.

You have completed Lab 12 Exercise 1.

Lab 12 – Exercise 2 Multi Function RPGIV Payroll Register Program

There is no RPG/400 solution to this problem defined in this Lab.

The program in this lab, LAB12E4Y is mostly a renaming of the external RPGIV version of the PAREG3 program from Chapter 24 of the RPG Textbook. For a more detailed explanation of the decoding of this program, you may find Chapter 24 quite helpful.

Method 1: Not Recommended. Copy your Lab 9 result LAB09E4Y that you converted in Lab 9 into your source file as a starting point, This will give you an externally described RPGIV version of a new RPGIV program called LAB12E4Y. To this, you will have to add all of the code to support the new requirements. Don't do this until you are sure. The program LAB12E4S is the solution and it sits in your Source File in your library.

You would get to learn RPG by taking the program specs and comparing them with the program designed for method 2. This helps show you the steps necessary to take the Lab 9 result and make it into a powerful interactive, multipurpose program. So, you may want to start by looking at the solution and working it back into the LAB09 work. This would take longer and it would be lots more work. If you completed it, you would learn more than method 2. Remember after you use the recommended method 2, you can come back and try Method 1 and see how you do.

Method 2: Recommended... The RPGIV program shell LAB12E4 is ready in your library for you to do a PDM copy into member LAB12E4Y. Then bring up SEU from PDM using option 2 and make your modifications to these many statements so they function as a multi-purpose program providing menu capability, interactive access and update, batch reporting and updating and archiving. There are lots of XXs that need to be resolved and that means there is lots of learning inside.

After decoding LAB12E4Y, preparing it to compile, compiling it and making it work, you will have a great perception of the many capabilities in RPG and RPGIV and you will be ready for your own solo flight (with some help from the experts in the shop perhaps -- but you are on your way.)

As you know the Y in LAB12E4Y stands for you. The E means it is the externally described version and the 4 means it is written in RPGIV. To this, you will have to add certain codes that have been omitted and you will have to change the XXs in the code to the proper entries. Method 2 is by far the easier method. Please note that LAB12E4S is the solution and it works. If you need help, take a peek.

General Program Function

The major program options in Program LAB12E4Y which drives the four panel display file LAB12D1Y application are as follows:

F10 to Create New Master Payroll Records
F11 to Update Master Payroll Records
F20 to Run the Payroll Register
F21 to Accept this Payroll as Correct and Write History File
F22 to Create Archive History Report for Pay Period 66

In order to implement all of this function, several new files and a data area are introduced with this program. The screen definitions were reviewed in Exercise 1. Before you examine this program in more detail, take a look at the record layouts in DDS form as shown in the figures below:

Figure 12-7 Data Description for EMPMAST

```
Columns . . . :   1  71          Browse              YOURLIB/SOURCE
SEU==>                                                EMPMAST
FMT PF .....A..........T.Name+++++RLen++TDpB......Functions+++++++++++++++++++
      *************** Beginning of data ************************************
001.00     A          R EMPR
002.00     A            EMPNO         3S 0        COLHDG('EMP' 'NBR')
003.00     A            EMPNAM        30          COLHDG('EMP' 'NAME')
004.00     A            EMPRAT        5S 2        COLHDG('EMP' 'RATE')
005.00     A            EMPCTY        20          COLHDG('EMPLOYEE' 'CITY')
006.00     A            EMPSTA        2           COLHDG('EMP' 'STATE')
007.00     A            EMPZIP        5S 0        COLHDG('EMP' 'ZIP')
008.00     A            EMPSCD        1           COLHDG('SAL' 'CODE')
009.00     A            EMPDPT        4           COLHDG('DEPT' 'CODE')
010.00     A          K EMPNO
      ***************** End of data *****************************************
```

Figure 12-8 Query Listing of Major EMPMAST Fields

```
                      Display Spooled File
File  . . . . . :    QPRINT                   Page/Line   1/6
Control . . . . .                             Columns     1 - 78
Find  . . . . . .
*...+....1....+....2....+....3....+....4....+....5....+....6....+....7....+...
          THE DOWALLOBY COMPANY EMPLOYEE LIST      BY STATE        6/09/07
    ST    CITY                 ZIP     EMP#  EMPLOYEE NAME           RATE
    PA    WILKES-BARRE         18702   001   BIZZ NIZWONGER          7.80
    PA    WILKES-BARRE         18702   002   WARBLER JACOBY          7.90
    PA    SCRANTON             18702   003   BING CROSSLEY           8.55
    AK    FAIRBANKS            99701   004   UPTAKE N. HIBITER       7.80
    AK    FAIRBANKS            99701   005   FENWORTH GRONT          9.30
    AK    FAIRBANKS            99701   007   BI NOMIAL               8.80
    AK    JUNEAU               99801   008   MILLY DEWITH            6.50
    AK    JUNEAU               99801   009   SARAH BAYOU            10.45
    NJ    NEWARK               07101   010   DIRT MCPUG              6.45
    NJ    NEWARK               07101   011   BANDAID JONES           4.50
                   HASH TOTAL OF THE RATES                 78.05
```

EMPMAST is the employee master file. There is one record per employee. It contains pay rate & department and other information. Department comes into play in this program as there is a compile time table at the end that is used in the program to provide a lookup vehicle so that the department name can be obtained without it being stored in the PAYMAST record.

This program provides routines to add and/or update records in the EMPMAST file prior to running any of the reports and any of the dollar updates to YTDFILE or PAYHIST. Unlike the TIMCRD file which gets its transactions from a separate process, this program is all that is needed to process the registers and update the master file.

For salaried employees, Salary is in the SALFILE file

Figure 12-9 Salary File -- Processed by the Employee # as key

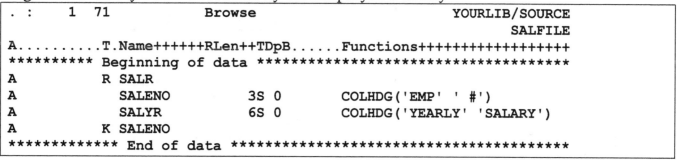

```
 . :    1  71            Browse                    YOURLIB/SOURCE
                                                          SALFILE
A..........T.Name++++++RLen++TDpB......Functions++++++++++++++++++++
********* Beginning of data ********************************
A          R SALR
A            SALENO        3S 0       COLHDG('EMP' ' #')
A            SALYR         6S 0       COLHDG('YEARLY' 'SALARY')
A          K SALENO
************ End of data ********************************
```

Figure 12-10 Data Records in Salary File (Salaried Employees v Hourly)

```
                              Display Report
                                        R
Position to line  . . . . .             Shift
Line      ....+....1....
          EMP     YEARLY
           #      SALARY
000001    3      23,000
000002    4      29,000
***** ********  End of report  ********
```

Figure 12-11 Data Descriptions for TIMCRD FIle

```
********** Beginning of data ******************************
A           R TIMR
A             EMPNO         3S 0        COLHDG('EMP' 'NBR')
A             EMPHRS        4S 2        COLHDG('EMP' 'HOURS')
A           K EMPNO
************ End of data ******************************
```

Figure 12-12Query Listing of TIMCRD File Data

```
          EMPNO   EMPHRS
000001      1      35.00
000002      2      40.00
000003      3      65.00
000004      4      25.00
000005      5      33.00
000006      6      40.00
000007      7      39.00
000008      8      40.00
000009      9      40.00
000010     10      35.00
***** ********  End of report  ********
```

The TIMCRD file is created / updated in a totally separate process from this program in an independent process. This file provides current time records for PAYROLL processing. Though this program falls short of actually calculating taxes, it does have room for taxes in the various history files. For salaried employees, no hours need to be provided on the time card but the TIME card must be present in order for the salaried employee to be paid in this pay period. If there is no Time Card on the random read (CHAIN) to the TIMCRD file, the respective salaried employee does not get paid.

Figure 12-13 Payroll Register Printed Output in Report Form

```
         THE DOWALLOBY COMPANY GROSS PAY REGISTER BY STATE        2/21/06

ST      CITY            EMP#    EMPLOYEE NAME        RATE    HOURS     CHECK

PA      Wilkes-Barre    001     Bizz Nizwonger       7.80    35.00    273.00
PA      Wilkes-Barre    002     Warbler Jacoby       7.90    40.00    316.00

                                TOTAL CITY PAY FOR Wilkes-Barre        589.00

PA      Scranton        003     Bing Crossley        8.55    65.00    555.75

                                TOTAL CITY PAY FOR Scranton           555.75

                                TOTAL STATE PAY FOR PA             1,144.75

AK      Fairbanks       004     Uptake N. Hibiter    7.80    25.00    195.00
AK      Fairbanks       005     Fenworth Gront       9.30    33.00    306.90
                        006 NO MATCHING MASTER               40.00
AK      Fairbanks       007     Bi Nomial            8.80    39.00    343.20

                                TOTAL CITY PAY FOR Fairbanks         845.10

AK      Juneau          008     Milly Dewith         6.50    40.00    260.00
AK      Juneau          009     Sarah Bayou         10.45    40.00    418.00

                                TOTAL CITY PAY FOR Juneau            678.00

                                TOTAL STATE PAY FOR AK             1,523.10

NJ      Newark          010     Dirt McPug           6.45    35.00    225.75

                                TOTAL CITY PAY FOR Newark            225.75

                                TOTAL STATE PAY FOR NJ               225.75

                                FINAL TOTAL PAY                    2,893.60
```

Figure 12-13 shows the same payroll register report that has been the mainstay of the labs since Lab 3.

Figure 12-14 Select Records for Pay Report -- QPRINT2

STATE NAME	CITY	EMP#	EMPLOYEE NAME	DEP NAME	Y GROSS	>HRS	SAL?
	THE DOWALLOBY COMPANY Select PAY History List					7/16/07	
PENNSYLVANIA	WILKES-BARRE	001	BIZZ NIZWONGER	PINGING	273.0	.35	N
PENNSYLVANIA	WILKES-BARRE	002	WARBLER JACOBY	MILLING	316.0	.40	N
PENNSYLVANIA	SCRANTON	003	BING CROSSLEY	GRINDING	442.3	.00	Y
ALASKA	FAIRBANKS	004	UPTAKE N. HIBIT	GRINDING	557.6	.00	Y
ALASKA	FAIRBANKS	005	FENWORTH GRONT	MILLING	306.9	.33	N
ALASKA	FAIRBANKS	007	BI NOMIAL	PINGING	343.2	.39	N
ALASKA	JUNEAU	008	MILLY DEWITH	SANDING	260.0	.40	N
ALASKA	JUNEAU	009	SARAH BAYOU	SANDING	418.0	.40	N
NEW JERSEY	NEWARK	010	DIRT MCPUG	MILLING	228.9	.35	N
NEW JERSEY	NEWARK	011	BANDAID JONES	PINGING	.0	.00	N

Figure 12-14 shows a new report that is to be generated by this program. It is a list by employee of the payroll data used for a particular pay period. This data also is to be written to the PAYHIST file to show the exact information about the time records and pay calculations and the year to date status of an employee on a particular pay period.

Figure 12-15 Error Report -- From ERROR Print file

```
                     Display Spooled File
  . . :    ERROR                      Page/Line   1/1
  . . .                               Columns     1 - 78
  . . .
...+....2....+....3....+....4....+....5....+....6....+....7....
  This Error Report is a result of reading the Time
  Card file completely and finding a missing employee
  master record. The time card record was either
  keyed wrong or the master has been inadvertently
  deleted.  Check payroll input data.
     Employee Number & HRS entered : 006   40.00
```

Figure 12-15 shows the ERROR report from the ERROR print file. It is the same as that shown in LAB09E4Y.

Figure 12-16 YTDFILE -- The Year-To-Date Payroll File (updated each payroll)

```
  . :     1  71              Edit                     YOURLIB/SOURCE
                                                             YTDFILE
.A..........T.Name++++++RLen++TDpB......Functions++++++++++++++++++
*********** Beginning of data ***********************************
  A         R YTDR
  A           YTDNO          3S 0      COLHDG('EMP' '#')
  A           YTDNAM         30        COLHDG('NAME')
  A           YTDPAY         11S 2     COLHDG('YTD GROSS' 'PAY')
  A           YTDHRS         6S 0      COLHDG('YTD' 'HOURS')
  A           YTDFIX         9S 2      COLHDG('YTD' 'FED' 'TAX')
  A           YTDSTX         9S 2      COLHDG('YTD' 'STATE' 'TAX')
  A           YTDCTX         9S 2      COLHDG('YTD' 'CITY' 'TAX')
  A           YTDFCX         9S 2      COLHDG('YTD' 'FICA' 'TAX')
  A           YTDDED         9S 2      COLHDG('YTD' 'DEDUCTIONS')
  A           YTDNET         9S 2      COLHDG('YTD' 'NET' 'PAY')
  A           YTDNOT         24        COLHDG('NOTE IN YTD FILE')
  A         K YTDNO
  A*
************* End of data ***************************************
```

The YTDFIlE is updated each payroll with the new calculated gross YTD amounts. The Tax amounts are provided but since taxes are not calculated in this program (they would be in a real payroll program), they have no real play in this sample program. If there is already data in the YTDFILE when your program runs, ask you system administrator to clear it. CLRPFM YTDFILE...

Figure 12-17 PAYHIST Payroll History File

```
  . :     1  71              Browse                    RPGOBJ/SOURCE
                                                            PAYHIST
.A.........T.Name+++++RLen++TDpB......Functions++++++++++++++++++++
********** Beginning of data **********************************
A              R PAYHR
A                HSTE#          3S 0      COLHDG('EMP'  '#')
A                HSTNAM         30         COLHDG('EMP'  'NAME')
A                HSTRAT         5S 2      COLHDG('PAY'  'RATE')
A                HSTCTY         20         COLHDG('CITY')
A                HSTSTA         2          COLHDG('STATE')
A                HSTZIP         5S 0      COLHDG('ZIP')
A                HSTSCD         1          COLHDG('SAL'  'CD')
A                HSTDPT         4          COLHDG('DEPT')
A                HSTHRS         4S 0      COLHDG('HOURS')
A                HSTSAL         6S         COLHDG('SALARY')
A                HSTPAY         7S 2      COLHDG('GROSS' 'THIS' 'PAY')
A                FILLH1         3          COLHDG('FILL 1')
A                HSTDAT         6S 0      COLHDG('PAY'  'DATE')
A                FILLH2         17         COLHDG('FILL 2')
A                HSTFIX         9S 2      COLHDG('FIT'  'THIS' 'PAY')
A                HSTSTX         9S 2      COLHDG('STATX' 'THIS' 'PAY'
A                HSTCTX         9S 2      COLHDG('CTYTX' 'THIS' 'PAY'
A                HSTFCX         9S 2      COLHDG('FICA' 'THIS' 'PAY')
A                HSTDED         9S 2      COLHDG('DED'  'THIS' 'PAY')
A                HSTNET         7S 2      COLHDG('NET'  'THIS' 'PAY')
A                HSTYPY         11S 2     COLHDG('YTD'  'GROSS')
A                HSTYHR         6S 2      COLHDG('YTD'  'HOURS')
A                HSTYFX         9S 2      COLHDG('YTD'  'FIT'  'TAX')
A                HSTYSX         9S 2      COLHDG('YTD'  'STATE' 'TAX')
A                HSTYCX         9S 2      COLHDG('YTD'  'CITY' 'TAX')
A                HSTYFC         9S 2      COLHDG('YTD'  'FICA' 'TAX')
A                HSTYDD         9S 2      COLHDG('YTD'  'DEDUCT')
A                HSTYNT         9S 2      COLHDG('YTD'  'NET'  'PAY')
A                HGP            66         COLHDG('GROSS' 'LAST' '5 YRS')
A                FILLH3         144        COLHDG('FILL 3')
A                FILLH4         56         COLHDG('FILL 4')
A                HSTRNO         3S 0      COLHDG('RECORD' 'NBR')
A                HSTYR          2S 0      COLHDG('YEAR' 'OF'  'RECORD'
A                HSTPWK         2S 0      COLHDG('PAY'  'PERIOD')
A                HSTNO          3S 0      COLHDG('EMP'  'NO'  'KEY')
A              K HSTYR
A              K HSTPWK
A              K HSTNO
```

Figure 12-17 shows the layout of PAYHST. This keeps growing and growing and growing as more and more payrolls are processed. There is one record per employee who got paid per pay period in which they got paid. Each payroll if 50 people are paid for example, the file increases by 50 records. PAYHIST is basically updated by adding records, including new master records to this file for each employee's detailed "what happened" history.

It serves as a full history for multiple years. Also serves as potential means of recreating a given pay period's payroll for verification. If there is data in this file when you begin and it is disturbing your learning, ask your system administrator to remove it. CLRPFM PAYHST.

Figure 12-18 STATES and State Abbreviations File for Lookups

```
. :    1  71            Browse                    RPGOBJ/SOURCE
                                                          STATES
A..........T.Name++++++RLen++TDpB......Functions+++++++++++++++++++
********** Beginning of data ***********************************
A          R EMPR
A            EMPSTR         2            COLHDG('EMP' 'ABR')
A            EMPSTN        20            COLHDG('EMP' 'ST NAME')
************ End of data ***************************************
```

The STATES file shown in Figure 12-18 is read in prior to the program start and it is processed internally as a memory table. This has the advantage of permitting changes to the table using DB file processing as necessary (though State Names and abbreviations rarely if ever change).

Additionally because it is read in quickly prior to payroll processing, the lookups in memory are substantially faster than from random reads to disk. Notice in Figure 12-14 that the state name is in the report, though the state abbreviation is stored in the employee master file..

Figure 12-19 Externally Described Data Structure Name is PAYPERIOD in your library

```
*************** Beginning of data ***********************************
    A          R EMPR
    A            WEEK#          2S 0        COLHDG('WEEK' ' #')
    A            NXTEM#         3S 0        COLHDG('NEXT' 'EMP' 'NUM')
**************** End of data ***********************************
```

For your program to work properly, your instructor or system administrator will create a data area with a beginning set of numbers. The first # that it contains is the pay period # and the program updates this data area with the next pay period. Since the program also adds new employees to the Employee Master file, the next employee number is also stored in this file. Unless your instructor / system administrator is testing you, she or he will preload this data area so that it is usable for your program. Data areas are very handy for holding this type of data. The command to do this is as follows

CRTDTAARA DTAARA(YOURLIB/PAYPER2) TYPE(*CHAR) LEN(5) VALUE('01001')

The PAYPERIOD DS contains the description of the data area. -- pay period # in pos. 1 & 2 as 2 digit numeric & in 3 to 5, the next employee # 3 digits, numeric. Your program needs to read it in from the data area each time the payroll register program is run. PAYPER is the name of the structure in the program. It comes from the data area PAYPER, which is a data structure which holds the current pay period. This structure gets loaded at program start from a data area. The code you should assure is in your program that references this and makes it all happen is shown below:

```
D*
D PAYPER          EUDS              EXTNAME(PAYPERIOD)
```

Once the compiler brings in the data structure, the program needs to work with the data that is retrieved. For example, code such as the following would help to increment both the WEEK# and the next EMPNO.

```
C...        ADD   1        WEEK#
C...        ADD   1        EMPNO
C...        Z-ADD EMPNO    NXTEM#
```

Of course, you might want to wait until the ADD routine to perform the increment to the EMPNO field since there is no need to increase the next employee number if you are not adding a new one.

Two fields are contained in the external file named pay period from which the definition of the data area structure comes forth. WEEK# represents the pay period and NXTEM# represents the next employee # to be assigned in the employee ADD process.

PAYPER is the name of the data structure in the program and the name of the data area on disk. The U means it is a data area data structure and that RPG will bring it in at the beginning of the program and write its updated from back automatically at the end of the program.

There is another very important DS that was introduced in the last payroll Lab 9. It is called HLDMST in the program since it holds the prior master record read and permits control break calculations

Figure 12-20 HLDMST (Hold Master Record) Data Structure

```
I*   HLDMST DS holds the last master record read
I*   It is used to mimic level totals for state and city
I*   values in this structure are compared to current record
I*
I*
IHLDMST        DS
I                                  1   30HLDNO
I                                  1   70 HREC
I                                  4   33 HLDNAM
I                                  4   23 HLDNM
I                                 34  382HLDRAT
I                                 39   58 HLDCTY
I                                 59   60 HLDSTA
I                                 61  650HLDZIP
I                                 66   66 HLDSCD
I                                 67   70 HLDDPT
```

There are other important data structures that are left whole in the LAB12E4Y program so that there will be no guessing. For example, EMPREC is a DS used to minimize MOVE operations. EMPMST in EMPREC holds this master record - HLDMST holds last one. MLHMST DS holds the updated records used for this payroll. It is a multiple occurrence data structure with 100 record slots. It stores entire payroll information before, record by record or occurrence by occurrence before it needs to be written to the history file (PAYHST) -- at the end of the payroll processing of the time card and master records .

Program Logic

Before you attack this program, it would be good to go to the LAB12E4Y program that is decoded in Chapter 24 of the System i RPG and RPGIV Guide as PAREG3 and study it. If that is not available for your use, there is a copy of PAREG3 in your Lab library in the SOURCE file that you might want to look at to get an idea on how to approach this solution. Also, the solution is in your Lab SOURCE file with an S at the end. All of these are there to help you "get it" when it appears too elusive.

Come back the next day if you need all this help. Try to do it yourself and if you succeed, you got it. If not, come back the next day.

Though you have program LAB12E4S (the solution in your SOURCE file) and the XXs in LAB12E4Y to work with as a guide, it would behoove you to scope this out yourself -- even in pseudo code so that you get more out of removing the XX's and adding some code to the LAB12E4Y than you otherwise would gain.

The LAB12E4Y solution is the reincarnation of LAB094EY with a number of enhancements to demonstrate the power of RPGIV along with powerful database and data structure capabilities.   Look at the Files in Figure 12-21. Now, if you can understand what they are all about, you may soon be calling yourself an RPG programmer. Yes, these are correct for the solution. OK, take a peek, but try to solve the problem by removing the XXs and substituting what you think is right. Look it up someplace rather than looking immediately at the solution. OK, sorry, I knew you wouldn't but I had to say it.

Figure 12-21 File Descriptions and Early Table Entries

```
 Columns . . . :    6  76              Edit              RPGOBJ/SOURCE
 SEU==>                                                  LAB12E4S
 FMT H   HKeywords++++++++++++++++++++++++++++++++++++++++++++++++++++++++++++
         *************** Beginning of data ********************************
0001.00 H* RPG HEADER (CONTROL) SPECIFICATION FORMS
0003.00 F*
0004.00 F* RPG FILE DESCRIPTION SPECIFICATION FORMS
0005.00 F*
0006.00 FLAB12D1Y  CF   E                WORKSTN EXTIND(*INU1)
0007.00 FEMPMAST   UF A E          K DISK
0008.00 FTIMCRD    IF   E          K DISK
0009.00 FSALFILE   IF   E          K DISK
0010.00 FYTDFILE   UF A E          K DISK      USROPN
0011.00 FPAYHIST   UF A E          K DISK      USROPN
0012.00 FSTATES    IT   F    22      DISK
0013.00 FQPRINT    O    F    77      PRINTER OFLIND(*INOF)
0014.00 FERROR     O    E            PRINTER
0015.00 FQPRINT2   O    F    77      PRINTER OFLIND(*INOA)
0016.00 D TABABR          S              2    DIM(52) FROMFILE(STATES)
                                              PERRCD(1)
0017.00 D TABST           S             20    DIM(52) ALT(TABABR)


 F3=Exit    F4=Prompt    F5=Refresh    F9=Retrieve    F10=Cursor    F11=Toggle
 F16=Repeat find         F17=Repeat change           F24=More keys
```

To note how much code is in the LAB124EY program and the other versions which exist in the RPG book and in your lab libraries, this lab does not cover the enhancements made in LAB 06 as LAB 09 since they were explained in prior labs. There are enough substantial enhancements to this program to make the explanation very long without rehashing the prior functionality. For example, if we included all of the code (available on your CD/DVD in this LAB for the three other versions of LAB 12, without one line of explanatory text, the code alone with no description would be over fifty pages in length.

The best place to start decoding what's new in LAB124EY is by taking a good look at the solution's File Descriptions as shown in Figure 12-21. This shows the entire set of files including those that are new to this Lab and it enables us to explain their purpose. The first new file (line 006) is a display file called LAB12D1Y, a workstation file. This has been explained in the prior exercise for Lab 12.

The second new file is the YTDFILE, (Line 10), which is the payroll year-to-date earnings file. This file is updated during this process and it has records added to it for employees new to a given payroll. Notice the U in column 15 of file descriptions. This, of course, means update, and it tells the compiler that the YTDFILE is capable of being updated during this run.

The input specifications for the YTDFILE begin at line 102 and go to line 113. In the program described version, you get to see all of the input specifications for all of the files. By examining the YTDFILE, you can see that there are a number of fields defined including some for tax purposes as one would typically expect in a payroll application. However, this sample program does not include any explicit tax calculations.

The next file at line 011 is the PAYHIST file. This is not a year-to-date file. It is a history file. As a program defined file, this 38 field file extends from line 60 to line 97 on the Input (I) specs. PAYHIST is defined in the program with a U in column 15, though there are no update operations in the program against this file. It would have been more correctly coded as input (I). When the employee master and the YTD file are updated, the history file reflects those updates as the new information is written (added) with a WRITE operation at line 516 as shown following this paragraph. Each pay period, the 38 fields of employee information, including updated year-to-dates are added as a new record to the history file. The sum total of all the records in PAYHIST serves as a full history for multiple years for each employees weekly payroll values. It also serves as a potential means of recreating a given pay period's payroll for verification purposes.

```
0367.00       C    33                    WRITE      PAYHR
```

The next file at line 12 is the STATES File. A sample of the data in the STATES file is included in Figure 24-2 from the RPG Text book, shown here as Figure 24-2.

Figure 12-22; Figure 24-2 States External Table in Database

State Abbreviation Positions 1 to 2	State Name Positions 3 to 22
AK	ALASKA
AL	ALABAMA
AR	ARKANSAS
AZ	ARIZONA
CA	CALIFORNIA
CO	COLORADO
CT	CONNECTICUT
DC	DISTRICT / COLUMBIA
DE	DELAWARE
FL	FLORIDA
Etc.	

Notice in line 12 of File descriptions that the type of file is T for table, In RPG/400, there would be an E in column 39 to indicate that an extension specification is used in the program. No extension is permitted in RPGIV since there is no extension specification. Instead, the new D spec is used to define the alternating table that is used in this RPG program. The code for the two entries in the alternating table are also in Figure 12-21 in lines 16 and 17. These are repeated below:

```
0016.00 D TABABR...   S...      2    DIM(52) FROMFILE(STATES)
0016.01                              PERRCD(1)
0017.00 D TABST...    S...     20    DIM(52) ALT(TABABR)
```

This condensed statement # 16 & 17 (for readability) shows that the "From File" name is STATES. This means that the table will be loaded from the database file named STATES as a pre-execution table – right before the program begins to execute. When it is loaded to memory, it is built as an alternating table with the abbreviation part going into TABABR and the state full name going into TABST. In the program, only the state abbreviation is stored in the data files so in order to print the state's full name on the history report, a table lookup of the abbreviation against the alternating table needs to be done in the program at condensed line 529 as shown below:

```
                                                           EQ
C...   HSTSTA        LOOKUP   TABABR...   TABST...          87
C...87              MOVEL    TABST...   SMSTAT... 15
```

In this example, the state abbreviation as stored in the PAYHIST file is used as the search argument against the TABABR table. When there is a hit, indicator 87 is turned on and the state full name is stored in the TABST name. Then, to preserve the result of the look up the contents of TABST is moved to SMSTAT.

While we are examining new tables in the program, another alternating table (compile time) is needed for this program. Suppose we call it TABDNO (department #) and the alternate table is TABDNM (department name). This is to provide a look up capability for department # to get the department name.

See the code below to get the proper perspective as to how this needs to be implemented. With this table, the dept # field is used to lookup in the TABDNO table and the results come back in the TABDNM. The compile records that are at the end of this program are shown below:

```
D TABDNO...   S             4    DIM(10) CTDATA PERRCD(1)
D TABDNM...   S            30    DIM(10) ALT(TABDNO)
```

Note the keyword CTDATA. This makes it a compile time array. The compile records that are at the end of this program are shown below:

```
MILLMILLING
PIGPINGING
GRNDGRINDING
SANDSANDING
```

There is also an array introduced in this program set called GRP. It is defined as follows:

```
D GRP               S               11   2 DIM(6)
```

GRP is an execution array of six elements, each 11 digits long with two decimal places. This array is prepared to be used as needed to store the year-to-date gross pay amounts for the last six years. Each of the years can be manipulated individually in RPG/400 as GRP,x and in this RPGIV program as GRP(x).

The DDS for the display file is repeated below for your convenience in writing this program

Figure 12-23 DDS for LAB12D1Y Display File

```
01.00 A*%%TS SD 20060613 134404   BKELLY REL-V5R3M0   5722-WDS
02.00 A*%%EC
03.00 A*%%FD LAB12D1Y
04.00 A...                              DSPSIZ(24 80 *DS3)
05.00 A...            R PROMPT
06.00 A*%%TS SD 20060613 134404   BKELLY REL-V5R3M0   5722-WDS
07.00 A...                              CA10(10 'Create New Payroll Master
08.00 A...                              Record')
09.00 A...                              CA03(03 'End Job')
10.00 A...                              CA11(11 'Update Payroll Master
10.00                                   Reco-
11.00 A...                              rd')
12.00 A...                              CA20(20 'Run Payroll Register')
13.00 A...                              CA21(21 'Accept Payroll Write Histo-
14.00 A...                              ry')
15.00 A...                              CA22(22 'Create History Report for
16.00 A...                              this Period')
17.00 A...                          2 25'The Dowallaby Company '
18.00 A...                          3 30'Payroll Input'
19.00 A...    PAYWK#...   2S 0O   4 34
20.00 A...                          6  6'Press F10 to Create New Master Pay-
21.00 A...                              roll Records'
22.00 A...                          8  6'Press F11 tp Update Master Payroll-
23.00 A...                              Records'
24.00 A...                         10  6'Press F20 to Run the Payroll
24.00                                   Regis-
25.00 A...                              ter'
26.00 A...                         12  6'Press F21 to Accept this Payrolla-
27.00 A...                              s Correct and Write History File'
28.00 A...                         14  6'Press F22 to Create Archive Histor-
29.00 A...                              y Report for Pay Period '
30.00 A...    WEEK#...   2S 0O 14 65
31.00 A...                         17  6'Press F3 to END THE JOB'
32.00 A*%%GP SCREEN1     01
33.00 A*%%GP UNTITLED    01
34.00 A.. R ADD                       TEXT('Add EMPLOYEE')
35.00 A*%%TS  DD  20060612  115746  Brian       REL-V5.0.1  WDSC
36.00 A...                              CA12(12 'End ADD Function - Return-
37.00 A...                              to PROMPT')
38.00 A...                          2 25'The Dowallaby Company'
39.00 A...                          3 24'Add to Employeee Master'
40.00 A...                          6 21'Employee Number'
41.00 A...                          7 21'Employee Name'
42.00 A...                          8 21'Employee Pay Rate'
43.00 A...                          9 21'Employee City'
44.00 A...                         10 21'Employee State'
45.00 A...                         11 21'Employee Zip Code'
46.00 A...                         12 21'Employee Salaried?'
47.00 A...                         13 21'Employee Dept Code'
48.00 A*                           16  8'Employee Number to update next'
49.00 A...    EMPNO...   3S 0O   6 41
50.00 A...    EMPNAM.. 30     I  7 41
51.00 A...    EMPRAT...  5S 2I  8 41
52.00 A...    EMPCTY.. 20     I  9 41
53.00 A...    EMPSTA..  2     I 10 41
54.00 A...    EMPZIP...  5S 0I 11 41
55.00 A...    EMPSCD..  1     I 12 41
56.00 A...    EMPDPT..  4     I 13 41
57.00 A*     EMP#...    3S 0I 16 41
```

```
58.00 A..                      19  8'Press Enter to continue... Pres-
59.00 A..                          s F12 to end the ADD'
60.00 A.. R UPDATE1
61.00 A*%%TS SD 20060613 134404 BKELLY REL-V5R3M0  5722-WDS
62.00 A..                          CA12(12 'End UPDATE Function - Ret-
63.00 A..                          urn to PROMPT')
64.00 A..                       2 29'The Dowallaby Company'
65.00 A..                       3 34'Payroll Input'
66.00 A..                       4 38'UPDATE'
67.00 A..                       7  9'Enter the Employee # you wish to U-
68.00 A..                          PDATE'
69.00 A..                      10 12'EMP NBR:'
70.00 A..   EMP#...    3S 0I 10 22
71.00 A..97...                 14 12'EMPLOYEE # NOT FOUND'
72.00 A..97..EM#OUT...  3S 0O 14 35
73.00 A..                      17  6'Press F12 to End The Update'
74.00 A.. R UPDATE              TEXT('Add EMPLOYEE')
75.00 A*%%TS DD 20060612 115746 Brian REL-V5.0.1  WDSC
76.00 A..                          CA12(12 'End UPDATE Function - 76.00 Ret-
77.00 A..                          urn to PROMPT')
78.00 A..                       2 25'The Dowallaby Company'
79.00 A..                       3 24'Update to Employeee Master'
80.00 A..                       6 21'Employee Number'
81.00 A..                       7 21'Employee Name'
82.00 A..                       8 21'Employee Pay Rate'
83.00 A..                       9 21'Employee City'
84.00 A..                      10 21'Employee State'
85.00 A..                      11 21'Employee Zip Code'
86.00 A..                      12 21'Employee Salaried?'
87.00 A..                      13 21'Employee Dept Code'
88.00 A..   EMPNO...   3S 0O  6 41
89.00 A..   EMPNAM.. 30     B  7 41
90.00 A..   EMPRAT..  5S 2B  8 41
91.00 A..   EMPCTY.. 20     B  9 41
92.00 A..   EMPSTA..  2     B 10 41
93.00 A..   EMPZIP..  5S 0B 11 41
94.00 A..   EMPSCD..  1     B 12 41
95.00 A..   EMPDPT..  4     B 13 41
96.00 A*    EMP#...    3S 0I 16 41
97.00 A*                      16  8'Employee Number to update next'
98.00 A..                      19  8'Press Enter to continue... Pres-
99.00 A..                          s F12 to end update'
```

Main Program Formats

The LAB12D1Y display file is used as a WORKSTN file in the program. It is a multi-format display file as shown in the condensed DDS in Figure 12-23. There are two formats, one each for the ability to add employee records (ADD) to the employee file and to update employee records (UPDATE) in the file. There is also a format called UPDATE1 that permits the user to enter the employee number of the database file record to be updated.

The PROMPT format in the PAYINPUT display file is the first format (screen panel) defined. Based on options that you select, the program behaves differently. For example, there are five main functions provided by the main menu. By giving you a picture of the main menu in Figure 24-4, you can see these functions as well as the circumstances that cause the options to be executed.

Figure 12-24 LAB12D1Y EXFMT Output

```
              The Dowallaby Company
                 Payroll Input

 Press F10 to Create New Master Payroll Records

 Press F11 to Update Master Payroll Records

 Press F20 to Run the Payroll Register

 Press F21 to Accept this Payroll as Correct and
                Write History File

 Press F22 to Create Archive History Report
                for Pay Period


 Press F3 to END THE JOB
```

The code for the workstation file in this program is as follows:

```
006 FLAB12D1Y CF  E...   WORKSTN ...    U1
```

This File Description coding says that LAB12D1Y is to be a combined file (C in 15) processed in a fully procedural fashion (F in column 16) and it will use the field definitions of the externally described display file (coded with the E in column 19). It is a WORKSTN file and it is conditioned with indicator U1.

The External switches such as U1 to U8 inclusively permits up to eight external indicators U1 to U8. These need to be set on with a CHGJOB command and a modification of the SWS parameter. From the console type in

```
CHGJOB SWS(10000000)
```

This command would set on switch 1 which RPG would take as U1. Only when U1 -- a.k.a. switch 1 is on when the program begins does the workstation file get used in the program. SO, if you want to be able to see the PROMPT panel, you must make sure that U1 is on. What does the program do if U1 is not on. If you check the code that is available to peruse, you will find the answer in calculations as follows:

```
225 C... *INU1      IFNE    *ON
226 C...            EXSR    RUNREG
227 C...            SETON                LR
228 C...            ELSE
229 C* Prompt for Options if U1 ON
230 C...            EXSR    OPENFL
231 C... *INLR      DOUEQ   *ON
```

This says that if U1 is not on, execute the subroutine RUNREG and then when that is done, SETON LR and go away. Otherwise (ELSE in 228) if U1 is on, the workstation file is in the game and is in control of the game. The first action is to open the files since they are all in play if the WORKSTN file is in play. The next step is to begin the mainline DO loop. This loop is to continue until LR is on and the program is about to end.

The RUNREG subroutine happens to be the code that has been repackaged from the LAB09E4Y program. It executes the instructions necessary to print the new payroll register just as in LAB09E4Y. So, with no U1 switch setting, only print the register using the RUNREG subroutine to pull this off. With the switch setting, you give the control of the menu options but they should be done in sequence since the output of one function is used by the next.   That last piece of information is very important.

Running the menu gives five options – as long as U1 is on. The first permits records to be added to the file. The mainline snippet that sends out the PROMPT panel tests the first three options is as follows in Figure 12-25:

Figure 12-25 Main Code Snippet - Top of Program

```
0079.00 C                     EXFMT       PROMPT
0080.00 C      03             SETON                          LR
0081.00 C* Add Employee to Master before register
0082.00 C      *IN10          IFEQ        *ON
0083.00 C                     EXSR        EMPADD
0084.00 C                     SETOFF                         10
0085.00 C                     ENDIF
0086.00 C* Update Employee Master before register
0087.00 C      *IN11          IFEQ        *ON
0088.00 C                     EXSR        EMPUPD
0089.00 C                     SETOFF                         11
0090.00 C                     ENDIF
0091.00 C* Run Employee Register from ROMPT Menu  (RUNREG is DEFAULT)
0092.00 C      *IN20          IFEQ        *ON
0093.00 C                     EXSR        RUNREG
0094.00 C                     SETOFF                         20
0095.00 C                     ENDIF
```

EXFMT sends out the prompt panel. The next statement tests indicator 03 which is turned on in the Display File DDS by the user pressing 03 to end the job. 03 sets on LR to get end of job processing started for the program

If F10 is depressed, indicator 10 is on and the employee Add subroutine is executed as you can see in the code between lines 82 and 85. With this option, users are permitted to add employees to the payroll file before the register is run. If F11 is depressed, the employee update subroutine is executed.

With this option, users are permitted to update employee master records before the register is run. If F20 is depressed, the payroll register (RUNREG subroutine) is called in exactly the same fashion as it would have been if U1 were not on and there was no prompt panel for the program.

When the register is being run, in the subroutine NETPAY, the multiple occurrence data structure - MLHMST is loaded with the history fields for this pay period and all necessary fields to update the YTDFILE. If U1 is on, meaning the register was run from the prompt panel, then it is expected that the other options will also be run. Therefore, the YTDUPD subroutine which updates the YTDFILE is run if U1 is on.

So, at the end of this third PROMPT option, the data for each employee is saved in MLHMST and the year-to-date information is updated. The next two options to be tested are in the code snippet below:

Figure 12-26 Continuation of Main Snippet Testing Menu Options

```
0096.00 C* Check out register printout without exiting - update files
0097.00 C      *IN21          IFEQ      *ON
0098.00 C                     EXSR      PAYOK
0099.00 C                     SETOFF                              21
0100.00 C                     ENDIF
0101.00 C* Run History Report after PAYOK.. Run before or after exit
0102.00 C      *IN22          IFEQ      *ON
0103.00 C                     EXSR      HSTRPT
0104.00 C                     SETOFF                              22
0105.00 C                     ENDIF
0106.00 C                     ENDDO
0107.00 C                     ENDIF
0108.00 C*    MAIN PROGRAM FUNCTIONS ARE OVER - SUBROUTINES FOLLow
```

If F21 is pressed, the payroll register has been approved and the history file can be prepared for the history report. See Figure 24-5 for a condensed sample of the History Report. Notice that the state name is printed in full from the lookup operations. Indicator 21 is on and the PAYOK subroutine is executed as you can see in the code between lines 254 and 257. With this option, the PAYOK Subroutine reads the Multiple occurrence master DS and writes out the History File, PAYHIST.

If F22 is depressed, the history report subroutine HSTRPT is executed. With this option, the program prints from the PAYHST file that has received the new payroll data for this period. See Figure 12-14 for a look at the history list.

The ENDDO in line 106 in the sample code ends the mainline DO loop. During the HSTRPT subroutine, LR needs to be turned on. A loop needs to start when LR is on so the prompt is not displayed and the program ends peacefully. The rest of the code in the program is commented and is thus self-explanatory for an RPG programming decoder such as those of us who have endured more than eleven Lab exercises to this point.

In this Lab, we made another dramatic change in programming from programs we had been studying. In this last program, there is no RPG program cycle yet the program accomplishes the mission of matching records and control level processing,

A number of RPG innovations were fortified with examples in this Lab. The uses conditional file descriptions with the workstation file being in the program only if the external switch U1 is on. Additionally, two new files were introduced: an YTD file and a History file. The YTD file shows how databases get updated and the History file shows how databases have large records added.

Additionally, this program introduces the use of interactive programming to add and update records to the employee file based on separate options from a menu panel within the workstation file.

Two alternating tables are introduced for lookup operations for state names and department names. The one table is pre-execution, loading from a database file and the other is compile time, loading from the back of the program source code. We also introduced an execution time array for the future for holding up to six years of yearly gross pay information in the record.

This program also uses a data area data structure that automatically gets loaded at program startup and gets written back at program end. The next pay period # and the next employee # fields are maintained in this data structure by this program.

A multiple occurrence data structure is introduced that holds the current payroll information for up to 100 employees in its current form. When the register is finished, this gets used as the basis for building the history records in the PAYHST file and. As a final option in this program the entire PAYHST file gets printed in a report that uses a third printer file to keep the three reports produced by this program separated.

Detailed Instructions for Method 2

1. Use PDM / SEU to edit the LAB12E4Y program.

2. Remove all X's from the program and make changes to code at the point of the X as appropriate to support the program logic.

3. Save your work as LAB12E4Y.

4. Compile LAB12E4Y and place the object in your current library.

5. Run the program with no switch settings to see how it behaves.

6. Type CHGJOB SWS(1000000) on the command line to turn on switch 1.

7. Run the program again and select each option on the menu.

8. Look for three print files QPRINT, QPRINT2, and ERROR in your output queues and examine the output compared to the samples presented in this chapter.

9. When you are satisfied that everything has worked, you have completed Lab 12 Exercise 2.

10. When you have completed Lab 12 Exercise 2, you have completed all of the exercises in this Lab book / tutorial.

11. Feel free to back through all the programs that you successfully compiled and if you can explain why the X became something else, you will be that much closer to be an accomplished RPG programmer.

12. When you are working in the cubby holes with your peers, feel free to ask them questions. They know they know more than you do, and if they are anything like good people, (most are) they will e tickled to lift you out of any mud into which you might fall.

That's All Folks!

Congratulations.

Lets Go Publish! Books by Brian Kelly

(Sold at www.bookhawkers.com; Amazon.com, and Kindle.).

LETS GO PUBLISH! is proud to announce that more AS/400 and Power i books are becoming available to help you inexpensively address your AS/400 and Power i education and training needs: Our general titles precede specific AS/400 and other technology books. Check out these great patriotic books which precede the tech books in the list.

IBM i Technical Books

I had a Dream IBM Could be #1 Again
The title is self-explanatory

Whatever Happened to the IBM AS /400?
The question is answered in this new book.

The All Everything Operating System:
Story about IBM's finest operating system; its facilities; how it came to be.

The All-Everything Machine
Story about IBM's finest computer server.

Chip Wars
The story of ongoing wars between Intel and AMD and upcoming wars between Intel and IBM. Book may cause you to buy / sell somebody's stock.

Can the AS/400 Survive IBM?
Exciting book about the AS/400 in a IBM i World.

The AS/400 & IBM i Pocket SQL Guide.
Complete Pocket Guide to SQL as implemented on IBM i. A must have for SQL developers new to IBM i. It is very compact yet very comprehensive and it is example driven. Written in a part tutorial and part reference style, Tons of SQL coding samples, from the simple to the sublime.

The AS/400 & IBM i Pocket Query Guide.
If you have been spending money for years educating your Query users, and you find you are still spending, or you've given up, this book is right for you. This one QuikCourse covers all Query options.

The AS/400 & IBM I RPG & RPG IV Developers Guide.
Comprehensive RPG & RPGIV Textbook -- Over 900 pages. This is the one RPG book to have if you are not having more than one. All areas of the language covered smartly in a convenient sized book Annotated PowerPoint's available for self-study (extra fee for self-study package)

The IBM I RPG Tutorial and Lab Guide
Your guide to a hands-on Lab experience. Contains CD with Lab exercises and PowerPoint's. Great companion to the above textbook or can be used as a standalone for student Labs or tutorial purposes

The AS/400 & IBM i Pocket Developers' Guide.
Comprehensive Pocket Guide to all of the AS/400 and IBM i development tools - DFU, SDA, etc. You'll also get a big bonus with chapters on Architecture, Work Management, and Subfile Coding. This book was updated in 2016..

The AS/400 & IBM i Pocket Database Guide.
Complete Pocket Guide to IBM i integrated relational database (DB2/400) – physical and logical files and DB operations - Union, Projection, Join, etc. Written in a part tutorial and part reference style. Tons of DDS coding samples.

Getting Started with The WebSphere Development Studio Client for IBM i (WDSc).
Focus is on client server and the Web. Includes CODE/400, VisualAge RPG, CGI, WebFacing, and WebSphere Studio. Case study continues from the Interactive Book.

The IBM i Pocket WebFacing Primer.
This book gets you started immediately with WebFacing. A sample case study is used as the basis for a conversion to WebFacing. Interactive 5250 application is WebFaced in a case study form before your eyes.

Getting Started with WebSphere Express Server for IBM i
Step-by-Step Guide for Setting up Express Servers
A comprehensive guide to setting up and using WebSphere Express. It is filled with examples, and structured in a tutorial fashion for easy learning.

The WebFacing Application Design & Development Guide:
Step by Step Guide to designing green screen IBM i apps for the Web. Both a systems design guide and a developers guide. Book helps you understand how to design and develop Web applications using regular RPG or COBOL programs.

The IBM i Express Web Implementer's Guide. Your one stop guide to ordering, installing, fixing, configuring, and using WebSphere Express, Apache, WebFacing, IBM i Access for Web, and HATS/LE.

Seniors, Social Security & the Minimum Wage
The impact of the minimum wage on Social Security Beneficiaries

How to Write Your First Book and Publish It With CreateSpace
This books teaches how to create a book with MSWord and then publish it with CreateSpace. No need to find a traditional publisher.

Healthcare & Welfare Accountability The Trump Way
Why should somebody win the Lottery & not pay back welfare?

The Trump Plan Solves Student Debt Crisis. .
This is the Trump solution for new student debt and the existing $1.3 Trillion student debt accumulation.

Take the Train to Myrtle Beach The Trump Way.
Tells all about the Donald Trump Plan to restart private passenger railway systems in America while it tells you how to get to Myrtle Beach by Train.

RRRRRR The Trump Way.
This book represents the overarching theme of the Trump campaign with verbs ready to reign in the excessive policies of the Obama Administration. These are the six verbs for the RRRRRR plan: Reduce, Repeal, Reindustrialize, Raise, Revitalize, Remember

Jobs! Jobs! Jobs! The Trump Way!
All about the jobs mess we ae in along with a set of Trump solutions

The Trump Plan Solves the Student Debt Crisis
Solution for new student debt and the existing $1.3 Trillion debt accumulation

101 Secrets How to be a High Information Voter
You do not have to be a low-information voter.

Why Trump?
You Already Know… But, this book will tell you anyway

Saving America The Trump Way!
A book that tells you how President Donald Trump will help America so that Americans wind up on top

The US Immigration Fix
It's all in here. Finally an answer to the 60 million interlopers in America. You won't want to put this book down

Obama's Seven Deadly Sins.
In the Obama Presidency, there are many concerns about the long-term prospects and sustainability of the country. We examine each of the President's seven deadliest sins in detail, offering warnings and a number of solutions. Be careful. Book may nudge you to move to Canada or Europe.

Taxation Without Representation Second Edition
At the time of the Boston Tea Party, there was no representation. Now, there is no representation again but there are "representatives."

Healthcare & Welfare Accountability
Who should pay for your healthcare? Whose healthcare should you pay for? Is it a lifetime free ride on others or should those once in need of help have to pay it back when their lives improve?

Jobs! Jobs! Jobs!
Where have all the American Jobs gone and how can we get them back?

Great Moments in Penn State Football
Check out the particulars of this great book at bookhawkers.com.

Great Moments in Notre Dame Football
Check out the particulars of this great book at bookhawkers.com or www.notredamebooks.com

WineDiets.Com Presents The Wine Diet
Learn how to lose weight while having fun. Four specific diets and some great anecdotes fill this book with fun and the opportunity to lose weight in the process.

Wilkes-Barre, PA; Return to Glory
Wilkes-Barre City's return to glory begins with dreams and ideas. Along with plans and actions, this equals leadership.

The Annual Guest Plan.
This is a plan which if deployed today would immediately solve the problem of 60 million illegal aliens in the United States.

Geoffrey Parsons' Epoch… The Land of Fair Play
Better than the original. The greatest re-mastering of the greatest book ever written on American Civics. It was built for all Americans as the best govt. design in the history of the world.

The Bill of Rights 4 Dummmies!
This is the best book to learn about your rights. Be the first, to have a "Rights Fest" on your block. You will win for sure!

Sol Bloom's Epoch …Story of the Constitution
This work by Sol Bloom was written to commemorate the Sesquicentennial celebration of the Constitution. It has been remastered by Lets Go Publish! – An excellent read!

The Constitution 4 Dummmies!
This is the best book to learn about the Constitution. Learn all about the fundamental laws of America.

America for Dummmies!
All Americans should read to learn about this great country.

Just Say No to Chris Christie for President two editions – I & II -- Discusses the reasons why Chris Christie is a poor choice for US President

The Federalist Papers by Hamilton, Jay, Madison w/ intro by Brian Kelly
Complete unabridged, easier to read, annotated version of the original Federalist Papers

Companion to Federalist Papers by Hamilton, Jay, Madison w/ intro by Brian Kelly
This small, inexpensive book will help you navigate the Federalist Papers

Kill the Republican Party!
2013 edition and edition #2)
Demonstrates why the Republican Party must be abandoned by conservatives

Bring On the American Party!
Demonstrates how conservatives can be free from the party of wimps by starting its own national party called the American Party.

No Amnesty! No Way!
In addition to describing the issue in detail, this book also offers a real solution.

Saving America
This how-to book is about saving our country using strong mercantilist principles. These same principles that helped the country from its founding.

RRR:
A unique plan for economic recovery and job creation

Kill the EPA
The EPA seems to hate mankind and love nature. They are also making it tough for asthmatics to breathe and for those with malaria to live. It's time they go.